# BREAST CANCER

D1571094

# BREAST CANCER

*Poisons, Profits, and Prevention*

---

LIANE CLORFENE-CASTEN

COMMON COURAGE PRESS

LIBRARY OF CONGRESS CATALOGING-IN-PUBLICATION DATA

Clorfene-Casten, Liane.
Breast cancer : poisons, profits, and prevention / Liane Clorfene-Casten.
    p. cm.
    Includes index.
    ISBN 1-56751-095-7 (cloth). – ISBN 1-56751-094-9 (pbk.)
    1. Breast–Cancer–Environmental aspects. I. Title.
  RC280.B8C596  1996
  362.1'9699449–dc20                        96-29233
                                                CIP

Common Courage Press
PO Box 702
Monroe, ME 04951
207-525-0900
Fax: 207-525-3068

First Printing

To Paul, my rock and fighter, who holds on because life and our love is so special.

# CONTENTS

# ACKNOWLEDGMENTS

I gratefully acknowledge all the women who have contributed to this book—those I've met, learned from, networked with, cheered, with, and cried with. You are fighters all. With your leadership, power, vision, and energy, we will surely win the fight for justice and a cleaner, healthier world.

A special thanks to Greenpeace, whose dedicated researchers, especially Charlie Cray, were always there with a vast fund of valuable data.

Thanks to Greg Bates, publisher of Common Courage Press, who immediately saw the need to get this information out to the public. Your help and encouragement have been invaluable in making my vision a reality. And thanks to my editor, Robert Weisser, for distilling a mountain of data, testimony, and theory into a compelling discussion of the hidden villains of the breast cancer epidemic.

# 1

# THE CASSANDRA MICHAELS STORY

**H**er name is Cassandra Michaels—Cass for short. She used to be a full-bodied, broad-shouldered woman with an open, alert face. Her ruddy cheeks showed the time she spent outdoors. She is 35 years old, thin, and ghostly pale. She is dying from breast cancer.

Cass was one of six children raised on a dairy farm in the middle of Iowa not far from Des Moines. The family raised their own feedstock, too. One of Cass's earliest memories were the planes flying over their farm, coasting low up one end and down the other end of the grain fields, dusting with something that smelled so bad. Her daddy said they had to do it or the bugs and weeds would come, and they couldn't afford to lose a crop. Year after year, the planes had to spread more and more of the pesticides to get the job done.

After the dustings, from the early spring through the summer, there was the drift from the fields gliding over her mother's vegetable garden, coating the tomatoes, peppers, lettuce, and cucumbers. When it rained, the residue washed off into the ground—not just from her mother's garden, but from thousands of acres surrounding them. The water from the well on the farm had an acrid smell to it—not even a double dose of cherry drink mix could mask that odor.

Cass was an early developer, and started menstruating before she was eleven. During her junior year at Jefferson Consolidated High School, it was time; her mother took her to a well-respected Des Moines gynecologist for her first female exam. The doctor interviewed them about their family medical history. The year before, Cass's mother, then forty-five, and her older sister Helen, then twenty-six, had both been diagnosed with breast cancer. This had rocked the family, but their doctor had told them it wasn't so unusual: women were getting breast cancer younger and younger.

After hearing the family history, the gynecologist told Cass and her mother that he was participating in a nationwide drug trial sponsored by the National Cancer Institute. He admitted the drug was experimental and the results so far were speculative, but he felt comfortable recommending it because a prestigious federal agency was behind the study. There was some evidence that the drug helped prevent breast cancer in women who had a family history of the disease. There were some possible side effects; for instance, Cass could develop endometrial cancer, although the doctor maintained that the chances were very slim. Cass's mother, deeply concerned about her daughter and trusting this doctor and his good reputation, eagerly gave her consent. The drug was tamoxifen.

Cass stayed on tamoxifen all during her college years, confident that it was helping her avoid breast cancer. In addition, she had a mammogram every other year, starting at age 20. Her doctor mentioned that she was a little on the young side to be doing this, but with her history, it seemed like a good preventive measure.

She had married Tom, whom she had met in her senior accounting class. His daddy was a farmer, too, and so they had to choose whether to follow the family path or to become city folk. When Tom was offered a job at a large accounting firm in Des

Moines, the decision was made. In their new apartment in the city, Tom and Cass decided to put off having children for a while so they could save up to buy a house.

When she was twenty-six, Cass had a shock. Her fourth mammogram revealed a lump in her right breast. Since the cancer was already at Stage II—no longer a tiny speck—her doctor recommended a complete mastectomy followed by radiation therapy, and Cass agreed. And after nine years of medication, her oncologist took her off tamoxifen. It had prevented nothing.

Even though she trusted her doctor's advice, Cass approached the mastectomy with great anxiety; so much so that her mother drove in from the farm to be with her. Tom and her mother took Cass to the hospital to give her the love and support that she needed.

The surgeon removed only the breast tissue; the underlying muscles and the lymph nodes were left alone. The breast tissue is a large mass; it goes from the collarbone down to the edge of the ribs and then from the breast bone out to the muscle in the back of the armpit. After the doctor removed the entire breast, he sent the tissue to the pathologist whose job is to examine it for cancer. The report indicated her nodes were clear. The result, from Cass's point of view, was one very flat chest.

Cass remained in the hospital for several days while the build-up of fluid was drained. She was told by her surgeon to start moving her arm around normally as much as she could. Putting it in a sling would create a stiffness which might mean physical therapy later. She was exhausted, having been through not just the surgery and anesthesia, but the anxiety of knowing she would be forever different. It took a long time before she was able to look at herself in the mirror and an even longer time before she was able to stand anyone's touch in the scar area. She felt her nerve endings were on fire.

Of course, her doctor recommended localized radiation after the surgery while there were comparatively few cells to attack. About a month after surgery, when sufficient healing had taken place, she started the treatment. The radiologist took great pains to measure just the right spot (including the lymph nodes) so the rays could be targeted accurately. The regimen, which lasted five weeks, wasn't so bad—it was painless really, although during the last couple of weeks the skin surrounding the breast turned an angry red and Cassandra developed a slight cough. A total of about 4,700 rads of radiation were used. (In comparison, a chest x-ray involves just a fraction of a rad.) If there were any microscopic cancer cells remaining, the radiologist assured her, such a mighty dose would surely get rid of them.

Cassandra was glad when the treatment was over. She was a worn-out young woman, barely able to cook a proper dinner for herself and Tom.

A half a year later, with the trauma behind her, Cass began to wonder if she would have kids.

She and Tom were making a good living, and had saved enough for a down payment on a house. They had even picked out the development they wanted to live in, and were looking at the builder's plans. It was time to start a family, and Cass was looking forward to it. She loved the idea of a big family! Oh, the memories they would have . . .

A year after her mastectomy, Cass had still not conceived. Another year went by, and her frustration and self-doubt gnawed at her. Her mother had had six kids, and each of her sisters had had at least two. What was wrong with her? The stress was taking its toll on Tom, too, and they were arguing more often. Cass began to wonder about the very essence of her femininity, and whether Tom had begun to see his one-breasted wife as unattractive. She became obsessed with looking "normal."

Fortunately, Tom's firm was doing well and could afford good health insurance. She drove herself to a plastic surgeon who was highly recommended by her gynecologist, and inquired about an implant. The next week, Cassandra—28, childless, scarred, and scared—had a silicone implant surgically inserted into her right chest cavity.

Cass was a happy woman again. She and Tom seemed to be closer. She still had not conceived, but Cass figured that children would arrive in good time. They took romantic trips to exotic places, went out on the town, and started to build their dream house.

A few months after moving into their new home, Cass woke up tired and achy. She had felt this way for a long time, but had always convinced herself that it was because of all the work in getting the new house decorated. The symptoms were subtle. Some days she would drag through her work with a headache that no amount of aspirin could erase. The pains in her joints made sleep difficult, and even the occasional full night's rest didn't lift her malaise. She rubbed herself with a drugstore full of anti-arthritis ointments, but the pain persisted. What finally sent her to her doctor was the sensation that she couldn't swallow anymore—she felt as if her throat was closing up.

The internist her insurance plan sent her to examined Cass, but could find no physical cause of her problems. He put her into the hospital for observation, administered standard blood and urine tests, ordered x-rays and even a mammogram, but was unable to offer a conclusive diagnosis. The mammogram on the left breast was negative; the one on the right was inconclusive. In his final consultation, he strongly suggested that her problems were mental—an unconscious cry for help due to her inability to become pregnant.

Cass knew she wasn't a mental case—she knew absolutely that something was wrong with her body. She had been so happy and optimistic after her implant, and now her health was deteriorating monthly. Desperately, she spent the next two years going from one doctor to another, practically begging for help. The pain became so bad that she had to quit her job and go on disability. All thoughts of children were gone—the mildest exertions exhausted her, and she spent most of her days lying down.

While in bed one day, she rolled over onto her right side. Something didn't feel right. A glimmer of recognition . . . and then a paralyzing fear gripped her, constricting her throat. With her eyes closed, she felt her right breast. It was flat again.

When Tom came home that night, Cass was rocking in her chair. She could barely stammer out her discovery. Could this stuff be leaking? The next day, she and Tom went back to the plastic surgeon and demanded that he check the implant. Within the week, Cass was scheduled for surgery and the misshapen, nearly empty implant was taken out. Too late for Cass, of course, for the silicone from the leaking sack had long since been distributed around her pain-wracked body. But that wasn't the only reason she felt so sick. In removing the implant, the surgeon had noticed a large lump, which he sent to the lab for analysis.

The lump was malignant. She had had several mammograms in her search for an answer to her sickness, but the silicone capsule had hidden the growing lump from the x-rays. It had gone undiagnosed for too long, and more tests revealed the cancer had metastasized.

With the cancer invading her lungs, Cass was put through a regimen of chemotherapy so powerful that all of her hair fell out and she couldn't eat. She lived for weeks in the hospital with chronic nausea, massive weight loss, infections in the lining of her stomach, and exquisite joint pain from the silicone. When her thirty-fifth birthday arrived, Cass knew she was dying. In fact, she wanted to die. Hooked up to tubes and an apparatus to help her breathe, the only drug that could control her pain was morphine.

Cassandra Michaels had been poisoned to the point where her wasted body could no longer repair itself. Who did this? A closed-minded medical system; physicians experimenting with dangerous substances whose use national authorities support; profit-driven corporations; federal agencies that allow corporations to continue dangerous practices; all worked together to kill her. Was their goal to kill this one woman? It never is. But Cassandra was a profit opportunity, and the major goal of our political, social, and economic systems is to make more profits. If the consequences of reaching that goal include sacrificing human life, so be it. For the corporations and powerful people who run our society, that's an acceptable risk.

These claims might at first seem outlandish, but they are supported by reams of testimony in court cases and before government agencies, and backed up by many scientific studies. The poisons that killed Cassandra started early, with the cancer-causing pesticides that were sprayed on her family farm during her youth. The EPA supports this practice, despite its knowledge of the toxicity of the pesticides. The poisons continued with frequent mammograms at an inappropriate age ("just to be safe"), when she was vulnerable to radiation, and with the prolonged administration of tamoxifen (which may have rendered her infertile). The tamoxifen was wrongly prescribed in the hopes that it would prevent breast cancer, given Cass's family history. However, the source of her family's cancer was more likely in the contaminated water and food the family ate, and not in its genes. The problems with silicone breast implants are now widely publicized—the casings leak recognized poisons into the bodies of the victims. This had been known for many years to the various implant manufacturers and the agencies that regulated them, but this knowledge was kept from plastic surgeons and the public.

The last step was the administration of chemotherapy, profoundly toxic substances for the "treatment" of cancer, and the only cancer therapy officially sanctioned by the cancer establishment. These drugs not only poisoned Cass further, they wreaked havoc on an immune system already depressed by the silicone. Yes, Cass was killed.

Cassandra Michaels is not a real person. She—and what she went through—is a composite of what thousands of breast cancer patients have experienced. And without a major change in how we view the disease, countless thousands more will experience the same agony.

The cancer epidemic is a twentieth-century legacy. With the modern onslaught of toxic contaminants, imposed through our industrialized environment and protected by very profitable systems, all of our lives are at stake. We all carry a burden of toxic substances and the damage of unnecessary radiation in our bodies. In our lifetimes, we will recognize that we will not be unlucky if we get cancer, but rather that we will be lucky not to get it.

And despite what politicians, nationwide fundraising campaigns, corporate-funded research, and drug company officials say, we are not "winning the war on cancer." In fact, the war hasn't even been properly fought, since the concentration has been on treatment rather than prevention. The American public has been diverted by powerful American Cancer Society/corporate/National Cancer Institute mantras and the subconscious messages they relay: "Take your hormone replacement therapy (because your hot flashes are a disease, not a normal bodily function)." "Milk is good for you (even milk laced with bovine growth hormones)." "Implants can help breast cancer patients (because you'll be unattractive after your mastectomy)." "Early detection is the key to successful treatment of breast cancer (and we're not researching how to prevent it)."

These slogans, reinforced by media talk shows and print reports and brilliant public relations campaigns, program our national thinking about breast cancer. We can treat—not cure—cancer, but let's not think about what we have to do to prevent it. Thus, millions of homeowners willingly put toxic pesticides and herbicides on their lawns so the grass will be forever green, never questioning the connection between these chemicals and our cancer epidemic.

Also unquestioned is the trail of profits involved. Although billions of dollars are spent yearly on "cancer research," who will profit from the research? Not the public, which supports the research with tax dollars and contributions. And certainly not the doctors who propose nonconventional preventive and treatment methods.

Those who will profit include chemical companies that make not only the cancer-causing pesticides but also the chemotherapy drugs used to fight cancer. Others are major cancer research centers whose well-connected directors shape the national dialogue on cancer. Still others are officials of government agencies who enjoy revolving-door access to top industry positions when they leave government service.

This book is about the cancer establishment and its awesome power: oncology training at traditional medical schools and prototype cancer treatment centers such as Memorial Sloan-Kettering Cancer Center in New York; institutions like the American Cancer Society and the National Cancer Institute that either fund cancer research or establish research/treatment priorities; federal oversight agencies—such as the Federal Drug Administration, the Environmental Protection Agency, and the Department of Agriculture—whose leadership, corrupted by personal ambition, politics, and corporate clout, fail in their duties and compromise their mission. This book is also about those companies that poison us, with full knowledge that their toxic products and processes do us harm. These companies—chemical manufacturers and nuclear polluters—now own the major media, control the news stories, and enjoy a tight, interlocking relationship with the powerful. Systems are in place.

In essence, this book is about exposing systems that serve those who stand to profit from the application, sale, administration, and disposal of toxic substances to the detriment of the public health. We do not have to stand by helplessly as these forces endanger us. There are other ways.

# 2

# ARE YOU THE ONE IN EIGHT?

The Cassandra Michaels story may sound terrible to you, or it may sound terribly familiar. Because of the prevalence of cancer in our industrialized society, most people in the United States know of at least one person who has been afflicted with cancer. Many have lost close relatives and friends to the deadly disease, and others have watched neighbors of all ages wither and die from it.

Cancer is a silent disease, stealthily gripping in its lethal claws millions of humans around the world. In the United States, the American Cancer Society (ACS) projected that over 1.2 million new cancer cases in general were diagnosed just in 1994—not including skin cancers, which would add 700,000 more to the statistics.

Over half a million people die from cancer annually in the United States according to ACS's pamphlet *Cancer Facts and Figures—1994*; that translates to 1,400 people a day. Sources differ on the percentage of overall deaths caused by cancer: ACS says one out of every five deaths in the United States is from cancer; the Women's Community Cancer Project states the number is one in four. Devra Lee Davis, former senior advisor to the

Assistant Secretary of Health and Human Services and noted cancer researcher (now with the World Resources Institute), wrote in the February 9, 1994 issue of *JAMA*, "Recent birth cohorts of Americans aged 20 years and older are developing higher rates of all forms of cancer compared with those born just before the turn of the century." Since 1950, the overall cancer incidence has increased by 44 percent.

Breast cancer is now at epidemic proportions. One in eight American women has a lifetime risk of the disease. Each year, more than 44,000 women, or nearly one quarter of the 182,000 diagnosed, die from the disease. According to the advocacy group Breast Cancer Fund, an additional 1 million American women probably have the disease and do not know it. This means that, for hundreds of thousands of women, the disease will remain undiagnosed until much later in its development.

Since 1960, more than 950,000 American women have died from breast cancer. To put this in perspective, only 617,000 Americans died in all the wars our country has fought in this century! And shockingly, almost half of these deaths have occurred in the last ten years, according to the 1994 Breast Cancer Health Project Fact Sheet, sponsored by the Massachusetts Department of Public Health. Between 1981 and 1991, about 446,000 women died of breast cancer, according to the Cancer Prevention Coalition; in that decade, annual breast cancer deaths increased by approximately 32 percent.

But these overall numbers mask the dangerous trends that have been developing. The advocacy group Breast Cancer Action states that breast cancer is now the leading cause of death for women between the ages of 32 and 52. (It is a close second to lung cancer for all women.) Studies indicate that tumors in young women tend to be larger and recur more often, and scientists speculate that the cancers of young and old women may be different diseases because the tumors in young women are so much more aggressive. A woman diagnosed with breast cancer in her twenties or thirties is more likely to die from the disease than is a woman in her sixties or seventies.

And when you break the headlining statistics down even farther, the story they tell becomes even more frightening.

- In 1994, ACS stated that while lung cancer has been the leading cause of cancer increase in general, breast cancer leads the statistics in women.
- Breast cancer has become the most common form of cancer in North American women. In 1989, 142,000 women were diagnosed with breast cancer; in that year, 42,836 women died from the disease. In November 1993, *U.S. News and World Report* reported that 2.8 million American women were victims of breast cancer.
- According to ACS, of the approximately 180,000 women diagnosed in 1992, 57.8 percent were between 40 and 70 years old. Women older than 70 make up the next largest group—36 percent.
- From 1940 to 1980, breast cancer rates increased by an average of only 1.2 percent each year. But more recently, rates have skyrocketed, according to ACS. Since 1980, the rate of diagnosis in women has increased about 2 percent a year, reaching a level of about 108 per 100,000 (*Cancer Facts and Figures*, ACS, 1994). From 1980 to 1987 alone, the number of breast cancer cases reported in the U.S. rose by 32 percent.
- Breast cancer incidence is growing rapidly in virtually all of the world's industrialized countries. In 1980, an estimated 500,000 women worldwide died of breast cancer. By the year 2000, that figure is expected to double.
- In 1993, the National Cancer Institute (NCI) had the unpleasant duty to report that breast cancer rates among younger women are rising. Although women under the age of 40 still make up only 6.5 percent of those diagnosed, the long-range effects of this particular increase are devastating. Breast cancer patients under 35 have the poorest sur-

vival rate of any age group. And those who do survive live with the constant fear of recurrence and early death.

- NCI researchers state that increases in breast cancer incidence appear to be real—not mere artifacts of improved diagnosis, classification, or recordkeeping. In fact, a growing number of scientists are acknowledging that better screening simply cannot account for the steady increase in incidence.
- Fifty years ago, a woman's chance of getting breast cancer in her lifetime was one in 20. Thirty-five years ago, it was one in 15. A few years ago, when breast cancer began to garner some publicity, the chance was one in nine. Now it is one in eight.

One in eight. In the United States today, there are more than 130 million women of all ages. More than 16 million of them will develop breast cancer.

One in eight. On a typical suburban block with perhaps 25 families, three mothers will develop breast cancer. If each family has two daughters, six of them will develop the disease. In cities, these numbers will be duplicated in just one high-rise.

One in eight. In most elementary schools, the great majority of teachers are women. Assuming two teachers per grade, at least two teachers in any school will develop breast cancer. (In 1994, the American Federation of Teachers reported that teachers have nearly twice the rate of breast cancer deaths as the general population.)

One in eight.

What's behind this explosion in breast cancer incidence? If you listen to the pronouncements that issue from ACS, NCI, the drug companies, and other mainstream agencies, it is our fault. Our family history is to blame, or reproductive/hormonal factors, or fatty diet and alcohol. But the truth is that 70 percent of women with breast cancer are getting their disease from causes other than genetics, chemical imbalances, and lifestyle. For more than 120,000 American women a year, their cancers are caused by environmental poisons—manmade chemicals and radiation that have been produced and distributed worldwide. And the leaders of the "war on cancer" have known this for decades and have refused to deal with this information.

Since the dawn of the chemical age and the production of carcinogenic and hormone-manipulating substances, breast cancer has risen steadily. In 1964, the World Health Organization (WHO) concluded that 80 percent of cancers were due to human-produced carcinogens. In 1979, the National Institutes of Health (NIH) identified environmental factors as the major cause of most cancers. This information is not filtering through to the public.

Annual production rates for synthetic, carcinogenic, and other industrial chemicals exploded from 1 billion pounds in 1940 to more than 500 billion pounds annually during the 1980s. Since cancer has a latency period, it is safe and altogether logical to say the growing incidence corresponds to increased exposure to a variety of carcinogens found nearly everywhere. Despite official denials from NCI and ACS and studies generated by polluting industries, despite the billions of dollars in breast cancer research that ignores the causal connection between our toxic environment and breast cancer, the connection between certain toxins in our environment and the decline of women's health has become more and more obvious.

Industry, farms, and our very own well-kept lawns are the sources of discharges of hundreds of persistent, toxic chemicals into our food, water, and air. Both common chlorine-based organochlorines and low-level radioactive pollution have the potential for compromising the immune system.

The 1994 Environmental Protection Agency (EPA) reassessment of dioxin, another organochlorine, links exposure to this chemical to immune disfunction. Dioxins (there are actually more than 200 chemical cousins in this family—all of them toxic) are considered the chemical equivalent of nuclear radiation, and they are regularly produced as unwanted waste products of hundreds of industrial processes and products. They are endemic to our environment; they enter our bodies right along with the very elements we need to survive, and go right to work destroying our natural defenses. EPA analysts admit that every person in the United States has a body burden of dioxin that is reaching the potential for a health crisis.

Whatever new statistics each year brings, whatever "breakthrough" drug or treatment plan is ballyhooed in the media, the trend is plain: the epidemic of breast cancer will continue because our exposure to toxins continues.

As more and more women are understanding, a tiny lump in the breast is not the beginning of breast cancer. It is only the first tactile proof of the disease that has been growing for years. Because of the toxins in our environment, we all carry the seeds of our own sorrow.

The conclusion that toxic contaminants are significant (in fact, overriding) causes of breast cancer is one that the cancer establishment is reluctant to address. Industry condemns the studies pointing to environmental causes, and NCI has only recently started to focus on them. Here, according to the Women's Environment and Development Organization (WEDO), the advocacy group founded by Bella Abzug, are some of the conclusions of careful, professional, scientific studies that the cancer establishment is not telling you.

- In a Connecticut study, levels of PCBs and DDT were 50-60 percent higher in the breast tissue of women with breast cancer than in women without breast cancer.
- The EPA found that U.S. counties with waste sites were 6.5 times more likely to have elevated breast cancer rates than counties that did not have such sites.
- A Colorado study reported an association between electro-

magnetic field (EMF) exposure and female breast cancer. Male breast cancer (an extremely rare disease) may be linked to occupational exposure to EMF.

- Exposure to ionizing radiation can increase the risk of breast cancer, as shown by the increased breast cancer risk among Japanese atomic bomb survivors.
- In Israel, a ban on three carcinogenic pesticides may have been responsible for a 30 percent drop in breast cancer rates from 1976 to 1986.

Other groups have provided evidence from different perspectives. Greenpeace, for instance, in a 1992 release entitled "Breast Cancer and the Environment: The Chlorine Connection," noted several occupations that contribute to the breast cancer epidemic: "Women working in the petroleum, chemical, pharmaceutical, and electrical equipment manufacturing industries had significantly higher rates of breast cancer than the general public. . . . A study of 347 female chemists found breast cancer rates 63 percent higher than expected."

And a 1994 report sponsored by the NAACP and the United Church of Christ offers a geographical connection between breast cancer and environmental carcinogens. "Racial minorities are increasingly more likely than whites to live near hazardous waste sites in America," says Benjamin A. Goldman, co-author of the report. The report contained the following analysis:

In 1980, 25 percent of the people living in a neighborhood that contained one or more hazardous sites were non-white. By 1993, that figure had risen to 31 percent. Nationally, the average neighborhood is 14.4 percent minority. . . . The situation is getting worse as more people become aware of the controversies surrounding waste facilities. Fewer people want them in their communities, which, in some cases, forces plants to cluster in areas already hosting a facility. . . . Looking at Zip Code plots, the study found that about one-fourth of the 530 commercial hazardous waste treatment, storage, and disposal facilities in the U.S. were in neighborhoods where people of color were in the majority. Some 310 neighborhoods, or close to 60 percent, were above national average in terms of minority populations.

Why is this significant? NCI says the overall increase of 2.7 percent for female breast cancer among all races combined during the period 1973-1989 appears to be primarily due to a nearly 18 percent increase in the disease among black women. And for women younger than 40, blacks are 12 percent more likely than whites to get breast cancer, and 52 percent more likely to die from it. Common sense dictates that geography must be factored into any analysis of breast cancer.

There are many more studies that bring us to the same conclusion: it's the environment. The connection between our toxic, industrialized environment and cancer is compelling. Cancer-causing materials have been dumped into the environment and onto people for the past five decades—and today's statistics reflect the long-term development of cancer that exposure to these materials produces.

Accepting this basic principle means our attention must turn to prevention. As Devra Lee Davis stated in *JAMA*, "Preventing only 20 percent of all cancers in the United States each year would spare more than 200,000 people and their families from this often disfiguring and disabling disease."

# 3

# THE RISKS OF LIVING
# IN THE
# MODERN WORLD

**D**r. Judah Folkman, professor of cell biology at Harvard University, showed that cancer cells can survive in a dormant state. Years later, something triggers a sort of switch inside the cells, causing local blood vessels to multiply, nourishing the cancer.

What causes the switch to be thrown is critical to every woman.

## The "Thirty Percent" Crowd

Most women carry around a major misconception about breast cancer—that it is somehow their "fault" that they have or might get the disease. This belief is abetted by official pronouncements that breast cancer is correlated with genetics (family history) and lifestyle. There are certain *risk factors* acknowledged by all authorities that show up in approximately 30 percent of all breast cancer patients.

The factors are often separated into two divisions:

### *Risks That Cannot Be Controlled*

- Familial history

- Early onset of menarche
- Late onset of menopause
- Never becoming pregnant
- First full-term pregnancy after age 30
- Not breastfeeding an infant
- Obesity
- Timing of weight gain
- Height
- Personal history of ovarian or endometrial cancer

### Risks That Can Be Controlled

- Oral contraceptive use (especially in young women)
- Excessive alcohol consumption
- High-fat diet
- Abortion (not spontaneous); a controversial but reportable issue

But a risk factor is not a cause—it simply means that a woman's chance of getting breast cancer increases with the number of factors that she has.

So what is the connection between the risk factors and breast cancer? Strong evidence indicates that it is the levels of hormones—specifically estrogen—in women's bodies.

The word *hormone* comes from the Greek *hormon,* meaning "to excite," which is the role hormones play in the body. They produce the physical changes of adolescence, the sexual desire leading to reproduction, the hot flashes and mood swings of menopause in females, and the day-to-day energy production and metabolism of our lives.

Hormones are potent chemicals that serve as messengers from your brain telling your organs how to function. In *Natural Hormone Replacement,* Dr. Julian Whitaker states, "Over 50 individual hormones have been identified, and they stimulate, regulate, and control our vital bodily functions." They travel in the bloodstream, turning on and off critical bodily functions to maintain health and well-being. They control growth, development, and behavior. Taken together, the tissues and organs that produce and respond to hormones are called the endocrine system.

Whitaker goes on to explain the role of estrogen:

> Although we think of estrogen as a single hormone, it's actually an entire group or class of steroid hormones with very similar properties. The three major forms of estrogen that are active in the female body are estrone, estradiol, and estriol. Estradiol is the primary estrogen produced by the ovaries. Estrone is made by the adrenals and is also converted from estradiol in the intestinal tract. Estriol is primarily converted from estrone in the liver and from estradiol by a different route.

The class of estrogens is the common thread running through all of the risk factors of the 30 percent crowd.

*Familial history.* A history of breast cancer within a family may indicate a genetic connection, although this may be true in only 5-10 percent of cases. (Family history also seems to multiply other risk factors.) It is more likely that multiple incidence of breast cancer in a family arises from common exposure to a nearby source of contamination: the family might live downwind from an incinerator, a toxic dump, farm fields that are sprayed with pesticides, or a former nuclear installation, and the entire family certainly might be eating the same contaminated food. These contaminants, once in the body, act as toxic estrogens. (See below.)

*Timing of childbirth (or not having children).* Iris Schneider, an assistant director of NCI, says that those women who delay having their last child until 38 or later or who have no children have twice the risk of getting breast cancer compared with those who complete their families in their early twenties. (Lesbians, who are mostly childless, have two or three times the rate of breast cancer as heterosexual women do.) If your first pregnancy is after age 30, you are twice as likely to develop breast cancer as women who give birth before 30.

Your overall risk of breast cancer falls with the number of full-term pregnancies. Pregnancy is a detoxification route for the mother because of the transfer of chemicals to the fetus. So too is breastfeeding, since hormonal substances are passed to the infant through the mother's milk. (The flip side is that this may be one reason women are getting breast cancer at younger ages; they were nursed by their mothers who passed on dioxins, PCBs, and DDT.)

*Early onset of menarche.* Since the turn of the century, the average age at menarche in developed countries has fallen steadily. If you start menarche in your teens, rather than before the age of 12, your chances of getting breast cancer are lower. The primary issue is the activity of estrogen.

*Early menopause.* Ovarian function is also tied to breast cancer. Normal nonsurgical cessation of menses before the age of 45, or the surgical removal of a woman's ovaries before 40 confers a decreased risk of breast cancer. One study of 1,000 Brazilian women discussed by Dr. Graham Colditz of Harvard (*The Network News,* May/June 1994) showed that women who had natural menopause between 30 and 39 had a 32 percent reduction in risk compared with women who had a natural menopause between 45 and 54. Women who had a natural menopause by age 55 or older had twice the risk compared with those who had menopause before age 45. The common link again: hormones.

*Obesity, timing of weight gain, height.* Obesity is a serious national disease that contributes to more than 300,000 deaths a year. An article printed in the December 5, 1994 *Chicago Tribune* quoted former Surgeon General C. Everett Koop as saying, "More than a third of all [American] adults are obese. . . . Eleven percent of breast cancer can be attributed to obesity."

The timing of your weight gain also seems to be important. At the May 18, 1994 meeting of the American Society of Clinical Oncology, a group of researchers from the E. Lee Moffitt Cancer Center at the University of South Florida presented a paper entitled "Weight at Age 30 and Breast Cancer Risk." The study was conducted by Dr. Noreen Aziz and her colleagues, who stated, "We found that the most important decade in a woman's life was the third decade. . . . The significant association observed between excess weight in the third decade of life and beyond, with increased breast cancer risk, suggests that weight gain during this time period may be particularly important as a risk factor."

Height of greater than 68 inches has been associated with breast cancer for both young and old, according to an article by Dr. Louise Brinton, an epidemiologist at NCI, in a 1992 issue of *Annals of Epidemiology.* What factors are involved in increased size? Nutrition and hormones.

*Ovarian or endometrial cancer.* These cancers, linked to hormonal influence, have been confirmed with exposure to tamoxifen, DES, and postmenopausal hormones.

*Oral contraceptive use (especially in young women).* "If you stay on oral contraceptives for five years or more, know the increased estrogen levels are considered as associated with breast cancer," states Dr. Brinton. Since earlier preparations had higher levels of both estrogen and progesterone than do current products, the ultimate incidence and distribution of breast cancer linked to these products will not be revealed until the users reach menopause. However, increased risk with longer duration of use has been reported in most studies. (See C. Chilvers, "Oral Contraceptives and Cancer," *Lancet* 344, 1994.)

*Excessive alcohol consumption.* Two reports, both appearing in the *New England Journal of Medicine* of May 7, 1987, state that if you are over 40 and have more than two drinks of alcohol a day, you may have a 50 percent higher risk for breast cancer; three or more drinks a day and you may double your chances. Preliminary studies have proposed that increased alcohol consumption raises the concentrations of estrogen in the body.

*High-fat diet.* The foods from which most Americans get a high percentage of their daily calories are the fattiest foods—

meat, cheese, oils, fatty fish. These are the very foods that store poisons we unwittingly eat at our tables.

*Abortion (not spontaneous).* Information on this risk factor is not available from most breast cancer advocacy groups because abortion is so political. But the December 1995 issue of the conservative magazine *National Review* included a story on the connection between abortion and breast cancer with sufficient scientific backing as to be mentioned here.

The author, Joel Brind (professor of biology and endocrinology at Baruch College) speaks of a study by Dr. Janet Daling, et al., that "found a significant overall increase in breast cancer among Washington State women who had one or more induced abortions (as opposed to spontaneous abortions or miscarriages, which were not associated with increased risk)." Brind says that this study is not isolated, noting corroborating evidence from four Japanese epidemiological studies dating back to 1957.

Again, hormones play a crucial role in this story. Brind explains:

> The first trimester of a normal pregnancy is marked by a surge of hormones from the mother's ovaries, including progesterone, to maintain the pregnancy, and estrogen, which makes the breasts grow. Most known breast cancer risk factors act via some form of overexposure to estrogen. Normally the high estrogen levels of early pregnancy are counterbalanced by other hormones late in the pregnancy, which differentiate the breast into milk-producing organs, thus rendering them permanently less susceptible to cancer. However, if the pregnancy is artificially terminated, the growth-stimulating effects of the estrogen surge help primitive and/or abnormal cells to grow into potential cancers.

Spontaneous abortions are characterized by subnormal secretion of ovarian hormones, including estrogen, and Brind states, "The failure to distinguish between spontaneous and induced abortion is a fatal weakness in any study."

We could add all these risk factors together and still have to deal with the fact that more than *70 percent* of the women who develop breast cancer have none of these factors! While many officials at ACS, NCI, and other institutions that determine the national dialogue about breast cancer believe the increased numbers of breast cancer are merely the result of better screening and earlier detection, something else is going on.

## The Other Seventy Percent

What's going on is that for 70 percent of breast cancer patients, the cause of their illness is outside their bodies! Evidence compiled since 1990 points toward our environment and specific toxins that do serious damage.

### *Environmental Estrogens*

Certain environmental contaminants act like toxic hormones. These hormone-mimicking chemicals, when taken into the body through our food, water, and air, can trigger unnatural cell growth that can progress to cancer. We don't set out to ingest these chemicals; rather, we cannot escape them in our modern world.

Since 1990, evidence has been accumulating that a host of industrial chemicals—including many plastics, pesticides, and byproducts of combustion—mimic hormones. These hormone mimickers are capable of disrupting reproduction and development of humans and animals. Equally strong is the evidence that these same toxic estrogen mimickers can cause some of the most common cancers: prostate and testicular cancer in men and breast cancer in women.

The American Chemical Society reported on this in the April 19, 1993 issue of *Chemical & Engineering News*. Then came studies published by the National Institute of Environmental Health Sciences (NIEHS), in the October 1993 issue of *Environmental Health Perspectives*. And in its February 9, 1994 issue, *JAMA* published a study which stated, "Estrogen and [chemical] agents that mimic it appear to be more pervasive and problematic than ever suspected."

In the February 17, 1994 issue of *Rachel's Hazardous Waste News,* Peter Montague explained the danger:

> Hormones are chemical messengers, essential to the body's healthy operation and internal communication. Hormones are present at very low levels (parts per billion or even parts per trillion), and often for only short periods of time, yet they have very powerful, long-lasting effects on growth, development, and metabolism.
>
> The female hormone, estrogen, and chemicals that mimic estrogen, operate inside cells by fitting themselves into "estrogen receptors" (proteins) the way a key fits into a lock. Once the key is in the lock, the key-and-lock together can move into the nucleus of a cell and attach to the DNA, releasing messenger RNA which then causes a cascade of changes in cells, tissues, and organs throughout the body.
>
> . . . Examples of estrogen mimickers are DDT and its breakdown byproduct DDE; Kepone, dieldrin, methoxychlor; some PCBs and alkyl phenols from penta- to nonylphenol, as well as bisphenol-A (the building block of polycarbonate plastics), which is used in many common detergents, toiletries, lubricants, and spermicides. Many estrogen mimickers are persistent (they resist breaking down in the environment) and highly soluble in fat (causing them to accumulate in the bodies of fish, birds, mammals, and humans). Many of them cross the placental barrier and pass from the mother to the developing fetus. . . . Estrogen chemicals have a cumulative effect.

A number of established factors have emerged that are basic to understanding the effect of estrogenic compounds on our bodies:

- The higher the daily dose of estrogen, or estrogen-like compounds, the less time required for a cancer to develop. (This is true for exposure to other carcinogens as well.)
- The more constant the absorption of estrogen, the less time

it takes to develop cancer, and the smaller amount of hormone required.

- The greater the estrogenic potency of the chemical absorbed, the less time required to develop breast cancer.
- Estrogenic chemicals of radically different chemical structures can be similar in their hormonal action and are similar in their cancer-producing action.
- A variety of breast cancer cell types, all with the ability to metastasize, are produced by estrogen administration.
- Long-term, repeated administration of relatively small doses may intensify tissue response to hormonal substances.

During the 1980s, United States industries manufactured over 500 billion pounds a year of synthetic organic chemicals, many of which are carcinogens. By comparison, in 1940 only 1 billion pounds were produced. Thanks to modern industrial practices that place profit before public health, we are exposed to thousands of industrial emissions that are toxic and carcinogenic. Most of these compounds have never been tested for their safety or their effects on the human body.

The industries involved have littered the entire landscape of the United States with some 50,000 toxic waste landfills (20,000 of which are recognized as potentially hazardous), 170,000 industrial impoundments (ponds, pits, and lagoons), 7,000 underground injection wells, and some 2.5 million underground gasoline tanks, many of which are leaking. These industries manufacture products and use processes that are taken for granted in our modern industrial state: plastics (especially PVCs), products bleached with chlorine, metal mining and processing, nuclear fission products, and petrochemicals.

Due to the action of wind and water, toxic pollutants can now be found almost everywhere, even the most remote areas of the globe. And thanks to the accumulative exposure to thousands of toxic contaminants, all beings are imperiled. We can no longer hide from the stark reality that the air we breathe, the water we drink, the food we eat, and the places where we work may be profoundly contaminated. As the contamination increases, so will the cancer statistics.

How has all this contamination come to be? During the past two decades, the American people have put their faith in federal and state laws and regulations that limit, but do not stop, the release of toxic pollutants. This philosophy is euphemistically called "pollution control," and it permits releases of toxic chemicals into the environment as long as the amount of each release stays below the levels considered "acceptable" by regulators— government and industry officials who work hand in glove together.

The release of toxins below permitted levels—once—is one thing. But this philosophy does not admit the actuality that many pollutants persist in the environment, remaining harmful for decades and accumulating in the bodies of all living things. For instance, dioxins bioaccumulate in fish at concentrations 159,000 times higher than in the water they swim in. Those beings who are higher up on the food chain accumulate ever-higher concentrations. Humans, of course, are at the top of the chain, and so reap the greatest share of this toxic harvest. According to Greenpeace, we carry in our bodies toxins at concentration levels thousands or even millions of times greater than in the surrounding environment.

Devra Lee Davis is one of many researchers who thinks it's time to put more emphasis on the environmental causes of breast cancer. "We're spending $22 billion on the war on cancer and the bulk of that is in treatment," she says. "And as of 1993, the five-year survival rate for advanced breast cancer has not improved in two decades. It's time we changed public policy to ask how to prevent cancer. It makes sense to say the environment may be playing a role in human breast cancer. The weight of evidence, the hundreds of articles on experimental animals and the growing literature on humans all point in the same direction."

A large number of the articles that Davis mentions report on independent research done in the United States, Finland, Sweden, and Israel that have identified a specific group of chemical pollutants as being particularly dangerous to humans. They are called *organochlorines:* compounds in which chlorine is bonded to the carbon-rich organic matter of which living things are made. (They are also called *chlorinated organic compounds* and *chlorinated hydrocarbons.*) They include thousands of persistent chemical products and byproducts. These compounds resist breakdown for decades and even centuries.

They concentrate in fatty tissues and multiply in concentration as they move up the food chain. Greenpeace reports that at least 177 organochlorines have been identified in the fat, breast milk, blood, semen, and breath of the general American and Canadian population, and many of them have been shown to cause or promote breast cancer. As Greenpeace notes, "The worldwide increase in breast cancer rates has occurred during the same period in which the global environment has become contaminated with industrial synthetic chemicals, including the toxic and persistent organochlorines."

These industrial chemicals that mimic human hormones are called *xenoestrogens,* and they have the potential to disrupt the human endocrine system. (The Greek root *xeno-* means "foreign.") DDE for example, has the same chemical structure as a hormone. It stimulates estrogen, which in turn stimulates breast cells, which then proliferate rapidly. Other chemicals mimic hormones, tricking the body and promoting cell growth. Once inside our bodies, they weaken our defenses and wreak their harm: cancer, hormonal disruption, immunological abnormalities, and birth defects. They are silent, insidious enemies.

### DDT and Its Cousins

DDT (dichloro-diphenyl-trichloro-ethane), a colorless, odorless chemical compound, was discovered in 1939 to have powerful insecticidal properties. The military used it during World War II to combat the malaria that was affecting troops in the Pacific theater. The results were sensational, and the disease was virtually eradicated in many areas in which it had been endemic.

In 1944, the Geigy Corporation patented DDT and touted it to agricultural interests and the general public as an easy way to rid themselves of insects—disease-bearing or not. Eventually, the use of DDT was expanded to nearly all foodstuffs, vegetable and animal, as well as into commercial and home pest-control and moth-proofing. Women living in Long Island, New York and other suburban areas now showing a high incidence of breast cancer well remember the DDT trucks lumbering down their streets spraying everything in sight during the 1960s.

However, like all powerful insecticides, DDT's negative aspects began to appear early on. DDT killed "good" insects as well as "bad." And the insects that survived were resistant to the pesticide. Pest control agencies fought back, increasing the amount of chemical used and developing new formulations, causing new rounds of mutations in the insects. All too soon, the insects began developing resistance to all chemical pesticides. Despite this trend, chemical dependency eased out traditional methods of pest control.

By 1969, the results of the DDT blitz had become so damaging that a blue-ribbon Department of Health, Education and Welfare commission on pesticides recommended that the use of DDT be discontinued because of insect resistance and the chemical's toxic effects and persistence. Three years later, DDT use was banned in the United States. (Sweden banned DDT in 1970; by the mid-1970s, Japan and most European countries had banned it too.) However, production of DDT and its relatives continues worldwide, and it is readily available today, even in the United States. The 1995 *Farm Chemical Handbook* identifies at least three international companies with offices in the United States that continue to manufacture DDT. Even if it were not available, it is still with us. The compound has a half-life of seven years, at which time it has decomposed to the compound DDE, which is useless but also highly toxic. It takes up to 30 years to eliminate these compounds from the environment.

Repeated moderate doses of DDT can result in greater total storage in the fat than a single fatal dose, reports W. J. Hayes in his 1982 book *Pesticides Studied in Man.* And DDT and associated organochlorines can be excreted in the breast milk of all animals tested, including cows and humans. This load of hormonally active chemicals is transferred via the placenta to the developing fetus, and via the milk to the nursing infant.

### *Polychlorinated Biphenyls (PCBs)*

PCBs are another group of organochlorines that are extremely dangerous to humans. Like the other organochlorines, PCBs behave as toxic estrogens, can pass the placenta into the developing baby, are concentrated in breast milk, and are directly connected to breast cancer. According to researchers Chris Waller, Deborah Minor, and James McKinney, writing in the July 1995 issue of *Environmental Health Perspectives,* PCBs and related compounds should be considered "environmental toxicants due to their interaction with hormone receptors."

Manufactured in the U.S. by Monsanto at its plants in Sauget, Illinois and Anniston, Alabama, PCBs have been sold under a number of trade names, including Arochlor, Clophen, Fenclor, Inerteen, Kanechlor, and Phenoclor. Because of their resistance to deterioration and fire, they have been used extensively in electrical transformers and capacitors in large electrical power systems, such as those in locomotives and generating plants, as well as in many smaller devices, such as electric utility lines, air conditioners, and fluorescent lights. But this doesn't begin to describe their presence in the environment—PCBs were also incorporated into hydraulic and heat transfer systems, gas turbines, vacuum pumps, plasticizers in adhesives, textiles, sealants, paints, printing inks, and carbonless carbon paper.

PCBs may contain one or more chlorine atoms. The more chlorine atoms in the compound, the more resistant it is to breakdown—and the more toxic it is. Because of their wide-spread industrial and commercial use, PCBs are now considered ubiquitous in the environment. That is one reason why firefight-ers are so careful when battling fires in electrical generating facilities—the PCBs in the burning material is released into the air and can be breathed into the body.

An important study by Drs. Frank Falck, Mary Wolff, and associ-ates was published in the March 1992 issue of *Archives of Environmental Health*. It further identified the connection between organochlorines and breast cancer. It was a pilot study to measure and compare levels of chemical residues in breast fat tissue from women with malignant and nonmalignant breast dis-ease. Forty women who had been seen for palpable breast mass-es in 1987 were examined by the investigators. They found that the tissues of women with breast cancer showed concentrations of PCBs, DDT, DDE, and other hydrocarbon-based pesticides 50-60 percent higher than normal. "The results," the team wrote, ". . . suggest a role for environmentally derived suspect carcino-gens in the genesis of mammary carcinoma. . . ."

The levels found in this study (DDT, 216 parts per billion; DDE, 2,200 ppb; PCBs, 1,965 ppb) are about 1,000 times higher than the levels the FDA considers safe in food. Falck concluded, "Perhaps it wasn't fat that was the culprit [in breast cancer] but what was *in* the fat."

Mary Wolff repeated the study and published similar results in the April 21, 1993 issue of the *Journal of the NCI*. Her conclu-sions:

> Environmental accumulation of DDT and PCB residues has been documented for at least three decades. Levels in the U.S. and Europe have diminished since the late 1970s as a result of government regulation, but human exposure is still common. Since elimination of body burden is slow, taking several decades, consequent health risks may continue for a long time after exposure; therefore cancer, with its long latency, has

been of particular concern. Our observations provide important new evidence relating low-level environmental contamination with organochlorine residues to the risk of breast cancer in women. Given the widespread dissemination of organochlorines in the environment, these findings have immediate and far-reaching implications for public health intervention worldwide.

A landmark Israeli study corroborates Falck's and Wolff's conclusions. In 1976, Dr. M. Wasserman and colleagues, publishing in the *Bulletin of Environmental Contamination and Toxicology,* showed that three organochlorine pesticides that produced over a dozen types of cancer in 10 different strains of rats and mice were present in extraordinarily high concentrations in Israeli milk and dairy products. The three—BHC (benzene hexachloride), lindane, and DDT—were present for 10 years or more at concentrations up to 100 times higher than those found in American dairy products. Concentrations in Israeli breast milk were possibly 800 times greater than in American breast milk.

BHC and lindane had been shown to be carcinogenic at dietary doses as low as 10 and 80 parts per million, respectively. DDT had been shown to be carcinogenic and mutagenic in repeated animal studies. Workers exposed to DDT were found to have significant increases in chromosomal aberrations in their lymphocytes. Embryos, fetuses, and infants are particularly vulnerable to the carcinogens. One report indicated that organochlorine pesticides accumulate in the fetus to levels more than 100 percent higher than those found in the mother.

Despite the research, Israel continued to allow almost unrestricted use of both lindane and BHC. By 1975, lindane concentrations in human milk averaged more than 850 ppb. (By contrast, levels of lindane in American breast milk were 8 ppb, still a dangerously high amount.) The primary source of breast-milk contamination was cow's milk.

Neither the Ministry of Health (MoH) nor the Israel Cancer Association (ICA) made any moves to warn the public or change the situation. In fact, the MoH and the Director of its National Food Administration withheld the findings from the public for more than a year and denied the existence of any problems, despite numerous attempts to get access to the data by Consumer Shield, a small, feisty Israeli consumer organization.

The information did finally get out, and the public outcry forced the government to ban these three organochlorines. The result was a precipitous drop in the concentrations of these substances in Israeli cow's milk. By 1980, concentrations of lindane had dropped 90 percent in breast milk in Jerusalem, DDT levels had decreased 43 percent, and BHC had dropped an estimated 98 percent.

Breast cancer rates also went down dramatically. Of 28 European and Middle Eastern countries surveyed, only Israel recorded a true decrease in rates between 1976 and 1986. "Epidemiological and laboratory findings are consistent with the possibility that the dramatic drop in breast cancer mortality rates that occurred in Israel subsequent to the pesticide ban is a direct result of that ban." This dramatic drop—more than 30 percent—in age-specific breast cancer mortality rates among women below 44 years old "suggests the occurrence of a dramatic change in the environment or in lifestyle, especially coming, as it does, in the wake of a 25-year period of continually increasing rates," according to Jerome Westin of Hebrew University Hadassah Medical School. He also pointed out that "if action had been taken earlier, the lives of hundreds if not thousands of Israeli women might have been saved."

The scientists who studied pesticides in Israel made one more powerful observation: all known factors contributing to breast cancer affect estrogen. The connection is stated by Greenpeace:

Exposure to hormonally active organochlorines early in life, especially in utero when hormonal feedback systems are being imprinted, can result in permanent alteration of systems that control estrogen and other sex hormones. Studies show increased risk of breast cancer among women born to mothers with indications of high estrogen levels during pregnancy. [Thus,] the transfer of accumulated organochlorines from mother to daughter may indeed contribute to breast cancer.

## *Dioxins*

Dioxins—chemical compounds that always include chlorine— are profoundly toxic, even at the smallest concentrations. They affect the body in many ways.

Dioxins are a factor in breast cancer because they affect hormones. Since dioxin is extremely toxic, the minutest amounts can damage cells. It possess anti-estrogenic properties, binding to a critical portion of a cell called the Ah receptor, altering the function of the cell. Several chemicals act similarly on the Ah receptor, displaying both carcinogenic and anti-estrogenic effects, as reported by Dr. K. Chaloupka and colleagues in a 1992 issue of *Carcinogenesis.*

The latest evidence on this toxic compound is that it attacks the immune system at extremely low doses and that, acting like an environmental hormone, it can disrupt normal cell physiology, enhancing abnormal cell growth. It also appears to cause cancer by amplifying the activities of other carcinogens.

A study by Manz, et al. on 1,583 dioxin-exposed German workers, published in the October 19, 1991 issue of *The Lancet,* revealed a cancer rate 39 percent above the norm. Among German workers 20 years on the job, the rate was 82 percent above the norm, and among the most heavily exposed German workers, the cancer rate was three times the norm. In female workers, the risk of breast cancer was doubled.

And the evidence keeps amassing. The February 1996 issue of *Environmental Health Perspectives* published a study by Kang, Wilson, and associates identifying DDT, dieldrin, and toxaphene as having potential for promoting tumors in human breast tissue by suppressing the body's natural anticarcinogenic actions. The authors identified these chemicals as "pollutants in the Great Lakes [that] have found their way through the food chain into humans because of their environmental persistence...."

In the early 1990s, the pulp and paper industry—under pressure from mounting lawsuits—had prodded the EPA to reassess its analysis of dioxin. The EPA hired independent scientists to study dioxin's properties on a number of levels. To the manufacturer's dismay, in September 1994, the EPA published its reassessment, admitting that the family of dioxins is extremely toxic, and that the dioxin TCDD (tetrachlorodibenzo-p-dioxin) is the most toxic substance known to man. The 1994 report not only affirms its carcinogenic properties, it states that in the most minute quantities, dioxin is capable of disrupting the immune, endocrine, and reproductive systems, including decreased sperm counts in male animals. (A 1992 article in *Science News* stated that TCDD's suppressive effect on the immune system may possibly be more important than its carcinogenicity.)

The research done by the independent scientists was damning. The final EPA report, however, took into consideration the political aspects of the issue and softened the findings. Carefully worded though the EPA report was, the evidence is still compelling, and a reading of it still produces the strong sense that the dioxin in our bodies is creating a national health crisis.

Dioxins are an entire family of chemicals, most of which are formed during the manufacture or burning of chlorinated products. Although TCDD is the most toxic of the group, it is by no means the only harmful family member: there are at least 209 other forms of dioxin. However, government regulators and industry scientists frequently test only for TCDD in their products and in the environment. Therefore, the total biological effect on our population is greatly underestimated.

The EPA considers the main sources of dioxins to be medical and municipal waste incinerators, although all incinerators spew out dioxins along with host of toxic heavy metals. The burning of any chlorine-containing materials—municipal, household, or medical—generates dioxins. These toxic emissions leave the smokestack and are carried by wind and rain to earth, where they are absorbed by soil and plants. The plants are fed to cattle, sheep, and poultry, polluting the human food chain. (The EPA quietly admits that beef is a significant avenue of contamination.) Once dioxins are in a woman's body, they are concentrated even more in her body fat. Because breast tissue is so fatty, the poisons are passed on to nursing infants through the breast milk. And one of the most insidious actions is the concentration in breast milk in higher levels than are found in the foods adults eat, as noted by Beth Baker in the Fall 1994 *Environmental Action.*

A great hue and cry was made over Agent Orange, the herbicide that was used during the Vietnam War and which affected thousands of American soldiers. This product is composed of two chemical compounds known as 2,4-D and 2,4,5,T. Dioxin is the inevitable contaminant in these compounds—when you produce these compounds, dioxin is an automatic byproduct. What was not acknowledged is that these herbicides have been used worldwide on rangelands, forests, crops, and rice fields for defoliating unwanted growth. Closer to home, other dioxin cousins are employed as antibacterial and preservative agents, including the popular wood preservative pentachlorophenol, which is commonly used to treat lumber. Thus, the wood on your backyard deck may be full of dioxin. Other common household products that may contain at least trace levels of the compound include cotton garments (pentachlorophenol having been used in growing and processing the cotton, according to Greenpeace), disposable diapers, tampons, and paper coffee filters, and most other items that have been bleached during production.

All of these toxins are bad enough alone, but when they are combined (as they are in our environment), there effects are enhanced incredibly. A study published in the June 7, 1996 *Science* showed that combinations of these compounds can be up to *1,000 times as potent* in producing breast cancer as the individual compounds. Presently, EPA monitors environmental chemicals one at a time.

## Synthetic Hormones

There are other chemicals that were and are manufactured by drug companies, administered by physicians, and approved by the FDA that serve to create the same toxic responses as do environmental estrogens. These are the synthetic hormones.

Why would anyone produce synthetic estrogens? Because these products are salable and on the surface appear to answer an entire panoply of medical needs that women may have—despite their known negative effects on human and animal health.

### *DES*

Since the epidemic in breast cancer seems to be the result of an accumulation of past carcinogenic exposures, the best place to start is with the toxic synthetic hormone diethylstilbestrol (DES). This is a particularly significant compound because for a time it was considered the answer not only to various "female" problems, but was one of the first synthetic hormones to be given to animals. DES was prescribed for the prevention of miscarriages, the treatment of postmenopausal "complications," headaches, dizziness, nervousness, depression, frigidity, insomnia, muscle and joint pains, vaginitis, gonorrhea, and infertility. It was also prescribed to prevent conception, and was given to cattle, pigs, and poultry to promote weight gain.

And it was a public health disaster.

DES is no longer on the market. However, it still has potential to cause breast cancer because of the disease's latency period—the time between initial exposure to a carcinogen and the discovery of a cancer. Thus, women who took DES (or whose mothers took DES) may discover that they have breast cancer 20 or more years after the exposure.

DES was very cheap to make, affording huge profits to those companies that sold it. As a consequence, before it was finally banned, DES had crept into the lives of hundreds of thousands of women who have become victims of corporate greed and a compliant FDA.

Synthetic hormones are not a recent phenomenon. As early as 1929, scientists had isolated estrogenic substances from urine, and by 1934 two English doctors, Cook and Dodos, showed estrogenic activity in at least eight different forms of a stilbene preparation, a forerunner of DES. Once researchers understood the basic formula of the stilbenes, it was a relatively simple matter to add other chemicals to make the compound more potent and more marketable. The diethylstilbestrol form of the chemical showed activity 400 times greater than that of any natural estrogen, lending itself to attractive commercial development.

There were major risks, though. More than 50 years ago, researchers found DES to have dangerous properties in animals, including cancer of the breast and testes. DES-dosed rabbits developed genital cancers. Additional DES studies carried out by NCI produced breast cancer in animals. Nobel laureate Dr. Hans Selye had noted abnormal liver findings, as well as a high rate of mortality among DES-treated mice. He wrote in a 1939 article in the *Canadian Medical Association Journal,* "it is well for the physician to realize that estrogens do not only affect the sex organs but have general systemic effects, and that weight per weight, diethylstilbestrol proved more toxic in the majority of our experiments than" the natural estrogens. Over the years, research has shown that DES can cause cancers at many different sites: breast, ovary, vagina, uterus, testes, and kidney. Even so, the FDA approved DES for commercial use in 1941.

By 1947, Eli Lilly had submitted an application to use stilbestrol for the "prevention of toxemia of pregnancy and abortion," despite a published finding (*Lancet* 2:788, 1939) that a form of stilbestrol caused abortion in cattle. This was followed by many corroborating reports, citing nausea, elevation of blood cholesterol, and darkening of the breasts of babies born to mothers who had been give stilbestrol—an ominous sign of estrogen stimulation of the fetus.

Through the 1950s, evidence kept mounting that DES did not do what it was touted as doing. For instance, separate studies by J. Ferguson and by W. Dieckmann, et al., both reported in the *American Journal of Obstetrics and Gynecology* in 1953, indicated that DES did not alter the course of pregnancy. And in 1957, W. Meissner and associates at the New England Deaconess and Massachusetts Memorial Hospitals published a damning report in the journal *Cancer* concerning uterine disease that was developing postpartum in women who had been treated with "depot" estrogens during pregnancy. Meissner's team tested DES on rabbits, and found that the subjects developed the same genital diseases—polyps, hyperplasia, metaplasia, and cancer—as were seen in the DES-dosed women.

Despite this research, approximately 1 million pregnant women were given DES in the 1960s. In 1970, however, Harvard physicians Herbst and Scully tentatively linked the administration of DES to pregnant women to cancer in their daughters. Their report in *Cancer* discussed an extremely rare cancer of the vagina which had occurred in seven young women aged 15 to 22. The next year, two studies—one by Herbst, et al. and the other by P. Greenwald and colleagues, both in the *New England Journal of Medicine*—definitely confirmed the link between maternal DES exposure and cancer in daughters.

However, the one-size-fits-all attitude of the DES manufacturers kept expanding. Around the same time that DES was identified as a human carcinogen, it was being touted as a contraceptive by the directors of student health services in Canada at the University of Alberta and in the United States at the University of Michigan (Kuchera, *JAMA*, 1971). Suppression of lactation in women who did not breastfeed their babies became another goal, proposed as early as 1939 (Wenner, *Lancet*, 1939). Despite documentation showing the ineffectiveness of estrogens in preventing breast engorgement symptoms, these products are still recommended in commerce today.


By the 1950s, DES had become a major food additive. It was used in cows to increase milk production, and in steer, swine, and poultry to increase weight, despite reports of adverse effects on the animals. DES was promoted to fatten both chickens and cockerels to upgrade an entire market, although as early as 1947 a hormonal effect had been demonstrated in women who consumed poultry treated with DES (Bird, *Endocrinology,* 1947).

In 1971, Judah Folkman estimated that three-quarters of the 40 million cattle slaughtered yearly were treated with DES (Folkman, *New England Journal of Medicine,* 1971). DES had become a ubiquitous element in our food supply, distributed without caution.

It was not until December 1973 that Congress banned DES-laced food. (During congressional hearings that year before the Committee on Governmental Operations, it was revealed that the FDA had rejected the recommendations of its own Advisory Panel on Carcinogenesis, delaying the removal of DES from the food supply.) Despite this, more than a decade after its banning, tax-supported research into the use of DES in cattle was still being conducted (Rumsey, 1985). And although the use of DES has been banned, other synthetic hormones have taken its place.

### *Menopause and Hormone Replacement Therapy*

You've got hot flashes. You can't sleep at night although you're tired all day. You're a bit edgy, and you're feeling somewhat depressed. You may be losing bone density, you may be at greater risk for heart disease, and you're even suffering from some incontinence and vaginal dryness. According to an article in the May 1995 issue of *Natural Health,* you are one of the estimated 35 million American women who are experiencing the symptoms of menopause.

You enter menopause—a normal consequence of aging—when the estrogen in your body starts to diminish. Ovarian production of estrogen slows, and though adrenal production increases, the adrenal estrogen is much weaker than the ovarian. The resulting low estrogen levels increase your risks for a number of conditions, all part of the general menopause syndrome.

And that's when some doctor begins to treat you as if you have a disease. The recommended "treatment" is very often estrogen therapy, or hormone replacement therapy (HRT). The drugs of choice are the synthetic hormones Premarin and progesterone.

If you are approaching menopause, your doctor may give you a full-color videotape and booklet containing sample tablets of Premarin from the manufacturer, Wyeth-Ayerst, the corporation that bills itself as providing "worldwide leadership in female healthcare." They may be right on one level: more than 5 million women currently take Premarin, and the company's pamphlet "What Every Woman Should Know About Estrogen" claims that the drug is prescribed by doctors six times more often than any other estrogen product. (These products, including Amnestrogen, Conestron, Estrifol, and Genisis, have been identified as carcinogenic by the National Technical Program, Fourth Annual Report on Carcinogens, 1985.) But whether it promotes health care is subject to serious debate.

Traditionally trained doctors are usually happy to recommend Premarin or progesterone. Millions of women will take these synthetic hormones in the hopes that their symptoms will go away, that bone loss will be stopped, that their hearts will be stronger. And many of them will be able to avoid the symptoms of that natural life change.

But, these little pills are not risk-free. In bold print, the book touting Premarin states, "Majority of studies have not shown an increased risk of breast cancer with low doses of estrogen used after menopause." The fine print of the package insert, however, tells a different story:

Some studies have suggested a possible increased incidence of breast cancer in those women on estrogen therapy taking higher doses for prolonged periods of time. . . . The reported endometrial cancer risk among estrogen users was about fourfold or greater than in nonusers and appears dependent on duration of treatment and on estrogen dose. There is no significant increased risk associated with the use of estrogens for less than one year. The greatest risk appears associated with prolonged use—five years or more. In one study, persistence of risk was demonstrated for 10 years after cessation of estrogen treatment.

Contrary to what the company literature implies, there is a great deal of evidence linking HRT to breast cancer. According to Dr. Julian Whitaker, editor of the monthly alternative health newsletter *Health & Healing,* there have been at least 30 such studies, all of which have revealed an increase in breast cancer risk of from 1 percent to 30 percent. The adverse effects from postmenopausal use of estrogens have been well-documented, indicating an elevated risk after only two years of use and a twentyfold increase in endometrial cancer after 10-15 years of replacement therapy (Weiss, *JAMA,* 1979).

One study is especially telling. Prolonged use of HRT—more than five years—doubles the risk of breast cancer, according to a 14-year follow-up from an ongoing Nurses Health study conducted at the Harvard Medical School and reported in the April 1994 issue of *Oncology News.* In women who have used HRT for less than four years, the increased breast cancer risk is minimal, according to Dr. Graham Colditz, the lead researcher of the study. But five to nine years of hormone use raised breast cancer risk 59 percent, with an additional 35 percent risk in HRT users who are 55 or older.

Perhaps that's why Dr. Melody Cobleigh and associates of Rush-Presbyterian-St. Luke's Medical Center in Chicago maintain that it is time to study the effects of estrogen replacement therapy in breast cancer survivors. In the case of women with cancer, might there be an acceleration of cancer because of the introduction of estrogen into their bodies? Might the so-called benefit of estrogen replacement hasten the deaths of women already suffering with breast cancer? These questions must be answered before any more women plunge headlong into menopause "therapy."

Adding to the concerns about HRT is a 1996 report published in the *Journal of the NCI.* Epidemiologists at the University of Washington in Seattle looked at the medical records of 8,779 women over the age of 50 and found that the use of HRT seemingly decreased the efficacy of mammograms because of the increased breast density that HRT frequently promotes. The group found that four of 13 cancers in women currently taking HRT were not detected by mammogram, as opposed to only two of 34 cancers that went undetected in women who had never had HRT.

A more appropriate question is whether postmenopausal women without specific medical conditions that necessitate HRT need synthetic estrogens at all? The sellers of these products emphasize estrogen's role in osteoporosis and heart disease. These are undeniably significant problems.

For women who legitimately need HRT, Dr. Whitaker advises them to take a compound of estrogens made up of estriol (80 percent), estrone (10 percent), and estradiol (10 percent). Estriol is weaker than the other estrogens; thus the combination with small amounts of estrone and estradiol, which Whitaker feels will "dramatically improve its effectiveness." The combination is called "tori-estrogen" or "tori-est" and can be made by any compounding pharmacy. (A compounding pharmacy is one that actually formulates, or compounds, drugs. Contact Professionals and Patients for Customized Care, 713-933-8400).)

Also recommended is natural progesterone, not the synthetic Prover, the most popular brand of progestin, which is listed in the *Physicians Desk Reference* as having no less than 30 possible adverse side effects. Prover, the synthetic progestin, is unable to synthesize other hormones or help the body produce the other hormones it needs to function at full potential. Natural progesterone can be taken as a transdermal cream or by eating yams and soybeans—plants that contain large amounts of natural progesterone which are exact chemical copies of the progesterone produced by your body.

However, if your symptoms are not as severe as you may be led to believe, it's quite possible that postmenopausal heart disease and bone loss can be controlled with careful diet, calcium supplements, no smoking, and adequate exercise. (The August 1996 issue of *Women's Health Advocate* includes a concise table showing how to deal with menopause symptoms through diet, lifestyle changes, and supplements and herbs. Write to Aurora Publications, 3918 Prosperity Avenue, Fairfax, VA 22031.) The benefits of these noninvasive activities are just now being studied.

A recent study by Ettinger and Grady suggests it's better not to even start the HRT program. In the October 14, 1993 issue of the *New England Journal of Medicine,* the two researchers state that, in order to stop the normal thinning of bone mass that occurs with age, women who start HRT must continue therapy for the rest of their lives: "Discontinuation of hormone use results in rapid bone loss to the level that would have occurred had no hormones ever been taken."

And another study reported by the Associated Press in December 1994 indicates the way to avoid a broken hip is to pump some iron. The study, conducted at the Jean Mayer Human Nutrition Research Center on Aging at Tufts University in Boston, found that postmenopausal women who used exercise machines intensively only two times a week for a year built up their bones, increased the size and power of their muscles, and improved their balance. Physiologist Miriam Nelson, the study leader, said, "The study shows for the first time that a single treatment can improve several risk factors for spine and hip fractures in older women." Nelson also said that she and her colleagues have developed exercises that can be done at home using simple, low-cost leg weights and dumbbells.

As for heart disease, the advocacy group National Women's Health Network states, "The FDA has not approved any form of estrogen for heart disease prevention because the studies conducted to date do not measure up to the standards typically used to prove a drug is effective. Even less is known about the effects of progestons on heart disease. Many women with obvious risk factors for cardiovascular disease, including heart disease, were told not to take estrogen because of FDA labeling warnings about problems with blood clots and high blood pressure."

And as for your sex life, the Network adds, "The alternatives to drug therapy include the application of vitamin E oil, the use of water-soluble lubricants during intercourse, and . . . regular sexual activity [which] helps relieve vaginal dryness and prevents discomfort during intercourse." Hardly the stuff of profitable pharmaceutics.

## Bovine Growth Hormones

The latest and perhaps most insidious corporate threat to public health is Monsanto's 1994 license to manufacture and literally force farmers to use recombinant bovine growth hormones (rBGH)—called Posilac—in cows with the dubious rationale that the cows will produce more milk. It's the biggest FDA-licensed, untested experiment on human health ever. In this experiment there are no control groups, since nearly all Americans are ingesting hormone-laced milk either through milk and other dairy products, hamburger meat from contaminated cows, and various processed foods such as baked goods and baby formula.

The genetically engineered Posilac was approved by the FDA in November 1993 and went on sale in February 1994 despite opposition from the American Public Health Association and countless consumer groups because Posilac contaminates milk with excessive levels of insulin-like growth factor 1 (IGF-1). The FDA made its decision on the safety of rBGH milk in 1985, when there had been no consideration of the effect of IGF-1 on cell proliferation and inadequate studies. Since then, several other countries, including Norway, Sweden, Denmark, the Netherlands, and parts of Canada, have banned its commercial use.

Independent scientists have researched the literature and have found studies, many by industry itself, demonstrating some unpleasant side effects from the introduction of the hormones. Dr. Sam Epstein, professor of occupational and environmental medicine at the University of Illinois, reviewed the FDA's efforts at "studying" Posilac and has called the agency's studies "flawed" and tainted by a "misleading presentation of the data," as reported in an article in the *Los Angeles Times.* Among other criticisms, Epstein noted that the dose units for test and control animals were "incomparable." (In fact, after discovering these problems, the Hazelton Laboratories, which conducted the study on which the FDA based its opinion about the nontoxicity of IGF-1, refused to comply with a May 1994 Congressional request for an unabridged copy of its 1988 report.) Epstein, who is an internationally recognized authority on toxic and carcinogenic effects of environmental pollutants, has also suggested that rBGH milk would expose infants and young children to levels of IGF-1 substantially above safety margins, for when rBGH milk is pasteurized, IGF-1 levels are increased and the milk becomes more bioactive.

In addition, there is a very ominous potential connection to breast cancer, as Epstein pointed out in a February 14, 1994 letter to FDA Commissioner David Kessler:

> I am writing to express grave concerns about the risk of breast cancer from consumption of BST [another name for rBGH] milk. These concerns are based on the following scientific considerations:
>
> BST administration induces a sustained increase in levels of an uncharacterized insulin growth factor (IGF-1) in milk. . . .
>
> BST administration induces prominent uptake of IGF-1 by specific receptors in breast epithelium.

IGF-1 induces rapid division and multiplication of cultured human breast epithelial cells.

IGF-1 induces malignant transformation of normal human breast epithelial cells.

IGF-1 is a growth factor for human breast cancer cells, maintaining their malignancy, progression, and invasiveness. IGF-1 has been similarly associated with colon cancer. . . .

The undifferentiated prenatal and infant breast is particularly susceptible to hormonal influences. Such imprinting by IGF-1 may not only constitute a direct breast cancer risk factor, but may also increase the sensitivity of the breast to subsequent unrelated risk factors, such as carcinogenic and estrogenic pesticide contaminants in food and mammography.

On the basis of these data and women's right to know, I urge that minimally you revoke recent FDA restrictions on labeling of BST-free milk. More prudently, I further urge that you revoke approval of BST registration.

Dr. Epstein, other researchers, and activist organizations have done their best to keep this issue in the public eye. For instance, Epstein and the consumer group Food and Water held a Washington, D.C. press conference in January 1996 to publicize their findings. They were roundly lambasted not only by representatives of and scientists employed by the Dairy Coalition, but also by Stephen Sundlof, director of the FDA office that approved Posilac.

Six months after the introduction of Posilac, 8 percent of American cows had reportedly received the hormone, according to the September 15, 1994 *Washington Post. Rachel's Environment & Health Weekly* reported Monsanto's claim that it sold 14.5 million injections between February 1994 and January 1995, reaching almost 30 percent of the dairy herds in the nation. *Rachel's* also reported on February 29, 1996 that, "A survey published in October 1995 in *Dairy Today,* a respected midwestern farm journal, said 20 percent of the U.S. farmers have tried [Posilac]. But opposition appears to be hardening among farmers, according to the survey firm Rockwood Research. Among farmers who hadn't used [the hormone] 87 percent said they would never use it. . . . Of farmers who have tried the drug, 40 percent have since given it up. . . . In California, by the end of 1995, rBGH usage was down, according to two agricultural economists who track California's dairy industry." Perhaps this is why Monsanto is offering new discounts to farmers if they make a six-month commitment to buy Posilac.

Monsanto stands to earn $300-$500 million annually from selling Posilac. The nation will gain an estimated 12 percent increase in its milk supply. However, we already produce more milk than we can use, so the federal government will purchase the excess product at an additional cost to taxpayers of $200 million. Farmers are already reporting ill effects of Posilac on their herds. Who is to know, since this is such a massive public experiment, when ill effects will show up in human patients. That's the tradeoff: corporate profits or human health. It's a bad deal.

## Nuclear Radiation

Another industry involved in this terrible tradeoff is the nuclear industry. And as with chemicals, nuclear manufacturers stand to make great profits by protecting and expanding their markets.

Radioactivity exposure data supports a link between consumption of dairy products and cancer. Radioactive strontium (Sr-90) and iodine (I-131) concentrate in the non-fat part of cow milk and in human breast milk. There is ample evidence that fission products in the diet act synergistically with chemical pollution to cause harm to a person, resulting in cancer, birth defects, and immunological and neurological damage.(See Sternglass and Gould, *International Journal of Health Services*, 1993, and Sherman, *Toxicology and Industrial Health*, 1994.) Repeated exposure increases our risks, often in unanticipated ways. Exposure to both chemical toxins and radioactive materials have a compounding effect and increase the hazard of each.

The argument for the effects of dairy contamination is compelling. When 16 industrial countries were studied, only four—New Zealand, Australia, Hong Kong, and Israel—showed declines in breast cancer deaths between 1971 and 1986. None of these countries has nuclear power generators. And the threat goes far beyond nuclear power plants. There is uranium that is mined, milled, purified, and put into bombs and reactors. This material is transported by train and truck all across the country. Tailings, the radioactive rock left over from mining, was once used for fill and road construction, and is spread across the landscape. Radioactive materials are handled, transported, used, and stored throughout this country for myriad purposes.

Nuclear bomb testing adds to the burden: the United States, Russia, France, Britain, China, and unacknowledged others have all contributed their share of tests. Similar to bomb tests are various catastrophes that have occurred at nuclear power plants, including Chernobyl and Three Mile Island.

Radioactive releases from nuclear power plants are also a growing concern. It is not only the faulty plants that are troublesome—well-operated plants release low-level radiation into the environment as part of routine operations. Even more important is the fate of the spent fuel rods from these facilities. The U.S. and Canadian governments have mandated that these wastes be buried in deep underground dumps, creating a crisis for the nuclear industry, since neither country has made real progress toward constructing such a repository. As a result, dangerous radioactive wastes are building up on site at every nuclear power plant in the United States. Typically, the nuclear industry characterizes these storage pools as "temporary," but they are only temporary in the sense that they will be used until something better is available. Meanwhile, these storage pools and the newest "answer"—dry cement storage casks—can leak into the ground and our water supply. On May 28, 1996, a hydrogen flash fire caused an explosion that raised a three-ton shield off one of the casks at the Point Beach, Wisconsin nuclear plant. This is the same type of cask used at the Palisades storage site hard by the shores of Lake Michigan, where more than 100 tons of high-level radioactive waste, including 2,200 pounds of plutonium, are loaded into 13 concrete casks.

According to a 1994 press release from the Cancer Prevention Coalition (CPC), there is a "significant increase in breast cancer mortality rates among U.S. women living near nuclear facilities." This statement is based on a report by Drs. Jay Gould and Ernest Sternglass of a nationwide ecological survey of breast cancer mortality rates in 268 counties within 50 miles of five military facilities and 46 civilian nuclear power plants. From 1950 to 1989, age-adjusted cancer mortality rates rose from 24 to 26.4 deaths per 100,000 women, a 10 percent increase, compared with a 4 percent increase for the nation as a whole. Rates of increase around the five military facilities—Hanford, Washington; Idaho Falls, Idaho; Savannah River, South Carolina; Brookhaven, New York; and Oak Ridge, Tennessee—were even higher: 41 percent. Even more conclusively, for the seven counties within 40 miles of the Oak Ridge plant, breast cancer mortality rates increased by 39 percent for women living in three downwind counties, but *decreased* by 4 percent among women living in four upwind counties.

Dr. Gould concluded, "Nuclear emissions appear linked to increased breast cancer deaths among women living near these facilities. The public has not been informed of its risks."

A small two-column story in the December 7, 1994 *Chicago Tribune* added powerful affirmation to Gould's position, making the cancer connection a reality.

"Tons of Plutonium Stored Unsafely, U.S. Concedes," was the headline. The story explained that the Energy Department admitted that American nuclear weapons plants at 13 sites around the country maintain thousands of containers of plutonium that could leak before the material is properly disposed of, posing a significant risk to workers and the public. Little is being done to address the problem.

The plutonium—26 metric tons of it—was left over when

production of nuclear arms materials was stopped in the late 1980s. Much of the material is being stored in containers that can leak because few thought back then that the shutdown would become permanent. The Energy Department acknowledged Rocky Flats, near Denver, as the most vulnerable site, but also mentioned the Savannah River facility, Hanford, and other locations where the materials are leaking.

The report stated that "The material in tanks could concentrate itself in a way that could cause an accidental nuclear chain reaction and the plutonium in ducts and pipes also could come together accidentally into a 'critical mass' during cleanup operations. Such a chain reaction would not produce much of a blast but could give off a life-threatening shower of neutron radiation in the immediate area."

We are at great potential risk.

The world is still coming to grips with the toxic legacy of the nuclear age. In Russia, the true horror of the Chernobyl explosion is just beginning to be known. Nuclear fallout is now mixed with industrial pollution in the old USSR, and in the absence of any other available land, crops are being planted in irradiated soil. The head of Russia's environmental agency publicly admits this sad legacy, but can only watch in agony as growing numbers of Russian children die from childhood leukemia.

As Rachel Carson said in *Silent Spring* in 1962:

> The most alarming of all man's assaults upon the environment is the contamination of air, earth's rivers, and sea with dangerous and even lethal materials. This pollution is for the most part irrecoverable; the chain of evil it initiates not only in the world that must support life but in living tissues is for the most part irreversible. In this now universal contamination of the environment, chemicals are the sinister and little-recognized partners of radiation in changing the very nature of the world—the very nature of its life.

# 4

# AVENUES OF
# ENVIRONMENTAL
# EXPOSURE

In July 1994, leaders of 15 major environmental groups—including the American Oceans Campaign, Defenders of Wildlife, Friends of the Earth, Greenpeace, National Audubon Society, National Wildlife Association, the Sierra Club, and the Wilderness Society—sent a joint letter to all their members. It read, "You have never received a letter like this before. This is the first time the combined leadership of the nation's leading environmental groups have sent a single call to action to our combined memberships. Even during the Reagan/Watt/Gorsuch years, we have never faced such a serious threat to our environmental laws in Congress. Polluters have blocked virtually all of our efforts to strengthen environmental laws, but still they are not satisfied. Now they are mounting an all-out effort to weaken our most important environmental laws."

More than 170 activists and leaders from all over the country added their own warning in an open letter in September of that year: "People in neighborhoods across the country are suffering injuries to health and life, from chemicals, radiation, incinerators, power plants, . . . etc. And we know that nature is under attack, that many species, ecosystems and wilderness areas have been ravaged."

What do these letters have to do with breast cancer? Everything. Estrogenic chemicals, dumped, sprayed, spilled, poured, and exhausted into the environment by these polluters are wreaking havoc in women's bodies. Our exposure to hazardous chemicals multiplies each woman's risk of breast cancer.

## Pesticides

Chlorinated pesticides are dangerous in many ways to people who eat residues on their food, especially children. They are dangerous to farmers and farm workers; they are dangerous to wildlife. Yet, while pesticides are responsible for the deaths of an estimated 10,400 Americans each year (according to the February 22, 1996 issue of *Rachel's Environment & Health Weekly*), their use keeps expanding. (Assault rifles—a much hotter political issue—are responsible for only about 250 deaths each year.) The trade publication *Agrow: World Crop Protection News* reported in early 1996 that global pesticide sales in 1995 increased by approximately 4.3 percent to $29 billion—an all-time high. It also predicted that the market would continue to expand by almost 2 percent a year over the next five years.

There is no question that hazardous pesticides are dangerous to humans. The Northwest Coalition for Alternatives to Pesticides stated in the *Journal of Pesticide Reform* (Winter 1995), "Of the 25 most commonly used agricultural pesticides, 5 are toxic to the nervous system, and 18 can damage skin, eyes, and lungs. Long-term health problems are also a concern. About half of these commonly used pesticides have been classified as cancer-causing chemicals by EPA. Seventeen of these 25 pesticides cause genetic damage in laboratory tests, and 10 of them cause reproductive problems. Six of them have been shown to disrupt the normal function of hormone systems."

Richard Wiles, Director of Agricultural Pollution Prevention of the Environmental Working Group, a nonprofit research organization based in Washington, D.C., testified about pesticides before the House Committee on Energy and Commerce on October 1993. He offered the following:

> Since the 1940s, American agriculture has released about 30 billion pounds of pesticides into the environment. Today, Americans use about 2 billion pounds of pesticides each year in agriculture, forestry, as wood preservatives, in water supplies, and in our homes, gardens, and workplaces. About 850 million pounds of this is used in some way to produce food.
>
> As a result, everyone in the U.S. has some trace level of pesticides in their body fat, and everyone is routinely exposed to pesticide residues in food. Perhaps the most tragic consequence is the contamination of human breast milk with the estrogenic pesticide DDT and the carcinogens chlordane, heptachlor, and lindane. The breast milk of many American women has higher levels of DDT and its metabolites than allowed in cow's milk by the FDA; cow's milk contaminated at similar levels would be seized as adulterated and banned from interstate commerce.
>
> Of course this situation was unforeseen when these pesticides were first introduced, yet problems such as these linger on, or in the case of the association between DDT and breast cancer, have only begun to surface, over 20 years after DDT was banned. . . . The pesticide regulatory system presumes that all pesticides on the market are safe until proven unsafe. Meanwhile we are the guinea pigs.

The Environmental Working Group gave special attention to the Midwest farm belt. In its 1994 study on the herbicides and pesticides, the Environmental Working Group stated:

> Every spring, farmers across the Corn Belt apply 150 million pounds of five herbicides—atrazine [a chlorinated triazine and one of the most heavily used herbicides in the world, according to the International Agency for Research on Cancer], cyanazine, simazine, alachlor, and metolachlor—to their corn and soybean fields. [Atrazine causes breast cancer in laboratory animals. It has been found in virtually every Corn Belt water sample tested, as well as 90 percent of samples

taken from a Pacific Northwest river basin.] And every spring, rains wash a substantial portion of those chemicals into the drinking water of 11.7 million people in the Midwest and Louisiana. During sustained periods of peak spring runoff, up to 18,000 pounds per day of these herbicides flow down the Mississippi River into the Gulf of Mexico (U.S. Geological Survey, 1993.) Drinking water contaminated with these herbicides is a serious public health issue; the manufacturers's own laboratory studies show that these five herbicides cause nine different types of cancer, various birth defects, and heritable genetic mutations. None of these herbicides is removed by the conventional drinking water treatment technologies that are used by more than 90 percent of all water utilities in the U.S.

To analyze the extent of exposure and health risks associated with herbicides in drinking water, we examined the results of over 20,000 tests for five herbicides in finished tap water and in drinking water sources (rivers and reservoirs). The results of our analysis show that:

- 14.1 million people routinely drink water contaminated with the five major agricultural herbicides.
- 11.7 million of these people live in the heart of the Corn Belt and in Louisiana, including every major midwestern city south of Chicago. Within this population, an estimated 65,000 infants drink these herbicides from birth via infant formula reconstituted with herbicide-contaminated tap water. An additional 2.4 million people are exposed to these herbicides via drinking water in the Chesapeake Bay watershed.
- Drinking water is commonly contaminated with two or more of these five herbicides. For example, 61 percent of samples taken at the Kansas City, Missouri water utility intake contained two or more of these five herbicides; 47 percent of samples collected from four northern Ohio rivers that serve as drinking waste sources contained three or more, and 38 percent of samples from 27 Midwestern drinking water reservoirs contained four or more of these five herbicides.
- More than 3.5 million people in 120 cities and towns face

cancer risks more than ten times the federal cancer risk benchmark, based on average annual exposure to these herbicides in drinking water. This includes residents of Columbus, Ohio; Indianapolis, Indiana; Kansas City, Missouri; Springfield, Illinois; Cedar Rapids, Iowa; and Omaha, Nebraska.

- People in small rural communities are at particularly high risk; over 400,000 people in 98 rural communities face cancer risks from 10 to 116 times the federal benchmark. . . .
- 3.1 million individuals in 23 cities with populations over 100,000 are exposed to cancer risks from herbicide-contaminated drinking water that exceed federal cancer standards by a factor of 10 or more. (Springfield, Illinois leads the list with the highest lifetime risk.)

Another serious source of human contamination by pesticides as well as other pollutants is the Great Lakes. Millions of people live and work near their shores, eat fish taken from the lakes, or just drink the water. Yet levels of persistent toxic substances in the Great Lakes are dangerously high. And according to the 1992 report from the International Joint Commission (IJC), a U.S.-Canadian body charged with monitoring the health of the Great Lakes, the contamination problem is only getting worse.

The Sixth Biennial IJC Report on Great Lakes Water Quality states, "Persistent toxic substances have adversely affected human, environmental, and economic health and continue to do so. . . . Many compounds produced by human activity and released into the environment disrupt the endocrine systems of fish, birds, and mammals, including humans. . . . The potential hazard to humans is great because of the likelihood of repeated and continued exposure to those chemicals."

The IJC focused on 11 "critical" chemical pollutants it had identified in its 1985 report. These chemicals come from a variety of sources: contaminated ground water (pesticides and pulp and paper bleaching), surface runoff of pesticides and road chemicals; and airborne pollutants originating both within and without the Great Lakes basin. This includes emissions from incinerators that settle upon land and water. (EPA officials indicate that the source of 95 percent of the dioxin in our food is incinerators.)

Dr. Forrest Pommerenke works at the Early Detection Branch of NCI. He has identified the areas in the United States where the highest levels of breast cancer mortality are occurring. States bordering the Great Lakes—Michigan, Illinois, Ohio, Pennsylvania, and New York—show especially high numbers. And it's no wonder—organochlorines are found in very high amounts throughout the Great Lakes.

The 1992 IJC report states, "The principal problem is the presence and impact of persistent, toxic substances on all sectors of the ecosystem . . . in the Great Lakes-St. Lawrence Basin Ecosystem. . . . toxic substances such as lead, mercury, and PCBs have caused widespread injury to the environment and to human health."

The report adds more proof to the hormone connection theory: "Toxic chemicals found in the Great Lakes can have subtle effects on cellular metabolism. . . . The commission concludes that the use of chlorine and its compounds should be avoided. . . . The potential hazard to humans is great because of the likelihood of repeated and continued exposure to those chemicals known to disrupt the endocrine system."

Other sections of the country are equally vulnerable. According to Pommerenke's maps, the Northeast and other eastern states also show higher than expected breast cancer rates. Highest increase of all—33 percent—were in two New York locations: Nassau County in Long Island and Schoharie County in the center of the state.

Breast cancer mortality in Nassau County was higher than in 99 percent of the counties in the country, with 106 of every 100,000 women developing the disease between 1983 and 1987. Because of these statistics, the New York State Department of Health has conducted a number of studies in Nassau County.

For example, five teachers at an elementary school in North Woodmere were diagnosed with breast cancer from 1977 to 1982. Ground water contamination became the prime suspect. Almost all of Long Island's 2.5 million inhabitants get their drinking water from ground water, much of which is threatened with chemical contamination. Dozens of public wells in Nassau County and thousands of private wells in Suffolk County have been closed since suspected carcinogens were detected in the water in 1980.

The New York State Department of Health summarized its findings:"There is general concern about the deteriorating quality of the environment on Long Island and growing concern about possible health effects from various environmental exposures....There is some evidence that environmental factors may be related to the occurrence of breast cancer. However, these environmental factors have not been evaluated in most research on the causes of breast cancer."

Another significant source of exposure to carcinogenic pollutants, besides our drinking water, is our food. Fish are one major source; they may live in waters contaminated by pesticide-laden runoff or may eat contaminated plants. Grazing lands and animal feed treated with pesticides spread the contaminants to beef, chicken, and sheep. According to the EPA, we get about 90 percent of our daily dioxin dose by consuming meat, fish, and dairy products, including milk, cream cheese, and ice cream.

Just like in the animals we eat, the toxic chemicals in our food will be stored in our body fat for a long time after exposure, accumulating in parts per trillion, billion, and then million as our exposure continues. Eventually, the accumulated contaminants reach critical mass and are released from the fat to begin their destruction. Cancer has a latency period; it takes time—often 20 years or more—before it shows up.

Studies indicate that geography plays a very powerful role in breast cancer. First, there is a marked increase in women who move from a low-rate area to a high-rate area. For example, a study by Ziegler, et al., published in the *Journal of the NCI* in 1993, showed that Asian immigrants who had lived a decade or more in the West had a breast cancer risk approximating that of native westerners, and more than *80 percent* greater than more recent arrivals. (The time lapse took into account cancer's latency period.) This may be attributable to change in diet and food sources in their adopted land. A major portion of American caloric intake comes from fatty foods—meat, deep-fried foods, dairy products—the very ones that store the environmental poisons. None of these foods feature highly in Asian cuisine.

Second, proximity to hazardous waste sites is associated with breast cancer. In New Jersey, a research team led by J. Griffith found breast cancer mortality significantly correlated with chemical waste disposal sites. In three New Jersey counties with the highest rates (Essex, Monmouth, and Bergen), breast cancer mortality has been rising significantly. In an article published in the *Archives of Environmental Health* in 1989, the team exposed some alarming statistics: "High breast cancer rates are significantly correlated with a number of toxic waste measures nationwide.... Breast cancer is the only cause of death of the ten examined . . . that is significantly associated with toxic waste Superfund sites.... There are almost four times as many facilities that treat and store toxic wastes in counties with the highest rate of cancer than in the nation as a whole."

And in 1994, the New York Department of Health, in their ongoing search for reasons for Nassau County's high breast cancer rate, found more compelling evidence: "Women on Long Island have a greater chance of getting breast cancer if they grew up within a mile of a chemical plant than if they lived further away," stated a report titled "Residence Near Industries and High Traffic Areas and the Risk of Breast Cancer on Long Island."

\* \* \*

## Lawn Care Products

How many times have you stretched out on a perfect lawn, or walked barefoot through the lush green grass of a well-maintained park? Think of the serene feelings you get from a sun-dappled patch of grass—picture the picnics there, the infants crawling free, the students reading Dickinson.

Then think of the Vietnam War and the defoliant Agent Orange. At least 34 pesticides are commonly used for professional lawn care at application rates up to five times higher than used in agriculture. Ten of these pesticides are known to induce cancer in experimental animals according to NCI studies. One of these cancer-producing pesticides is 2,4,D—an extremely effective herbicide, a major ingredient in most lawn care products sold with confidence at garden centers everywhere, and one of the two chemicals comprising Agent Orange, the lethal herbicide used during the Vietnam War. (The other chemical—2,4,5,T—has been suspended for most domestic use but is still allowed in certain wooded areas and rice fields and under certain conditions.) Some studies indicate that 2,4,D contains dioxin. As the most deadly chemical known to man, there is *no* level, no matter how small, that does not confer negative responses in humans. Golfers, barefoot strollers, students, infants, children, and anyone who loves the look and feel of weed-free grass are at major excess risk from exposure to these lawn care chemicals.

Despite warnings, youngsters run over newly sprayed lawns, breathe in the spray (which can be blown by the wind well beyond the treated site), absorb the chemicals through their skin, put their fingers in their mouths after wrestling in the grass. Exposure is inescapable, and long-term deleterious effects almost a certainty.

Some localities have been taking measures to control exposure. For instance, in 1996, Nassau County, Long Island passed a law requiring commercial lawn care companies to give neighboring property owners five days' notice before spraying chemicals. But what will this mean for children or people from down the block, who will not read or even get these notices? How can this approach counter the effects of these chemicals when such minuscule quantities do such great damage?

## Workplace Contamination

Most workers are happy to learn that their jobs come with certain "perks"—a company car, a window office, an end-of-year bonus. However, many workers are starting to worry about one possible "perk" that might be showing up at their companies; more specifically, *perc,* or perchloroethylene, the chlorine-based chemical solvent used in dry cleaning. According to an article in *World Watch Magazine,* studies in the United States and Sweden have demonstrated that breast and liver cancer are particularly prevalent among dry cleaning workers. And these are not the only group of workers at danger.

## Nuclear Radiation

Mixing synergistically with the chemical pollutants in our environment are radioactive pollutants. This radiation comes from various sources, including bomb testing, uranium mines, reprocessing of radioactive ore, and leaking disposal sites. And the general population is also falling victim to planned and unplanned radiation releases from nuclear power and weapons manufacturing plants. Most of these plants were abandoned after major cutbacks in the production of nuclear weapons when the cold war ended. Left behind was massive nuclear contamination of sites all across the country now affecting the land, the water, and the air.

The dramatic increase of breast cancer over the past four decades is no coincidence.

This correlation has been downplayed for years by apologists for the nuclear industry, despite overwhelming evidence demonstrating the assault on our bodies. No matter how tiny the dose, there is no threshold below which exposure means no risk. As

Dr. John Gofman, former director of the Lawrence Livermore National Laboratories, stated at a 1994 Breast Cancer Action-sponsored conference:

> Do not be fooled by the strange silence about radiation and today's incidence of breast cancer. It may well turn out that low-dose radiation is the single most important carcinogen and mutagen to which large numbers of humans are routinely exposed. There is already proof, by any reasonable standard of scientific proof, that there is no threshold dose or dose-rate below which ionizing radiation is harmless.

Assuming that this world-class scientist and nuclear expert is right, the consequences for all of us are broad and deep. It compels us, citizen activists, health care professionals, and anyone interested in public policy to rethink a great number of medical procedures, from diagnostic to therapeutic, and to question our long-held beliefs that nuclear power is safe.

There are three types of nuclear radiation: gamma, which is high-frequency radiation that can penetrate deep into a body; beta, which can also penetrate far into the body; and alpha, which cannot penetrate very far but produces damage at low, prolonged doses. The genetic damage to a cell caused by alpha particles may be transmitted to the cell's offspring many cell divisions later.

Exposure to these rays may come from within our body as well as from without. We can inhale or ingest radioactive gases, dusts, food, and water, after which the radioactive material sends out its destructive rays.

Half-life is another crucial issue in understanding radioactive damage. Radioactive elements are unstable, and over time decompose into more stable forms. They have various half-lives—the time it takes for half of a mass of radioactive material to degrade into a lower-energy, but not necessarily less-harmful form. After a certain number of half-lives, the decay process is complete and the element becomes inert. As the material decays, energy is dissipated in the form of radiation, causing damage to nearby cells in the body.

One of the longest-lived radioactive isotopes is uranium-238, which has a half-life of 4.5 billion years. Therefore, this element gives off its alpha and beta rays essentially forever. In the human body, this element is most commonly deposited in the bones, kidneys, gastrointestinal tract, and lungs. Plutonium, which also shows up in the bones, has a half-life of 24,000 years.

### Medical Applications

For decades, doctors and hospitals overused x-rays and other radiation for diagnostic and therapeutic purposes. Today's physicians are far more aware that any sort of radiation treatment, even "routine" chest or dental x-rays, expose patients to cancer risks. Each and every incremental exposure to radiation carries an added risk.

While the use of medical radiation has prolonged the lives of many patients through diagnosis and therapy, its use has been a very mixed blessing. It was not so long ago—within the lifetime of many of today's breast cancer patients—that doctors and the general public were absolutely ignorant of the effects of radiation. For instance, the May 12, 1994 *Rachel's Hazardous Waste News* describes research by Dr. Gofman on the medical uses of radiation dating back to the 1930s and 1940s. At that time, Gofman learned, many physicians were fixated on enlargement of the thymus gland, imagining that the condition was a common and potentially fatal problem amongst American children. They prescribed frequent large doses of x-rays and fluoroscopic examinations, for both diagnosis and therapy. (A fluoroscopic exam is like a motion picture x-ray, and gives the patient a much larger dose of radiation.) Many parents, even of newborns, were convinced that their children were not getting the best medical care if they were not given x-ray treatments. Gofman highlighted a 1948 medical article that claimed, "The obstetrician or pediatrician should accede to the wishes of the parents who want neonatal roentgenograms [x-rays] of their children. It might even be wise to administer therapeutic doses over the thymus. Whatever assurance is gained by this apparently harmless and perhaps beneficial procedure will aid in alleviating any anxiety which occasionally becomes a thymus phobia."

Gofman also pointed out that between 1920 and 1960, unnecessary, excessive x-ray exposures of the breasts were received by females of all ages in connection with scoliosis, mammograms, tuberculosis, enlarged thymus, nonmalignant breast conditions, and by exposure during exams of their children. Fluoroscopies were even performed in shoe stores to check how the shoes fit.

There are abundant articles in the medical literature going back more than three decades, including such prestigious journals as the *American Journal of Epidemiology,* the *British Journal of Cancer,* and *JAMA,* linking the past misuse of radiation to present breast cancer.

In 1995, Gofman published *Preventing Breast Cancer: The Story of a Major, Proven, Preventable Cause of This Disease.* He presented compelling evidence that 75 percent of breast cancer is caused by exposure to ionizing radiation, principally from medical x-rays.

Gofman's research shows that when a woman receives significant radiation prior to the age of 20, she is more likely to develop breast cancer before the age of 35. The younger the woman, the greater her susceptibility, perhaps because radiation affects some early stage of the malignant transformation process. This was confirmed in a study of Japanese women exposed to radiation from the atomic bomb blasts when they were as young as 10 by D. H. McGregor, et al. Their results, published in the *Journal of the NCI* in 1977, showed that these younger women experienced a greater incidence of breast cancer than those similarly exposed at age 35 or older, suggesting "the breast tissues of adolescent females may be more sensitive than those of older women to the effects of ionizing radiation."

A quarter of a century ago, Gofman and associates outlined their observations concerning the effects of radiation, and their findings are still valid today: all forms of cancer can be induced by radiation; younger persons require less radiation to increase cancer mortality; higher levels of radiation cause higher incidences of cancer, but there is no threshold below which radiation does not cause cancer.

Like DES, x-rays seemed to be a one-treatment-fits-all answer to a number of diseases and female bodily afflictions. Here are some examples among many:

- A 1965 article by MacKenzie in the *British Journal of Cancer* reported on 800 women who had been treated for tuberculosis in one hospital between 1940 and 1949. Women who had had "artificial pneumothorax therapy" [which included about 200 fluoroscopes of the lungs] had a 1 in 21 chance of getting breast cancer. The chances for those who did not get this therapy were 1 in 510.
- A 1925 article by H. I. Bowditch, et al., in *JAMA* discussed 850 whooping cough patients (750 of them younger than 7 years) who were subjected to x-ray therapy by the Boston Floating Hospital in the 1920s.
- At the Mayo Clinic, more than 1,000 patients were radiated for treatment of asthma, according to a 1949 article by Leddy and Maytum in *Radiology*. Countless more patients with dermatological conditions were given either x-ray or radium therapy, with few records remaining.
- Postpartum breast radiation was used to treat breast engorgement.

Peter Montague sums up the evidence quite simply. "What should a reasonable and prudent person conclude from all this? Is radiation important in causing breast cancer? Without a doubt."

Exposure to radiation comes in two additional forms besides medical purposes: the deliberate release of radiation into the environment by government agencies, and proximity to nuclear sites such as nuclear reactors or military weapons sites.

### Deliberate Releases of Radiation

Since the dawning of the atomic age is such a dim memory for us, most people can't conceive of there being intentional releases of radiation. But that is exactly what happened with the early bomb tests in Nevada. The fallout from one test did some surprising traveling and intense radiation was measured in 1953 in Albany, New York. The fallout cloud had passed 40,000 feet overhead, but was driven to earth by a thunderstorm.

Dr. Harold Knapp, a member of the Atomic Energy Commission (AEC) Biology and Medicine staff, calculated that radio-iodine deposition in Utah from Nevada bomb tests would result in far higher doses to the public than the AEC was willing to admit. It appears Dr. Knapp was right. By comparing cancer incidence in a 1951 cohort with that from 1967-1975, Dr. Carl Johnson found a near doubling of breast cancer in Utah women living in the fallout path from the Nevada test site. (Reported in *JAMA,* 1984.)

However, there have been other deliberate releases of radiation into the environment by various branches of our government. "Experiments involved the intentional environmental releases of radiation that (a) were designed to test human health effects of ionizing radiation; or (b) were designed to test the extent of human exposure to ionizing radiation," states an October 1994 report of the Congressional Advisory Committee on Human Radiation Experiments.

While it is unlikely the public will ever know the true number, extent, or kind of intentional releases, the advisory committee found solid documentation for more than 300 such releases, and indicated that there were many more.

Which governmental departments were in on these intentional exposures? According to the Advisory Committee's report, the CIA, with its MKULTRA program of experiments concerned with development of chemical, biological, and radiological materials for use in clandestine operations to control human behavior. The Director of Central Intelligence ordered MKULTRA files destroyed in 1973. The Naval Radiological Defense Laboratory (NRDL) was involved from 1947 until 1969, when its research reports were dispersed and its basic records were destroyed. The Department of Energy was involved also; it's Intelligence Division's "critical data on intentional releases and work done for others . . . revealed that these files were essentially purged during the 1970s and as late as 1989." And NASA was also included in the experimental program. "In the 1960s, NASA contracted with DOE's Oak Ridge operations to perform a retrospective study of whole body radiation [which] encompassed over 3,000 radiation exposures at over 40 institutions. . . . In 1981 congressional testimony, NASA stated that the data had been destroyed in the routine course of business."

Information about these intentional releases were uncovered during 1994 Senate hearings under the leadership of Senator John Glenn, who said in his opening statement, "It is becoming increasingly clear that all too often the overriding reasons for the classification of many of the radiation experiments records was not national security, but instead fear of lawsuits and personal culpability."

And in November 1993, Eileen Welsome of the *Albuquerque Tribune* published her breakthrough story identifying victims of a vicious experiment that smacked of the medical experiments Nazis performed on concentration camp prisoners during World War II—the injection of plutonium without the knowledge or consent of the victims. Hazel O'Leary, President Clinton's Energy Secretary, was at the time in the process of opening up much of the secrecy that characterized the Department of Energy and its predecessors. After Welsome's articles were published, O'Leary announced that the record of all such human experimentation was going to be examined openly in an effort to make "the victims and their families whole."

Two years later, on October 3, 1995, a presidential Advisory Committee on Human Radiation Experiments admitted to some 4,000 radiation experiments sponsored by the U.S. government from 1944 to 1974. "Hundreds would be eligible for compensation," according to Stephen Klaidman, a committee spokesman. The report will go to a cabinet-level group that will figure out who should be compensated and for how much.

### Nuclear Power Plants

Nuclear power remains a heavily supported but increasingly dangerous answer to our nation's energy needs. Although massive public relations efforts have tried to make the public believe nuclear power plants are safe, they are not. Instead, they are significant and continuing sources of radioactive pollution because of normal operations and unintentional leaks from the power plants themselves, and contamination of the environment from the production and transport of radioactive materials.

Dr. Ernest Sternglass, Professor Emeritus of Radiological Physics at the University of Pittsburgh School of Medicine wrote the following in *News & Views,* a publication of WEDO:

> Since the beginning of the century we have known that radiation of all types induces cancer. What was not known was how nuclear reactors and nuclear testing would create such sudden, great changes, that radiation produced by the process of fission would act very differently from natural radiation processes or x-rays. Very small amounts of protracted radiation are 1,000 times more toxic than a short-term x-ray, because it affects bone marrow and the immune system. Around one nuclear facility after another, there has been an increase in cancer.

As far back as 1947, in an article in *JAMA,* P. D. Keller described delayed effects upon immune competency and blood formation in men and women exposed at Hiroshima, an effect confirmed in the 1970s by Dr. Sternglass.

More recent evidence of the adverse effects of radiation upon immune function has been provided by Dr. Jay Gould, director of the New York-based Radiation and Public Health Project and a former member of the EPA Science Advisory Board. During the summer of 1986, he found an excess of between 35,000 and 40,000 deaths, primarily amongst the elderly and those with infectious disease, in the areas receiving the greatest fallout from the Chernobyl explosion. And infant mortality and stillbirths rose in areas of Germany receiving the greatest Chernobyl fallout, according to a 1989 article by G. Luning, et al. in *The Lancet.*

A common emission from the nuclear power plants and other nuclear sites is radioactive strontium (Sr-90), which a number of years ago was shown to concentrate in cow's milk and becomes deposited in our bones. Sr-90 decays by the release of powerful beta radiation, which damages the bone marrow, the site of blood cell and immune cell formation. Also released from nuclear power and bomb systems is radioactive cesium (Cs-137), another beta emitter. Cs-137 concentrates in soft tissues, including breast, liver, spleen, and muscle, resulting in near total-body radiation as it decays. Enhanced effects have been demonstrated at very low levels of radiation exposure. Independent studies by Gofman, Sternglass, and A. Petkau have shown that damage from low-level radiation includes changes in red blood cells, susceptibility to infection, and reduced antibody response and production. When the immune system is compromised, the body becomes more vulnerable to many diseases, including cancer.

In 1994, Joseph Mangano published shocking findings in the *International Journal of Health Services.* Mangano found from Department of Energy data that Oak Ridge National Laboratory had released Sr-90, Cs-137, and I-131 into the local water supply and other radionucleides into the air and water, mostly before 1960. Examining death records in Tennessee, Mangano discovered a 31.8 percent increase in cancer deaths between the periods 1950-1952 and 1987-1989, well ahead of the age-adjusted rate of the entire country. In Anderson County, home to Oak Ridge, cancer deaths rose 39.1 percent compared to a 29.5 percent increase in the 12 counties surrounding the facility up to 40 miles distant. In the mountainous counties, where rainfall is greater, the increase in cancer mortality was 40.4 percent, compared to 30.3 percent in the lowland regions. Three downwind counties recorded cancer death rate increases of 50.8 percent, compared to a 7.1 percent increase in four upwind counties.

Sadly, before the Oak Ridge facility was built, cancer mortality in the region was uniformly below the national average.

The evidence of health effects from nuclear installation comes from other areas, too. Breast cancer in five counties adjacent to the Three Mile Island reactor increased markedly following start-up of the reactor, as well as after the accident, according to a 1987 study. This implies risk not only from an accident, but from normal operations as well. The investigation was conducted by volunteer canvassers working with Drs. Carl Johnson and Bruce Moholt, who determined that the cancer rate in that area was seven times that of similar rural areas.

The high rates of breast cancer incidence and mortality in Connecticut and suburban New York counties, especially Nassau and Suffolk counties in Long Island, have been associated with the consumption of milk and water contaminated over the last two decades with nuclear fission products—the short-lived radioactive iodine and the long-lived, bone-seeking Sr-90 coming from the Millstone, Connecticut and Indian Point, New York nuclear reactors.

Sternglass and Gould give compelling evidence linking the release of nuclear materials and the elevated breast cancer incidence there. They reviewed the releases from nuclear reactors located closest to Long Island and New York City. These included the reactors at Indian Point, New York, which began operation in 1961; Haddam Neck, Connecticut, starting in 1967; and Millstone, Connecticut, starting in 1970, whose combined releases between 1970 and 1987 was more than three times the 14.2

curies reported for the Three Mile Island reactor in 1979. According to these scientists, the Millstone reactor, 10 miles from Suffolk County across Long Island Sound, "released 32.6 curies of airborne I-131 and other fission products, and 581 curies of liquid fission products by 1987, most of it in the period 1972-1979."

Other environmental risk factors in Nassau and Suffolk counties include a long history of contamination of air and water by pesticides and other xenoestrogens. Thus, women living on Long Island receive a double whammy: the effects of nuclear radiation multiplied by the effects of chemical pollutants. Such exposure leads to deaths. Peaks in mortality appear to have occurred seven to nine years after the start-up of the Haddam Neck and Millstone reactors. And when comparing the periods 1970-1972 and 1987-1989, Sternglass and Gould found a 39 percent increase in breast cancer deaths in Suffolk County alone, as reported in the *International Journal of Health Services* in 1993.

The most dramatic data comes from San Francisco, home to the most concentrated cluster of breast cancers in the nation. One in seven women in the Bay Area has breast cancer, reports the December 1995 issue of *News & Views*. A December 5, 1994 *Chicago Tribune* story headlined "Bay Area's Breast Cancer Rate Highest" led with the following:

> San Francisco-area white women have the highest rate of breast cancer in the world—a rate 50 percent higher than that of most European women and five times higher than women in Japan, according to a report from an international research agency. Bay Area scientists could not identify a cause of the high rates but said several factors, including diet and exposure to toxic substances might be to blame. . . . In 1994, the nine Bay Area counties will have about 4,500 new cases and about 1,000 deaths—about 12 new cases and three deaths every day.

The scientists interviewed for this article may not have had an inkling what was causing this concentrated epidemic, but Nancy Evans does. She is former president of Breast Cancer Action and co-chair of the Working Group to Implement National Action on Breast Cancer under Health and Human Services Secretary Donna Shalala. Evans has created cluster maps of the Bay Area that paint a frightening picture. The first map identifies confirmed and suspected birth defect clusters in the area. An overlay for this map identifies where the cancer clusters are. Not surprisingly, the map indicates considerable overlap for the two different clusters—leading to the very reasonable assumption that environmental factors are responsible for both. The second map identifies where major radioactive material sites and earthquake faults lie. The fault lines are dangerously close to the radioactive material. Evans suggests that the Livermore National Laboratory nuclear site, located on the east side of San Francisco Bay, is a prime suspect as the source of radioactive material affecting the Bay Area's women.

Epidemiological studies have demonstrated a link between proximity to radiation-emitting facilities and breast cancer. Volumes of human case reports, animal experiments, and biological data show the causal relationship between radiation exposure and breast cancer. To paraphrase Bill Clinton's winning slogan from his 1992 presidential campaign, "It's the environment, stupid."

Ordinarily, when so much concurrent proof is available, scientists and regulatory agencies would announce, "We know enough. We have identified the problem. Now we can get on with solving it." But our representatives are not moving on this issue—there are too many powerful, monied interests with a stake in the polluted status quo. It will be up to citizen pressure to make a difference for present and future breast cancer sufferers.

# 5

# PROFITING
# FROM GENES

**F**or the past two decades, an integral part of the "war on cancer" has been the search for genes that might predispose a person to the disease. Tens of millions of public and private dollars have been poured into this quest, hundreds of high-level researchers have been dedicated to it, and thousands of potential breast cancer patients have been anxiously awaiting results.

Preliminary results of the search for the elusive breast cancer genes—BRCA1 and BRCA2—are in, and they are tantalizing, confusing, and frustrating.

In 1993, researchers at the University of Michigan Medical Center announced they hoped to locate a defective gene that causes the disease within a year. Dr. Barbara Weber, scientific director of the breast oncology program, claimed they had already found genetic signposts or markers in several families with a high incidence of breast cancer. Weber's goal, according to an article in the April 5, 1993 *Chicago Sun-Times,* was to find the breast cancer gene, a task "comparable to checking every household in the country to find a single light bulb that's out."

Such a daunting search seemed worthwhile, Weber maintained, since women who inherit this gene have an 85 percent chance of developing breast cancer. Finding the gene would open up two avenues of research: studying the gene's properties and developing a blood test so women with family histories of breast cancer could learn whether they carry the gene.

Soon thereafter, more information on BRCA1 was made public and was greeted with fanfare. One of the major researchers, geneticist Mary-Claire King (formerly of the University of California, Berkeley and now at the University of Washington, Seattle) reported earlier research in the mapping of BRCA1 to a large region of human DNA, narrowing its location to an area of about 1,000 other genes.

After King had found the approximate location of the gene, she set about pinpointing its exact location. In April 1993, King and two other researchers published a report in *JAMA* anticipating the isolation of the gene behind early-onset (before the age of 50) breast cancer.

In October 1994, a group of no less than 45 researchers penned their names to the study "A Strong Candidate for the Breast and Ovarian Cancer Susceptibility Gene BRCA1" published in *Science*. This battalion of collaborators from five North American medical institutions pinpointed the genetic flaw associated with some 5 percent of all breast cancers. Scientists around the world had hoped that this gene—a mutant form of BRCA1—would provide insight into the causes of most other breast cancers as well. Those hopes were dashed, however, when BRCA1 proved to be an unusually complex gene associated with only a small proportion of inherited forms of breast and ovarian cancers. (See Seachrist, *Science News,* September 2, 1995.)

The researchers pointed out that BRCA1 appears to encode a tumor suppressor, a protein that helps to block tumor growth. Thus, the normal form of this gene appears to help control cell growth and maturation throughout the body. If it is damaged, it cannot do its job, and the chances of developing breast cancer skyrocket. As the article in *Science* stated, "Women who inherit a flawed version of the BRCA1 gene not only face an 85 percent chance of developing breast cancer at some point during their lives, but also experience a substantial increase in ovarian cancer risk."

This information, which was prominently reported by the national media, seemed to signal a new age in breast cancer treatment. However, not so well reported was a comment in a companion piece by P. A. Futreal, et al., in the same issue of *Science:* "The data from primary tumors . . . raise the possibility that BRCA1 may have only a minor role in sporadic breast and ovarian tumor formation." Making the issue more complicated was a November 1994 announcement by the National Center for Human Genome Research at the National Institutes of Health (NIH) that they had found numerous mutations in a gene linked to breast cancer, which would probably make it harder to swiftly develop a genetic test for a hereditary form of the disease.

The researchers at the University of Utah, part of the team of 45 who got credit for the *Science* article, admitted that they had also mapped a second hereditary breast cancer gene known as BRCA2 (located on a different chromosome arm), and that neither gene covered all the hereditary patients studied by the teams. The new defect, according to Mark Skolnick, one of the principal researchers, could cause "a malformation in tumor-suppressing proteins that would otherwise keep breast cells from turning cancerous as they divided." (See Gorner, *Chicago Tribune,* September 15, 1994.)

In an unrelated study, biologist Ruth Sager at the Dana-Farber Cancer Institute in Boston had identified more than 40 possible tumor-suppressor genes (A. Campbell, *University of Chicago Magazine,* August 1994). In further work reported by E. Pennisi in the *Science News* of January 29, 1994, Sager may have found a tumor suppressor gene—the maspin gene—that may play a role only in breast cancer. In general, however, most such research seems to point to the fact that a damaged gene resulting in malignancy is not unique to breast cancer.

Another piece of the gene puzzle was also revealed in 1993. The cover of the final 1993 issue of *Science* proclaimed the molecule p53 to be the "Molecule of the Year," adding that it was "a genetic key to cancer." In 1994, the same journal repeated the tribute with a cover proclaiming "DNA Repair—Molecule of the Year."

P53 is a normal component of life and is a tumor-suppressor protein. It must be intact and functional to perform its intended function: protection. If it is damaged, it will not work as it should and cancerous cells will grow unchecked.

According to an article by E. Pennisi in the November 1993 *Science News,* p53 exerts its tumor-suppressing effect indirectly by regulating the activity of other genes. It does appear that alterations of p53 are "involved, directly or indirectly, in the majority of human malignancies," states the same article. As a result, stated Dennis Breo in the May 11, 1994 issue of *JAMA,* scientists have been "stimulated in an intense search for the biochemical functions of p53 and the effects of mutations on these properties."

About 40 percent of breast cancers show mutations in the p53 gene. Breast cancer tumors with mutations in the p53 gene recur more quickly and prove more deadly than tumors with normal copies of the gene. But the p53 gene mutation differs with different cancer sites, according to M. Hollstein, et al. (*Science,* 1991), and is not constant even for cancers of a single organ. For example, people with liver cancer in China showed an entirely different pattern from those with the same cancer in the United States, reflecting a difference in carcinogenic stimulus (Aguilar, et al., *Science,* 1994).

What difference does this variation make for the genetic approach to cancer? Simply, without identification of the specific carcinogenic stimulus that sets in motion the malfunction of the p53 gene, it is unlikely that the "magic bullet" of gene identification for cancer will ever be more than another expensive laboratory operation that will strike fear into potential breast cancer patients but do little to prevent the disease from occurring.

In the meantime, money and attention will be diverted from more crucial issues.

For instance, it has been established that most mutations occur in a lipophilic (fat) portion of the p53 gene. Many environmental carcinogens involved in breast cancer are lipid (fat) soluble. Thus, there appears a possible link between environmental toxins and breast cancer genes.

And how do cancer mutations come about? Through interference with and damage by chemicals and/or radiation. P53 has been altered by such diverse agents as ultraviolet light and cigarette smoke. Damage is common, judging by the fact that 90 percent of the p53 damages are mutations which change the identity of a single amino acid (C. C. Harris, *Science,* 1993).

Unfortunately, precious little research, time, and money are going into strengthening the link between exposure and gene mutation. If science were free of politics, determining a possible link between gene mutation and body burden of carcinogenic chemicals would have been eagerly addressed already. Considering the potential threat to the status quo, and the negative financial consequences to the producers of carcinogenic chemicals—should the gene connection be documented—it is highly unlikely that such research will be undertaken unless there is concerted pressure to do so. (A large percentage of research these days is funded by corporations with a financial interest in the outcome.)

It seems likely that a great deal of money is going to be spent on developing screening tests for BRCA1, BRCA2, and whatever other cancer genes are discovered in the near future. These tests will not be easy to create because of the variations in the genes that have been documented. For instance, BRCA1 is recognized to have five different sites where alterations have occurred. Alterations include deletions, an addition, a substitution, an alteration, and a regulatory mutation. Which alteration—or which combination of alterations—is responsible for changing the function of the cell?

The families from whom blood samples were collected lived in Utah, a fact raising significant questions about the study. As discussed in chapter 4, people living in Utah may have been exposed to unnecessary nuclear radiation due to atomic bomb testing. That means the defective gene may have resulted from environmental causes and not heredity. Families with the BRCA1 gene had been identified in the Utah Population Database as having a cluster of premenopausal breast cancer. In addition to the breast cancer link, women with altered BRCA1 seemed to have a greater likelihood of developing ovarian cancer as well. However, the mutation was detected in only 3 of 32 breast and only 1 of 12 ovarian cancers, according to P.A. Futreal, et al., writing in *Science* in 1994.

The size of BRCA1 also makes screening a very complicated issue. It is about ten times as large as an ordinary gene. It offers up more sites to be damaged, and thus can be altered by a number of stimuli received during the person's lifetime. The researchers at the University of Utah found four different mutations in the eight families they studied. As of this writing, scientists have found more than 100 mutations—all of which cause cancer.

Neither the BRCA1 gene test nor any other gene test will be simple or inexpensive. Complicating the finding of a unique mutation is the fact that some women have variations in their BRCA1 even in the absence of breast cancer. Finding a unique mutation in the mass of the large gene will be difficult. When that is done, the task of comparing defective genes from different families may prove to be even more elusive. And BRCA2 and other breast cancer genes, not yet fully identified, make the task even more daunting.

It may be more reasonable to investigate what causes the alteration in the genes. Can we postulate that the cause of the altered genes and the high incidence of cancer in these women may indeed be from the potential contributions of hormonally active chemicals such as DES, DDT, PCBs, dioxins, and other unidentified factors? Considering that the BRCA1 findings were made in Utah, it is completely logical to suggest, as Carole Gallagher does in *American Ground Zero: The Secret Nuclear War,* that radiation from the nuclear test sites in neighboring Nevada and New Mexico be considered as a causative factor.

The National Women's Health Network agrees with this theory. "Rather than concentrating on the role of genes in breast cancer, many women's health activists believe that more emphasis should be placed on identifying cultural, social, and environmental factors that might also play a role. The study published in *JAMA* (270(3):331-337), affirms that position. The findings indicate that even when there is a family history of breast cancer, genes play a smaller part in the development of breast cancer than scientists previously thought."

This elusive breast cancer gene—a hoped-for panacea—may be a less bright beacon than originally hoped. Since gene mutations are multiple, and appear on differing sites, it is difficult to tell if a single defect (and its unique cause) cause cancer. More than likely it is the sum total of various defects and assaults that allow unchecked cell growth. The continued unbalanced emphasis on genetic research omits the question of primary prevention, and the entire problem of more successful treatment of those already sick.

However, there is a silver lining to the cloud hovering over the breast cancer gene that offers a ray of hope to women with the potential for both breast and ovarian cancers.

"Normal Version of Cancer Gene May Reverse Disease," stated a headline in the March 1, 1996 issue of the *Chicago Tribune.* The story, by Peter Gorner, identified two concurrent studies. Gorner reported:

> Biologists at Vanderbilt University and the University of Washington have demonstrated that healthy copies of the gene BRCA1 may be as effective at suppressing development of tumors in breast and ovarian tissue as mutant states of the

gene are at causing them. . . . The new studies show that the power of BRCA1 extends beyond the relatively rare forms that are inherited. . . .

"This is the first proof that BRCA1 is a tumor suppressor gene and can inhibit the growth of the tumors," said the lead author of the two studies, Dr. Mary-Claire King.

Vanderbilt researchers Jeffrey Holt and Roy Jensen discovered that breast cancer cell lines contained much less of the protein produced by BRCA1 than did normal cells. When they added the gene to cancer cells, the cancer stopped growing. Holt and Jensen determined that the proteins produced by BRCA1 act on breast and ovarian cells exclusively. This is a major finding because it proves the function of the gene, which is found in every cell in the body. The proteins produced by BRCA1 prevent uncontrolled cell division and growth in a completely different way than other proteins that combat cancer.

Jensen explained: "The proteins are secreted by ovarian and breast cells, then seem to hook back onto the cells and tell them to stop dividing. And Holt added: "Other tumor suppressor genes can inhibit the growth of almost all tumor cells, but most also shut down the growth of normal cells, making them harder to use as therapeutics. This doesn't appear to happen with BRCA1."

Dr. King, who had waited for 20 years for results of her own gene research, put all these new findings into perspective:

> BRCA1 will turn out to be an important gene for breast cancer as a whole, but its role in the greater cascade of cancer-causing genes is not yet clear. These are very early days. . . . We are hoping that with both of them (BRCA1 and BRCA2) as tools, we can suppress the growth of virutally any human breast and ovarian cancer cell line.

There is a bottom line to all this: It will take time before these theories are thoroughly tested on animals and then in humans. The FDA approval process is complicated and lengthy. Any therapies derived from this potential breakthrough will probably come too late for those already suffering from the disease. And as Dr. King has said, "There may be something in the future that proves us wrong."

Why is there such a rush to exploit genetic research at the expense of disease prevention? The answer can be found in the trail of profits.

Skolnick and his colleagues at the Utah Medical Center in Salt Lake City used various techniques to isolate BRCA1. However, when they submitted the group's findings for publication, they purposely omitted two critical pieces of information for fear it would get into the hands of the competition. The crucial sequences had been deposited in GenBank and Myriad Genetics, a Salt Lake City biotechnology company in which Skolnick was a major stockholder. Based on this information, Myriad has licensed the use of its genetic know-how for the development of drugs and diagnostic kits to Eli Lilly, the pharmaceutical and chemical giant (R. Nowak, *Science,* 1994). The patent rights from this specific BRCA1 research will be held jointly by Myriad and Lilly (R. Weiss, *Washington Post,* September 20, 1994).

Eli Lilly contributed six scientists and $4 million to the study, with product licensing going to a Lilly subsidiary, Hybritech of San Diego. However, the gene's co-discoverers left the government off the patent, which means the NIH would lose any control over tests or therapies developed for BRCA1 (R. Nowak, *Science,* 1994).

This is a serious omission. First of all, six of the 45 scientists working on the project were supported by NIH, bringing with them $2 million in federal funds. According to a report in the October 29, 1994 *Boston Globe,* "NIH director Harold Varmus said that he has filed a counter application, adding NIH scientists to the patent . . . since the research was partially taxpayer funded."

Second, there are numerous ethical and economic questions about granting an exclusive patent to a technology with such widespread public health implications, especially when the research was partially supported by the public's money. Where is the public inquiry and debate about such a deal?

And granting Eli Lilly a patent on a breast cancer test may be the ultimate irony: Lilly is one of the purveyors of the cancer-causing chemical DES, and it currently manufactures pesticides that are linked to cancer, neurotoxicity, and hormonal effects. One of Lilly's must successful chemicals is their mind-altering drug Prozac, which has been linked to tumor promotion.

That genetic research has great commercial potential and significant power is becoming evident. Myriad Genetics went public at $18 a share and the stock has gone up. Dr. Skolnick's 12 percent stake in the company is now worth approximately $22 million. In the summer of 1996, Myriad announced they would introduce a BRCA1 screening test for about $900 later in the year.

Other companies are in the wings, waiting to compete for a market share. Estimates are that revenues from the BRCA1 test will reach $17 million in 1997 and $67 million in 1998. Recognizing the value of getting into this field, Merck, another giant drug company, announced in November 1994 it would make public, with no strings attached, any chemical codes it deciphered for human genes, stating that putting basic research into the public's hands will increase the chances that useful products will be developed from that information.

Other genetic research is controlled by another pharmaceutical/chemical giant—SmithKline Beecham, under contractual agreements with the Institute for Genomic Research (TIGR), a nonprofit organization, and Human Genome Sciences, Inc. (HGS), a for-profit concern (E. Marshall, *Science,* 1994). HGS will allow use of its proprietary data, but only after a researcher agrees to allow HGS first option to license any useful products, and only if the researcher grants prior review of any publication (E. Marshall, *Science,* 1993). HGS's founder, Craig Venter, holds stock in his company valued at $11.5 million (K. Day,

*Washington Post,* April 4, 1994).

Within two weeks after the announcement of the isolation of BRCA1, Eli Lilly announced an 8 percent increase in its third quarter net income, to $318.7 million, and SmithKline Beecham posted a 4 percent net increase, to $320 million, for the same period (*Washington Post,* October 19, 1994).

That BRCA1 and BRCA2 may be factors in fewer than 10 percent of the women who will be diagnosed with breast cancer raises serious ethical questions. First, does this small percentage justify the millions of research dollars that are going into exploring breast cancer genes rather than into environmental factors, which are much more prevalent? Funding gene research seems more like a scientific shell game than an attempt to solve a national health crisis.

As Bella Abzug, president of WEDO, wrote in a letter to the *New York Times* on May 26, 1996, "Any effort to patent the breast cancer gene (BRCA1) mutations . . . is a diversion of funds and focus from much-needed prevention programs. It makes more sense to direct funds, research, and prevention programs to the environmental pollutants that have been identified as major factors in the breast cancer epidemic."

In addition, if a woman's test is positive, will she be denied employment or health insurance? And the implications don't stop there. The National Women's Health Network addressed some of these issues in the September 1993 issue of *The Network News:*

> Most diseases involve both genetic and environmental factors. Even though we constantly read and hear about how genetic discoveries will provide firm answers, the reality is different. . . . Cultural, social, and environmental influences interact with genes and genes interact with the rest of the cell. Thus, scientific and medical predictions of the future for individuals with certain genetic conditions may not be accurate. When large numbers of individuals are genetically diagnosed as being "at high risk" of developing specific diseases, but with

no certainty that they will ever develop them, the stage is set for stigmatization and discrimination.

Clearly, any woman with the diagnosis of breast cancer becomes a commercial opportunity. And commercial exploitation might be the least of her worries. Would this very personal and unique information be used against her? It does not take much imagination to picture a computer screen with one's genetic information available to anyone with the know-how to access the data. Insurance companies, potential employers, persons involved in lawsuits, and hackers doing mischief are just the tip of a very invasive iceberg. This is a major fear of potential breast cancer victims, according to a study by Caryn Lerman, et al. published in the June 26, 1996 issue of *JAMA.*

Such considerations prompted Dr. Francis Collins, director of the Human Genome Project, to urge Congress in 1995 to enact a law protecting the privacy of Americans who undergo testing for genes that predispose them to diseases. Since scientists are rapidly creating tests that disclose whether now-healthy people have genetic mutations putting them at increased risk of cancer, people need protection. Collins reminded the Senate Cancer Coalition that medical records are not private. And in 1996, Collins was joined by Dr. Sidney Wolfe of the Public Interest Research Group who stated, "it is time for a strong federal law protecting . . . confidentiality."

Concerned about the issue of insurance, the National Breast Cancer Coalition is also advocating for insurance policies that include protection against discrimination based on genetic testing or predisposition to disease. Insurance providers must be prohibited from:

- using genetic information to limit any coverage or establishing eligibility, continuation, enrollment, or contribution requirements
- establishing differential rates or premium payments based on genetic information

- requesting or requiring collection of genetic information
- releasing genetic information without prior written authorization of the individual

In 1995, 37 House members co-sponsored the Genetic Information Nondiscrimination in Health Insurance Act. The bill never made it out of committee.

These critical issues, discussed by the scientific community and politicians, are yet to be addressed openly by the public, those whose lives may be most affected. In the meantime, commercial exploitation of biotechnology is ascendant, and is running full-speed into the future. A failure of privacy may be the patient's greatest impediment to using genetic testing—if she indeed is given a choice in the matter.

The extensive media attention to the breast cancer gene—from cover stories in mainstream magazines to articles in scientific journals—seems no more than a heady, self-congratulatory diversion from those most important issues about breast cancer that very few are addressing. Emphasis on the gene brings false hope to many women, with the potential for costing them considerable financial and emotional resources in a possibly futile quest.

In all the media excitement surrounding the gene discovery, what reporter reveals the more important fact that BRCA1 is a repair gene—one that ought to repair cellular genetic damage. Because it has been altered, it is no longer able to do so. Why aren't the leaders of the "war on cancer" asking the more basic question: What causes this damage to the repair gene in the first place?

If BRCA1 becomes an accepted clinical test, then a second test should be included to investigate for hormonally active foreign chemicals linked to breast cancer. Proponents of the current cancer strategies will undoubtedly wail that the cost of such a test will be prohibitive. Yet the BRCA1 test alone will cost $900, and it does not definitively say whether a person has or will get a certain disease. And scientists are hoping to incorporate a test for BRCA2, pricing the total package at around $1,000.

We know which manufacturers produced many of the hormonally active chemicals polluting our environment. These are profitable companies. Would it not be just to place a tax on these corporations to help pay for the assays? Such a program would go a long way toward defining the relative roles of genetics and environment: linking the tests makes scientific and economic sense, and could end the wrangling and deliberate obfuscation concerning what is a cancer risk and what is a cancer cause.

Undoubtedly, however, what will decide these issues will be money and control. The ongoing study of the breast cancer genes and the development and marketing of screening methods represent billions of dollars of income for pharmaceutical companies. In addition, there will be ancillary drugs, preparations, and processes that will produce untold other revenues. Other companies in the chemical-pharmaceutical complex will also benefit from administering the screenings and other procedures that will become necessary. So, more certainly than it will benefit breast cancer victims, gene research will benefit our powerful international conglomerates.

As for control, it will be removed further and further from the individual. Regulation of industry rarely keeps up with industry's ability to invade an individual's privacy. Unscrupulous profiteers will gain access to medical records, including those showing results of breast cancer assays, and will sell them for fast money. A worst-case scenario: Women may find their medical secrets posted on computer bulletin boards or showing up on computer screens at their offices. Although companies will say that they don't discriminate because of a person's medical predisposition, supervisors very often make hiring and promotion decisions based on their own attitudes, rather than on company policies.

So it appears that, absent a major upheaval from the citizens of our country, the breast cancer drama will be played out on a stage advantageous to the groups that stand to make the most money from the technology, not the groups that would gain the most in medical benefits. Gene research will accelerate. Expensive new cancer drugs will begin to fill the approval pipeline. The public will continue to be lulled into a complacent belief that "they" are taking care of us, that "they" will find a cure.

And we still will not be addressing the causes for 70 percent of breast cancers.

# 6

# TAMOXIFEN: POISON MASQUERADING AS PREVENTIVE

Although all women are at risk for developing breast cancer because of widespread environmental contamination, women with a strong family history of the disease are considered to be at special risk. Clearly one of the most important decisions for any woman and for our country as a whole is how to prevent this potentially lethal disease. An option proposed by NCI for preventing breast cancer in women with family history is the drug tamoxifen.

Tamoxifen is a synthetic hormone, similar in structure to DES. Since 1970, more than 3 million women have received tamoxifen for treatment of breast cancer—as part of their therapy after diagnosis. Some studies credit use of the drug with prolonged survival and decreased recurrence of the disease. The 1987 collaborative treatment trial, utilizing multiple therapies including tamoxifen, showed a 9.2 percent better disease-free state and survival in the first five years.

Dr. Andrew Arnold, head of Medical Oncology at Hamilton Regional Cancer Centre in Hamilton, Ontario, strongly advocates the use of tamoxifen in the treatment of breast cancer. "If a patient is dying of the disease, tamoxifen definitely helps prolong lives," he has said. "I've seen dying patients go into remission thanks to this drug. I use it as adjunctive treatment after mastectomy. It's certainly a better choice than chemotherapy." Unfortunately, studies also indicate that the therapeutic values do not persist after five years (Breast Cancer Trials Committee, *Lancet,* 1987).

However, the critical issue for us today is not which *treatment* path to follow, but whether or not to participate in an experiment touted as a breast cancer *prevention* trial—especially when the drug to be used for the trial—tamoxifen—poses well-documented and serious health dangers.

Tamoxifen was developed by London-based Imperial Chemical Industries (ICI), one of the world's largest multinational chemical corporations. Zeneca, an ICI subsidiary in the United States created in June 1993, is responsible for marketing the hormone.

Less than a year after Zeneca was established, the company achieved widespread negative publicity. A large Swedish study linking tamoxifen to uterine cancer forced Zeneca to send letters to 380,000 physicians across the United States defending the drug in April 1994. The Swedish researchers had studied 1,371 breast cancer patients who took 40 milligrams per day of the drug for 2-5 years, and found that there was a sixfold increase in uterine cancer among those patients who took tamoxifen when compared to the 1,327 patients who did not take the drug. A second study involving 20 milligrams per day of the drug also showed a marked increase in uterine cancer compared to a control group.

The Swedish study was not unique. Another study by van Leeuwen, et al., in the Netherlands reported a statistically significant excess of uterine cancer in women after 2-5 years of tamoxifen, correlated with both cumulative dose and duration of use (*Lancet,* 1994). And a Danish/British study "detected endometrial abnormalities at various times from the first tablet of tamoxifen" (R. P. Kedar, et al., *Lancet,* 1994).

Zeneca's efforts at damage control would have made barely a ripple on the surface of national consciousness except for the fact that in 1992, NCI had begun its Breast Cancer Prevention Trial. Planned since 1990, and coordinated by NCI's National Surgical Adjuvant Breast and Bowel Project (NSABP), the study initially enrolled 11,000 healthy women between 35 and 78 as human guinea pigs to test tamoxifen as a "prevention" against breast cancer. Half of the women were to receive tamoxifen and half a nonhormonal placebo. (A similar trial in England has been so far declined by Britain's Medical Research Council.)

Thus, at the same time as Zeneca's letter went out to physicians, a similar communique was sent by NSABP to all the women enrolled in the trial. Healthy patients who were taking tamoxifen as a preventive but who were not included in the official trial did not receive the warning.

Right from the start, critics focused on obvious problems with the trial. It requires subjects to enroll for a five-year period at one of 240 sites—from private doctor's offices to university clinics—around the country. The investigators' experience in the proper conduct of clinical trials varies widely, from those who have extensive experience to those who have none. Little oversight is provided by NIH (J. Cohen, *Science,* 1994). These challenges indicate grave doubts about the uniformity, accuracy, and objectivity of any results of the trial.

For the trial, recruits were defined as "high risk" if they had a family history of breast cancer. Such a history alone was advanced as a major risk of developing the disease, a concept that is highly suspect. No consideration was given to the overwhelming evidence that breast cancer grouped in families is just as likely to be the result of identical exposures to environmental toxins specific to a location or community as it is to be the result of genetics. If it had been considered, perhaps the trial would have been on therapies other than tamoxifen, such as detoxification, that rid the body of toxins.

Another basic consideration not covered by the trial is regular, comprehensive gynecological examinations of the subjects. These were not a required part of the NCI protocol, even though 23 women had developed uterine cancer in the earlier B-14 tamoxifen study managed by the NSABP, as reported by Dr. Bernard Fisher, et al. in an article entitled "Endometrial Cancer in Tamoxifen-Treated Breast Cancer Patients" published in the *Journal of the National Cancer Institute* in 1994. The data from the B-14 program demonstrated an increased endometrial cancer rate of 1.6 per 1,000 in tamoxifen-treated women. If the present tamoxifen trial reaches its full enrollment of 16,000, it will guarantee that an additional 12-13 women will develop uterine cancer among the 8,000 women treated with tamoxifen. The originators of the present trial obviously consider that to be an acceptable risk.

Given the protocol's stated risks of 62 breast cancers prevented while causing 38 uterine cancers and 3 deaths due to blood clots in the lungs, the arithmetic hardly makes sense. And Michael DeGregorio of the University of Texas Health Science Center in San Antonio, writing in the 1992 *Journal of NIH Research,* says that the official study underestimates the chances of fatal blood clot by more than two-and-a-half times and underestimates that of uterine cancer by 50 percent.

Despite the obvious problems with the trial's conceptualization and the warnings of researchers, the trial was launched. It seems absurd, but why would the powers that be willingly promote a trial that promises to substitute one cancer for another in otherwise healthy women?

In the case of tamoxifen, medical research has taken a back seat to profits. And as in the case of bovine growth hormones, it is the population that is at risk.

## Development of Tamoxifen

Early evidence indicated tamoxifen was loaded with problems. In its April 1994 letter to America's doctors, Zeneca stated, "In rodent models of fetal reproductive tract development, tamoxifen . . . caused changes in both sexes that are similar to those caused by diethylstilbestrol."

This was not the first time that deleterious effects of the drug had been seen by its creators. As early as 1967, ICI scientists noted that "tamoxifen persists for some days in the uterus." In rats, a tamoxifen metabolite (a breakdown compound almost similar in structure to the original) was found to influence the uterus to be more receptive to estrogen. (The more estrogen, the greater the chance of unnatural cell division leading to cancer.) ICI also reported liver carcinogenicity of tamoxifen and both ovarian and testicular tumors in mice in its description of the drug in the medical standard *Physician's Desk Reference.*

Despite these results, tamoxifen was first developed as a contraceptive. However, it actually functioned as an abortant, and in rats it prevented implantation of the fetus resulting in the termination of pregnancy. Even at that, it was by no means 100 percent effective, according to researchers M. J. K. Harper and A. L. Walpole (*Nature*, 1966 and *Journal of Endocrinology,* 1967).

Tamoxifen's carcinogenicity and teratogenicity were not sufficient detriments to make ICI drop its interest in the drug. Neither was its interference with immunological function in mice, found by Luster, et al. and published in the *Journal of Toxicology and Applied Pharmacology* in 1979. Nor were its effects on premenopausal women, with or without breast cancer, who experienced elevated estradiol and prolactin levels. (Abnormal prolactin release has been correlated with a number of chemicals that act as promoters of breast cancer.) Nor was the statement by I. S. Fentiman, publishing in *Drugs* in 1986, that "administration of tamoxifen to a patient with undiagnosed malignancy could lead to the emergence of an endocrine unresponsive tumor."

Possible reasons that ICI did not drop tamoxifen may be found in the corporation's annual statements.

From 1992 to 1993, Zeneca's Annual Report showed an increase of 42 percent in "profit before exceptional items and taxation." Its pharmaceutical and agro-chemical divisions accounted for 42 percent and 33 percent of its 1993 business. In 1995, Zeneca ranked fourth in dollar sales of worldwide pesticides, with sales valued at over $2.36 billion. That year, it enjoyed increases in both volume and value in all geographical regions and product categories, including a 10 percent growth in the United States. In its "current sales range" of pharmaceuticals for cancer are Nolvadex (trade name of tamoxifen) and Zoladex. The former is prescribed to women with breast cancer; the latter, an inhibitor of pituitary sex hormone release, is prescribed to men with prostate cancer. It sells eight other chemicals under the category of "cancer."

In 1995, a month's supply of Nolvadex—20 mg a day—was priced in the United States at $85.99. In 1996, the price went up to $98.99. Now the most widely prescribed cancer medication in the world, it generated U.S. revenues of $265 million in 1992. (See A. Rock, *Ladies Home Journal,* February 1995.) In 1993, worldwide sales of Nolvadex reached $400 million.

And Zeneca's profits come from both sides of the cancer road. ICI's agro-chemical division, which includes Zeneca, sells the following herbicides, among others: Ambush, Crusade, Demon, Eradicane, Force, Karate, Paraquat, Touchdown, and Tillam. All are poisons, and several have been linked to disruption of the endocrine system.

Zeneca is not the only major chemical corporation that plays both sides of the cancer industry. With few exceptions, the manufacture and promotion of products that cause disease in addition to those that treat disease are fundamental to almost every major chemical corporation.

## The Trial

Despite the evidence, NCI initiated the tamoxifen trial under the leadership of Dr. Bernard Fisher of the University of Pittsburgh (the same Dr. Fisher who had reported increased endometrial cancer in the B-14 program) in the belief that the drug would reduce breast cancers by 30 percent while also reducing heart attacks and preventing osteoporosis.

According to information uncovered by the National Women's Health Network (NWHN), there appears to have been a disregard or at least a glossing over of concerns about the toxicity of tamoxifen by those eager to obtain the clinical trials. Research by Network members has confirmed that even before the trial began, risks associated with tamoxifen use was known, including uterine cancer, blood clots, and damage to vision.

In the spring of 1991, NCI announced that it was going ahead with the prevention trial. NWHN representatives testified before the FDA Oncological Drugs Advisory Committee in an effort to persuade it to amend the protocol and address the hazards that had been observed. The three women who spoke on behalf of the Network—Adriane Fugh-Berman, Cindy Pearson, and Susan Rennie—specifically testified:

> There are no data on the safety of long-term use of tamoxifen in humans.
> The animal data are not comforting.
> Public health interventions should be health-promoting or at least non-toxic.

That the testimony came from eminently qualified professionals, one a physician and one a Ph.D., meant little to the FDA, and the trial was approved unamended. The Network met with NCI and FDA officials again in an effort to persuade them to amend serious problems in the trial that had been observed. One of its requests was to require NCI to give women entering the trial accurate information on the consent form.

When the consent form came out in January 1992, the most up-to-date information of uterine cancer related to tamoxifen was not included. The risks of developing life-threatening blood clots were understated, and the risk of liver cancer, produced in rodents, was misrepresented. This gave potential participants the impression that the risks of the trial were tolerable.

Disturbingly, the consent form also included this disclaimer: "Other medications and all physicians' or hospital costs will be charged to me in the same fashion as if I were not part of this study." In other words, the costs of any complications that arise from it will be paid out of the pockets of the participants and the general public—through taxes, insurance premiums, or direct payments to doctors. It appears the NSABP takes no responsibility for costs incurred if a woman develops cancer while in the trial.

In June 1992, barely two months after the trial had started, more information emerged about liver damage in women taking tamoxifen. And later that summer, researchers N.A. Pavlidis, et al., published data showing eye damage to humans after long-term, low-dose tamoxifen treatment (*Cancer,* 1992).

During the summer and fall of 1992, the Network cooperated with a Congressional committee to investigate the adequacy of the consent form used in the trials. This investigation revealed that 68 percent of the forms either omitted or altered one or more key points from the NCI-approved model form. Some of the forms did not meet minimum legal requirements for informed consent. In October, the findings were presented to Dr. Bernadine Healey, then-director of NIH. She defended the trial.

In early 1993, researchers reported evidence that women taking tamoxifen were getting both endometrial and gastrointestinal cancers. In January 1994, reporters learned that Dr. Fisher, the head of the NSABP, had been aware of new endometrial cancers in breast cancer patients. Several women had died as a result of these new cancers.

There were other concerns about Fisher. NWHM chair Jane Sprague Zones, Ph.D., wrote:

> Zeneca Pharmaceuticals had endowed a chair at the University of Pittsburgh in Dr. Fisher's honor. The company had made a $600,000 grant to the university in 1989 to establish a professorship. One official characterized this unusual situation best:

"I think it is difficult to maintain an appearance of propriety and the practice of propriety if one's own department has received a large endowment ... by the company that has supplied the drug that is being used in a clinical study being carried out by that investigator."

After this leak, the Women's Health Network asked their supporters to write to Dr. Susan Blumenthal, Deputy Assistant Secretary of Women's Health at the Department of Health and Human Services, and to Congresswomen Olympia Snowe and Patricia Schroeder, co-chairs of the Congressional Caucus on Women's Issues. They urged the women to support "an independent blue ribbon commission to examine the tamoxifen prevention trial and advise on whether it should continue." The Congressional Caucus was abolished by the 1995 Congress.

In the meantime, more information about Fisher's management style and potential conflict of interest emerged in testimony before the House Subcommittee on Oversight and Investigations on June 15, 1994. *Science News* reported in its July 9 issue that "Chair John D. Dingell sharply questioned Fisher's management of the NSABP," and that "NSABP was years behind in performing audits and in writing up and forwarding audit reports." The same article also reported that Zeneca had picked up the tab for "lavish receptions at NSABP's annual meetings. The tab for these meetings often cost as much as $80,000."

The tamoxifen trial is unique in undertaking experimental testing on humans—specifically women—in the face of known adverse effects in test animals. Usually, FDA requires that drugs be both efficacious and safe before they are allowed to be administered to humans. And when there is a risk of harm, it is considered appropriate to use a drug for treatment only when the benefit outweighed the risk. In the context of the tamoxifen "prevention" trial, this exception does not apply.

Nor is the trial primary prevention, for tamoxifen users are at risk for developing early symptoms of menopause, including accelerated bone mineral loss and osteoporosis, as some studies have found (A. Gotfredson, et al., *Cancer,* 1984). The male equivalent would be a trial of hormonal castration of testicular function to "prevent" prostatic cancer.

The tamoxifen trial, an ill-conceived idea, could very well become a disaster, for the potential consequences for subjects are life-threatening. The very design—enrolling women at different sites, under the control of so many different physicians from university centers to private practices—is fraught with logistical problems and inconsistency. There is no assurance that each woman enrolled in the trial is receiving regular and adequate gynecological exams, eye exams, liver function tests, and blood tests. At the very least, experimentation with a toxic agent that may result in disease substitution rather than disease prevention may be seen as unethical.

Seattle attorney Leonard Schroeter commented before the House Subcommittee on Human Resources and Intergovernmental Relations hearings, "Any person who is harmed . . . [by] these trials without first having been fully informed of [tamoxifen's] risks most probably has an appropriate lawsuit against both the dispensing doctor and the government." This concern was echoed by former NIH director Bernadine Healey. Ironically, she stated, "We do not conduct trials without believing, based on scientific evidence, that those [involved] will reap more benefits than undergo risk" (J. Raloff, *Science News,* 1992).

At least $60 million in U.S. tax funds have been awarded for the tamoxifen trial; these funds do not include expenditures from insurance charges or other medical aspects of the trials. But criticism of the trial is getting around. By the fall of 1994, at least one cancer clinic had dropped the tamoxifen trials. *The Network News* reported, "Citing concerns about the ethics of giving healthy women a cancer-causing drug, . . . press reports in June stated that doctors at the Hamilton Regional Cancer Centre in

Canada (HRCC) decided to halt the trial after learning that the likelihood of developing uterine cancer was greater than originally believed. The doctors also stated that 70 of the 85 women in the trial had dropped out on their own." HRCC physicians are continuing to provide follow-up care for all women who originally volunteered for the study.

Dr. Arnold of the Cancer Centre explains that the newer information about endometrial cancer made him and the staff uncomfortable. "We chose to withdraw, but we were sensitive to the fact that over 80 women were already on the trial. If, after more information, these women chose to continue, they were welcome. Seventy-two dropped out." But, Dr. Arnold adds, "There are thousands of women who have chosen not to be part of any trial, since being on the trial means half the women will be getting a placebo. So, they take tamoxifen anyway. These women take the drug because three of their sisters have died of the disease and they are terrified. They take tamoxifen although they know there's a chance one in a hundred might get endometrial cancer. They figure a hysterectomy is preferable to dying of breast cancer."

In 1994, Dr. Fisher came under intense scrutiny when NCI charged him with sloppy management of the NSABP, and he was forced to resign in March 1994. NCI then temporarily halted recruitment of patients into the prevention trial. Of the potential 16,000 subjects, over 11,000 had already signed up.

Nagging issues remain. Neither recruits nor experimenters know which subjects are receiving the active agent and which are receiving the placebo. Only after the trial is over will researchers learn who got which. NSABP does not plan to inform volunteers of their status when the trial ends.

Arthur Caplan, medical ethicist and director of the University of Pennsylvania School of Medicine's Center for Bioethics, argues that in studies like this one, where a potent drug is dispensed to healthy volunteers, there ought to be a scheduled disclosure to each subject. After all, he argues, "women have been placed at increased risk of certain health effects, enough so to warrant close medical follow-up in subsequent years" (J. Raloff, *Science News,* October 22, 1994).

Backlash is mounting. In 1994, most of the women who withdrew from the prevention trial at HRCC asked to have their status confirmed. However, the NSABP appeared reluctant to divulge the information. Dr. Donald Trump, acting executive director, ignored two requests for confirmation in May and June 1994, and it was only during a July 8 phone call that Trump finally agreed to disclose the information "only for those who requested their status in writing." (At least 60 request letters were forwarded to Trump within the month.) The October 22, 1994 issue of *Science News* reported Trump as saying, "We've operated under the assumption that if the patient does want to know, we would give her that information." However, "we're not advertising that."

In California, a significant move has helped those who oppose the trials. Under Proposition 65, the state must publish and maintain a list of all known carcinogens. In May 1995, the state's Carcinogen Identification Committee (CIC) voted unanimously to list tamoxifen. The action drew protests from NCI and Zeneca. Both argued that the benefits of possible breast cancer prevention outweighed the risks of endometrial cancer.

In October 1995, the California EPA convened a public forum bringing together critics of tamoxifen and representatives from Zeneca, NCI, and tamoxifen researchers.

Thomas Mack, CIC's chairman and an epidemiologist at the University of California, was quoted in the November 1995 issue of *Science News* as saying, "Unless something comes along that's a complete surprise, tamoxifen will be listed." Opponents of tamoxifen were hopeful that such a listing would help end recruitment for the trial. Despite Mack's statement, Zeneca and NCI prevailed after the forum, influencing the CIC to have an unprecendented second review.

In the January 1996 issue of *The Network News,* Cindy Pearson reported more trouble for the tamoxifen trial. Her article, "Tamoxifen Prevention Trial Faltering: NCI Faces Difficulty Recruiting, Additional Bad News on Tamoxifen," told this story:

> In October [1995], it was revealed at a closed-door meeting that tamoxifen failed to prevent heart disease in breast cancer patients. These data have not yet been published in a scientific journal, but they have been discussed in presentations at the National Cancer Institute and other leading cancer research institutions. NCI has made no public comment, though, probably because they face a very embarrassing situation: the prevention trial is based on the premise that it will prevent heart disease in addition to breast cancer. If NCI is no longer able to claim that taking tamoxifen will result in fewer heart attacks, they will have to admit that healthy women over 60 are more likely to be harmed by tamoxifen than helped and younger women won't get much benefit either.
>
> In a related move, the National Heart, Lung, and Blood Institute withdrew its financial support from the trial, explaining that even if tamoxifen does help prevent heart disease, the prevention trial isn't going to be able to find out, because not enough women at increased risk of heart disease have been recruited.

Pearson also reported that NCI had sent a clinical announcement to American oncologists in November 1995 advising them that breast cancer patients should not take tamoxifen for more than five years. The announcement cited two randomized trials which found that women who continue on tamoxifen more than five years actually do worse: 92 percent of the women who stopped tamoxifen after five years were alive and disease-free compared with 86 percent of the women who had continued with tamoxifen. In addition, the women who continued tamoxifen had as many new tumors as did those who had stopped.

Despite this, an independent oversight committee for the NSABP trial decided that because it limited tamoxifen use to five years, the trial should continue. As Pearson wrote, "NCI has announced that these results have no relevance for the prevention trial, since women are only scheduled to take tamoxifen for 5 years."

There are other problems for the trial. After NSABP halted recruitment in 1994, about 20 percent of the enrolled women dropped out because of fear of developing endometrial cancer. Since enrollment resumed in 1995, only about 600 new women have joined the experiment. Reportedly, NCI started a new recruitment program in early 1996, relying on current participants to recruit others.

A major target of the new recruitment drive are nonwhite women. According to Hazel Cunningham, a former journalist who lives in Hawaii, this emphasis creates serious problems since tamoxifen's alleged safety was based on the study of white women. Cunningham claims that the trial is a "perversion of prevention," and adds, "One of the first volunteers in the trial is now dead—after two years. She was a black women, a diabetic, suffered from hypertension and should not have been a candidate for any trial. But she was an available body."

What for most reasonable people should have been the final nail in the coffin of the trial came with the March 2, 1996 *Science News* report that the World Health Organization (WHO) has formally designated tamoxifen as a human carcinogen, grouping it with roughly 70 other chemicals, about one-quarter of them pharmaceuticals, that have received this dubious distinction. However, NCI, using its power and authority, ignored the WHO ruling, and in a statement prepared before the WHO report came out said, "It had reviewed the same data and [considered] it in the study designs and informed consent procedures in all tamoxifen trials." Despite all the scientific evidence and ethical questions, the trial continues.

# 7

# MAMMOGRAMS: POISONS MASQUERADING AS DIAGNOSTICS

**O**ctober 1995. In the center of a full-page newspaper ad appearing in suburban Chicago papers is the soft photo of a naked woman, her arms folded across her chest, her eyes turned to gaze upon her body. The ad extols the virtues of mammography.

Getting a mammogram is not a time for taking chances. You want expert, proven diagnostic care. You want comfort and privacy. Rush North Shore understands this. That's why we've built a spacious 3,000 square-foot, state-of-the-art Breast Imaging Center with a staff dedicated to maintaining your dignity and privacy. That's why all our radiologists are board-certified and on-site. That's why additional imaging testing such as special mammographic views and ultrasound is immediately available.

Since you're a busy person, you also want convenience. Thus through October 31 our Breast Imaging Center will be open seven days a week, on weekdays from 7:30 A.M. to 6:00 P.M. and on weekends from 9:00 A.M. to 3:00 P.M. Additionally, your results will be available within 24 hours.

Finally, we understand value is important to you. Thus

through October 31 you will receive a specially reduced mammogram price of $85.00 which includes both physician and hospital fees, plus a 10% off Bloomingdale's coupon redeemable at Old Orchard Center.

Quality, convenience, and value . . . the ultimate mammography offer . . . All physician-referred and self-referred patients are welcome.

At the bottom of the ad was this tagline: "This special promotion is being offered to encourage early detection of breast cancer during National Breast Cancer Awareness Month."

Breast Cancer Awareness Month: Step up, ladies, and have your picture taken. It's good for business.

The two methods presently recommended and accepted by the medical establishment for detecting breast cancer are breast self-exam (BSE) and mammography. Most hospitals and doctor's offices display stacks of colorful brochures explaining how and when to do self-exams and answering questions about mammography.

Regular self-examination is still a major screening tool despite serious limitations. Some women are reluctant to touch their own bodies, while other women simply don't know what to search for. Self-examination may be done irregularly or not at all, and many women avoid the procedure in terror that they may discover a lump. (Avoidance is a very common way of dealing with something we dread.)

As for mammograms, more and more women are accepting this procedure. Most insurance programs now cover the cost of at least some mammograms. Early detection can help to save lives, thus reducing the cost of covering a more advanced disease. Despite this, many women, especially those who are not covered by insurance, shy away from the procedure. They may feel they cannot afford it, or that they do not need it since breast cancer is not part of their family history.

Early enthusiasm for mammography was spurred by ACS, in

conjunction with NCI, which in the early 1970s established a program of free mammograms at 27 centers. However, as early as 1976, John Bailar, editor of the *Journal of the NCI,* wrote, "The possible benefits of mammography have received more emphasis in the clinical literature than have its defects. . . . Mammography may eventually cause more deaths from breast cancer than it prevents" (*AMA Medical News,* April 12, 1976).

Mammography must not be confused with cancer prevention. Sadly, the whole concept of cancer prevention has been twisted by the cancer establishment (including First Lady Hillary Clinton) into a program of early diagnosis and early treatment.

For a mammogram to be positive, the tumorous growth must already be present, and large enough to be felt or seen. In fact, that growing tumor may have been in the body for years before it was large enough to be detected. The Cancer Prevention Coalition states, "By the time breast cancers can be detected by mammography, they are up to 8 years old. By then, some will have spread to local lymph nodes or to distant organs, especially in younger women."

In addition, mammograms scan only the part of the breast that protrudes. Thus, if a woman's breast is small, the chances that a mammogram will pick up a mass plummet. The same holds true if a woman's breast tissue is dense, as it is for many woman younger than 50.

Mammography involves exposure to radiation, one of the factors in cancer causation. These days, mammographic technique has improved, facilities have upgraded their equipment, and doses of radiation delivered to patients are now relatively low. Historically, however, this was not the case. Early—and even relatively recent—mammography used far higher doses of radiation.

More than a decade ago, Dr. Edward Webster, a radiation physicist at Massachusetts General Hospital, commented, "When a woman arrives at a doctor's office for a mammogram, she has no way of knowing whether she is getting three hundred or three thousand millirads [of radiation]" (cited in E. Rosenthal, *Science Digest,* March 1984).

Dr. Sam Epstein, writing in the *Los Angeles Times* of January 28, 1992, said the following:

> Up to 40 percent of women over 40 have had mammograms since the mid-1960s, some annually and some with exposures of 5 to 10 rads in a single screening from older, high-dose equipment.

> Significant studies on radiation risks to the breast have been well known since the late 1960s, including evidence that mammography, especially in younger women, was likely to cause more cancers than could be detected. A confidential memo written by Dr. Nathaniel Berlin, a senior NCI physician in charge of large-scale mammography screening, in 1973 may explain why women were not warned of this risk: "Both [ACS] and NCI will gain from a great deal of favorable publicity [from screening, and] . . . this will assist in obtaining more research funds for basic and clinical research, which is sorely needed."

> Thus, once again, suspect technology was applied to women on a large scale, in spite of the clear warning signals and with insufficient knowledge of the likely consequences.

Epstein did note that new mammography machines generally use about 0.5 rads per screening, with some equipment delivering only 0.14 rads to the breast tissue.

But of course, radiation at any level causes damage. Dr. John Gofman, in his book *Preventing Breast Cancer,* gives this warning about mammography:

> About three-quarters of the current annual incidence of breast cancer in the U.S. is being caused by earlier ionizing radiation, primarily from medical sources. . . . The recently growing incidence is not mysterious, and if we wish to understand why the incidence has been growing, we must look to radiation events in the life of a women 15, 25, 35, 45, and more years before breast cancer diagnosis.

Another major problem with mammograms is that doctors are not uniform in their interpretations. Trained radiologists may miss potential malignancies when reading mammograms: 10-30 percent of cancers present in women who get x-rays are missed. "A doctor's ability to read a mammogram for breast cancer varies dramatically, and some may miss a high number of tumors," a study directed by Dr. Joanne Elmore at Yale Medical School found. An article in the December 1, 1994 *Chicago Sun-Times* described the study, in which 10 community radiologists interpreted 150 mammograms and gave their recommendations. There was a shockingly wide range in the radiologists' accuracy.

One of the radiologists recommended that 63 percent of the patients who were not known to have cancer undergo biopsy; another radiologist recommended biopsy for only 20 percent of these patients. The recommendations of the first doctor may result in unnecessary surgery in many patients; the recommendations of the second may result in many potentially lethal lesions going undiagnosed.

And in the *FDA Consumer,* published in March 1994, the FDA stated that, while mammography can discover a tumor up to two years before it can be palpated, and detect 85-90 percent of tumors in women older than 50, it fails to find between 10 and 15 percent of cancers.

Although most states required inspection, calibration, and certification of x-ray facilities, until October 1994 there was no national standard for mammography certification. In that month, the FDA promulgated certification standards for quality assurance and control; for radiological equipment; for personnel qualifications of technicians who perform mammographies, physicians who interpret films, and physicists who monitor equipment; and for record-keeping and report transmission. (The Cancer Information Service provides the names and locations of facilities that have been FDA-certified. Women can call 1-800-4CANCER on weekdays to find the nearest certified mammography facility.)

The accuracy and benefits of mammography may just be plain oversold, as well. In an article in the Summer 1992 issue of *Mothering*, Dr. Rosalie Bertell, a well-respected critic of radiation, raised these disquieting issues:

- Mammography provides 5-10 false reports of tumors for every correct report. Many false-positive results lead to re-examination, exposing women to additional x-rays. Some lead to unnecessary surgery.

- Mammography fails to detect advanced tumors measuring more than 2 centimeters in diameter. One major Canadian study reported a failure rate of 15 percent. In some instances, mammograms have missed lumps that were easily recognized manually. [Another study found 16.5 percent false reports where a negative mammogram missed a palpable cancer.] Even repeat mammograms have been known to miss advanced cancers spreading through both breasts.

- Physicians intent on "preventing death" often fail to inform women of the known and suspected risks of mammography.

Bertell concludes, "The public relations effort behind mammography conveys a false sense of benefit, security, and control and it does so by glibly overlooking the core question, `How much x-ray exposure is too much?'"

Recently, official policy toward mammography has shifted somewhat because of reports by several researchers that mammograms in premenopausal women may be part of the problem. A crucial Canadian study of nearly 90,000 women aged 40-49 at 15 hospitals across Canada found a 50 percent increase in deaths from breast cancer among women over 40 who had annual mammograms versus those given physical exams only (Elizabeth Neus, *Chicago Sun-Times,* November 14, 1992). This data was backed by other studies confirming the dangers of mammograms in premenopausal women. For instance, a group of Swedish researchers agreed that screening has little effect in finding cancer in women in their forties.

Dr. J. Mark Elwood of the University of Otago in New Zealand examined the Canadian study and other studies from the United States and Europe conducted over the last 30 years. Collectively, the studies had enrolled nearly 500,000 women. "Elwood consistently found that only mammography screening among women 50 and over was related to a substantial drop (20-40 percent) in breast cancer death rates" (Judith Randal, *Chicago Tribune*, March 14, 1993).

While many studies show poorer survival of younger women diagnosed with breast cancer, this may not simply be failure of mammography, but may reflect more aggressive tumors—in keeping with the more active hormonal state of younger women.

Armed with this newer information, both NCI and the American College of Physicians recommended beginning mammograms at age 50 and every two years after that. In October 1993, NCI announced revised guidelines for breast cancer screening:

- Women ages 50 and older should be screened every 1-2 years with mammography and receive annual clinical breast exams. Women ages 70 and above should be screened unless otherwise indicated by health status.
- Women ages 40-49 should discuss with a health professional the advisability of breast cancer screening with mammography, taking into account family history of breast cancer and other risk factors. Annual clinical breast exams are a prudent practice for this group.

NCI's proposed changes were based on the summary of the International Workshop on Screening of Breast Cancer, held in February 1993. Workshop participants reviewed the results of 30 years of screening and a panel wrote a summary statement: "It is clear that in the first 5 to 7 years after screening there is no reduction in mortality from breast cancer that can be attributed to screening. There is an uncertain, and, if present, marginal reduction in mortality at about 10 to 12 years." However, the panel also found that more than 30 years of randomized trials have strengthened the conclusion that women 50-69 benefit greatly from regular mammograms.

The NCI guidelines have been opposed by many medical groups and the guidelines are not binding on doctors and their patients. Making matters even more confusing, ACS advises women to have a baseline mammogram by age 40, and claims that the new recommendations will have a "chilling effect" on mammography use for women of all ages. Others say the NCI decision will create confusion and fear among younger women who have been told that regular mammograms are the best way to protect themselves.

A recent large study at the San Francisco VA Medical Center, published in the July 3, 1996 issue of *JAMA*, added more fuel to the fire. The study indicated that for women under 50, the reason that mammography is less successful is not because of tissue density, but because the tumors in younger women grow so rapidly. These tumors can go from too small to be detected to large in less than two years. The lead in the Associated Press story about the report stated that the study suggests "that those worried about cancer should get mammograms every year."

The Boston-area Women's Community Cancer Project summed up its strong opposition to mammograms. Culling their information from a number of professional journals, the organization lists the following "Appalling Facts About Mammography and Breast Cancer for Women Under Age 50":

1. Studies have repeatedly shown that mammography misses nearly half of all breast cancers in women under age 50. Don't assume that a negative mammogram means you don't have breast cancer.

2. There is no evidence to suggest that mammography screening reduces the chances of dying of breast cancer among women under 50. . . . There will be the same number of deaths from breast cancer in a population of women who have annual mammograms than in a population who have not, and in fact, there may be even more.

3. Women have been assured that mammography is safe, despite the fact that all responsible scientists agree that there is no safe level of radiation. Exposure to radiation from one mammography visit is more than ten times greater than that received from a typical chest x-ray procedure.

4. Mammography is big business. Since a mammogram in a women under age 50 may or may not pick up a lump a little earlier [and since discovery of the lump] does not alter the course of the disease in this age group, some people think that the real beneficiaries of the American Cancer Society/National Cancer Institute guidelines are the individuals, businesses, and institutions that derive huge profits from the manufacturing of mammogram machines and film, as well as those who own, operate, and read the film.

To suggest giving mammograms to younger women whose breast cancers are growing rapidly is thoughtless, and indicates the poverty in mainstream thinking about diagnosis. That younger women are experiencing a rise in fast-growing breast cancer is alarming; that yearly mammograms are the only early detection technique recommended ignores the fact that x-ray exposure adds to the toxic load in their bodies.

Remember, mammograms are embraced by Breast Cancer Awareness Month supporters: ACS, radiologists, giant mammography machine and film corporations which specifically target premenopausal women with sophisticated ads.

\* \* \*

## Alternatives to Mammography

Understanding that carcinogenic risks come from radioactive isotopes already released into the environment, and knowing that there is a cumulative risk from mammographic radiation exposures, other diagnostic procedures need to be explored.

The substance melatonin appears to be a useful adjunct to mammography. Melatonin is the new, over-the-counter discovery that has created a great stir among alternative advocates. In the October 1995 issue of *Alternatives,* Dr. David Williams reported, "Researchers recently irradiated two separate batches of white blood cells (lymphocytes), one incubated with melatonin and one without. The cells with melatonin sustained 70 percent less radiation damage than the untreated ones. Healthy tissue could be protected with melatonin before undergoing diagnostic x-rays."

Another alternative concentrates on improving self-examination. Dr. Henry Pennypacker of Gainesville, Florida founded Mammatech, a company that teaches examiners what to feel for and how to search real breast tissue. His techniques enable doctors, nurses, and women themselves to discover breast lumps as small as a quarter of an inch in diameter, a sixfold improvement over self-exams done by untrained women, who normally can identify lumps only after they have grown to more than an inch in diameter. The Mammacare Clinic has created curricula, a home practice kit, and a videotape designed to teach proficient manual breast exams. (Call Mammatech at 800-626-2273.)

Pennypacker is convinced these techniques are a major advancement in early detection:

> If we can teach fingers to read braille, we can teach women to find a lump smaller than a golfball. The fingers are extraordinarily sensitive instruments. When we show the fingers what they are feeling for, and then coordinate the fingers with the brain, we get excellent results. Over and over, we've had women tell us they don't know what to feel for. With proper

training, we can get women to find cancer that mammography missed. This works especially well with younger women, who should not be exposed to x-rays too soon.

Yet another possibility is thermography, a technique in which infrared-sensitive materials measure heat emitted by the body in order to observe differences in temperature distribution in a woman's breasts.

Thermography has been widely used in rheumatic and occlusive vascular diseases, although it has not been as successful in mammography for a number of reasons. Among these are issues detailed in regard to radiographic standards: standardization of procedures, quality assurance, and training. A unique issue is the thermological definition of a "normal" breast. However, combining mammography and thermography raises the breast cancer detection rate above that offered by either technique alone, according to S. Blume (*International Journal of Technological Assessment in Health Care,* 1993). If the medical establishment would address the inconsistencies of thermography, its advantages could be fully developed and made available to women.

After considerable testing and review, the Joint Working Group of NCI and ACS concluded in 1979 that, "thermography does not appear to be suitable as a substitute for mammography for routine screening." However, it also noted that "thermography has no radiation risk and is less costly than mammography, and continued developmental work on this procedure, as well as other techniques suitable for screening, is needed" (O. H. Beahrs, et al., *Journal of the NCI,* 1979).

Fortunately, some researchers have taken the positive recommendation to heart. In 1990, French researchers led by Dr. M. Gautherie reported on a 24-hour thermographic technique to monitor breast temperature changes, similar to a patient wearing a heart monitor. The technique is based upon evidence that breast surface temperature reflects metabolism in the interior of the breast. Evidence indicates that there is a relationship between tumor growth rate, thermal and vascular reactions, and an early appearance of thermovascular disorders associated with breast malignancy. Of great interest are the findings of "alteration of the circadian rhythm of skin temperature observed in animal and human breast cancers, even at the early stage of tumor growth" (M. Gautherie, et al., *Chronobiology International,* 1990).

Other nontoxic alternatives to mammography are in the wings, waiting for approval and support. There's Video Breast Imaging Technology, or Lintro-Scan, which was approved for marketing by the FDA in 1992. The video machine illuminates the breast with a high-intensity light source. The breast acts as a natural light filter which absorbs the infrared light in proportion to blood volume. An infrared camera and lens captures this image in real time and displays it on both black-and-white and pseudo-color monitors. The multiple images of the breast give physicians and radiologists a three-dimensional look at abnormalities that could prove to be cancerous without exposing the patient to harmful radiation. The test can be applied as often as necessary to all patients.

Tests conducted at the University of Miami School of Medicine showed Lintro-Scan to have a sensitivity rating of 96 percent—compared to mammography's 85-90 percent. Company spokespersons state that the response from the medical community has been "overwhelming." However, the cancer establishment seems to have buried this technique—nothing more has been heard about it since it was first introduced.

Then there's the CIA, which had developed a top-secret image-matching technology designed to detect military targets by comparing aerial images taken at different times. The digital images are superimposed on each other, and features that have not changed are removed, leaving only the differences, which an analyst can easily spot. This same technology may be able to find very early breast cancers, detecting pinpoint tumors one to two years before a lump is large enough to be felt.

The process was developed in 1985, but now Assistant

Surgeon General Susan Blumenthal, the government's top specialist in women's health says, "If we can image a missile 15,000 miles away, surely we should use this technology to detect a small lump in a woman's breast." According to Senate Intelligence Committee chair Arlen Specter, the technique is supposed to be available in 1997, after it is field tested.

Then there's ultrasound. In December 1995, an FDA advisory panel recommended that the agency approve an ultrasound device that can determine whether a suspicious breast lump is benign or cancerous. According to a report in *Science News* that month, "The technique, high-definition imaging (HDI), could reduce the 700,000 biopsies performed each year. Physicians routinely use mammograms to find small lumps in the breast. But mammograms can't tell if the lump is cancerous, so surgeons must perform a biopsy of the lump." In a test of over 900 breast lumps, HDI's manufacturer, Advanced Technology Laboratories of Seattle, reported 99.5 percent accuracy in diagnosing benign lumps. The technique effectively picks out benign, fluid-filled cysts but is less successful at distinguishing cancers from other kinds of benign growth.

And finally, there's the sensor pad. This device—essentially two impervious latex sheets surrounding a liquid silicone lubricant—is designed to enhance the tactile surface of the breast, making lumps easier to feel. This increases the sensitivity and accuracy of BSE. Twelve trials have found it be quite effective.

The pad's manufacturer, Inventive Products of Decatur, Illinois, had been trying to get FDA approval for a decade, spending over $3 million on studies in hospitals from Illinois to Colorado to Japan. (All have shown positive results.) The FDA finally approved the pad for distribution only through health-care providers, clinics, and other facilities where women could be taught how to use it.

This was only a partial victory, for the company had been trying to have the device approved for over-the-counter sales. Val Mullens, spokeswoman for the company, said, "This is an embarrassment to American women to say they don't know how to read instructions and do a breast exam."

As of January 1996, the pads were still not available to anyone. The stumbling block, says company president Grant Wright, is the FDA, which has put obstacle after obstacle in the way of a product that seems to serve everyone's best interests.

> When we introduced the pads to the FDA in 1985, they put it in Class 3 category, along with pacemakers, implant apparatus, and other radical life-saving devices. Now that's a pretty drastic move, considering that all the device does is reduce friction, enhance sensitivity for BSE, and help overcome resistance to touching your own body. We went for a legal opinion and were told that we should take the pads to market despite FDA rulings. We then sold it to 250 hospitals, and everyone, doctors, women, even industry loved it.
>
> The FDA took us to court and we lost. Then we testified at congressional hearings and remarkably, under the glare of public scrutiny, FDA removed the pads from Class 3 category and approved the device within two days, calling it an accessory to ultrasound. We thought we were home free, and waited for the official letter to move ahead.
>
> That FDA letter finally came and is so ambiguous and confusing, we've been stopped cold in our tracks. In one paragraph, FDA says women will need a prescription; in another paragraph, FDA says we don't. Nothing is clear and we're too frightened to do anything right now. If we do start selling the pads without a prescription, the FDA could keep it off the market, put us out of business, or put us on their blacklist—a list they keep on companies they have serious problems with. Yes, officially, there is no blacklist, but we all know it exists. Right now, I'm so disgusted I don't know what to do. It's become the theater of the absurd.

Why are these harmless, non-invasive, effective, and far less costly techniques of diagnosis not being supported in the United States? Is it because corporations like General Electric, a major manufacturer of x-ray equipment, are reluctant to give up any of the lucrative mammography market, and have the political and media clout to influence societal decisions affecting women's health? What is the role of hospitals and radiology clinics, which have spent hundreds of millions of dollars on massive radiology machinery and employ thousands of highly trained technicians? Are they afraid that they will lose an important revenue stream if lower-tech diagnostic options are publicized to women?

Safe, non-invasive, inexpensive, reliable methods of breast surveillance are more than ever a necessity, especially in this polluted world. We do not need to add any more burden to women who are already exposed to radiation through ignorance, accident, or arrogance of corporations and our own government. A compassionate government will invest the money, time, expertise, and support in less-dangerous techniques to diagnose and study breast cancer. Diagnosis should not add to the toxic burden of American women.

# 8

# SILICONE IMPLANTS: POISONS MASQUERADING AS REPAIR

The following is the actual story of Patty Lawrie, then age 36, who has gone through hell because of the silicone implants she received after mastectomy. Patty is not alone; there are thousands of women like her, women who experienced the pain and debilitating illness of the implants and then suffered from the gross ineptitude and in some cases malpractice of those doctors and psychologists to whom she went seeking diagnosis and treatment.

December 1989. Meme breast implants became infected. The breast incisions were opened and they began draining. Plastic surgeon Dr. Barnes said I was "allergic to the sutures," but he did not mention that infections were a common reaction to the Meme implants.

Incision on the left was closed with antibiotics—in the doctor's office. The right one was closed on February 20, 1990. The Meme implant on the right was open and draining and exposed prior to February 27. By January 1991, the incision on the right side spontaneously opened and implant was protruding a quarter of its entire size through the opening.

By January 1991, I changed to another plastic surgeon (Dr. Zambrano), and he recommended immediate right side implant removal. That month, the right Meme implant was removed and remained out for two months to allow infection to clear. By March 1991, another Meme implant was re-introduced. Dr. Zambrano failed to mention anything about Meme toxicity. Between December 1989 and the fall of 1994, I've had numerous bouts of bronchitis, hormone intolerance, and depression.

By January 1994, I began having drenching night sweats. My sheets were soaked. By April 1994, I began to experience acute right breast/chest wall pain. I saw an internist, Dr. Flavey, and finding nothing on the mammogram, he recommended anti-inflammatory medicine. By May 1994, I had a bout of sneezing and experienced two spontaneous rib fractures in the right side, at the place of the old open wounds and draining areas. At the same time, I developed severe allergies with chronic nasal drainage. Rectal bleeding began as well.

Between May and November 1994, I developed numerous health problems and saw a total of ten doctors. Except for my most recent and wonderful plastic surgeon, Dr. Karin Montero of Austin, Texas, and Dr. William Rea of the Dallas Environmental Health Center, all my symptoms were discounted as either of "no significance" or due to unknown origin with no suggestions for problem solving or relief.

For the sake of clarity, I'm enclosing a list of those symptoms: Prolapsed rectum; visual impairment—a steady decline in the last 6 months with an astigmatism diagnosis; deviated septum of unknown origin—probably severe allergies and acute inflammation with a loss of smell, taste, and feeling (in my left hand); high blood pressure; mild incontinence; abnormal nerve conduction studies (upper and lower extremity, polyneuropathies of the ulnar, median, and sural nerves; memory loss; word loss; confusion; energy and endurance loss leading to lethargy; weight loss; severe upper extremity tremors; inability to safely perform my job as a physical therapist.

In July 1994, I saw Dr. Loukas, an oncologist, because of the bowel/bladder changes and lymph node enlargement, along with the gamut of my other health changes. Dr. Loukas specifically wrote in his report to Dr. Falvey that my problems were not implant related. Between May and August 1994, I saw at least five doctors who said my breast implants were not a problem.

By August 1994, I found Dr. Karin Montero, a plastic surgeon. She is a miracle. A gift from God. She removed my implants beautifully. At the time of their removal, she also performed lymph node and bone biopsies and sent pericapsular fluid to a lab for a check for toluene diamine [TDA] 2,4 and 2,6, and silicone. The tests revealed a positive for both TDA and silicone, and the lymph nodes were nearly completely filled with foamy histiocytes due to the fact that silicone and polyurethane were in the entire lymphatic system.

In spite of my worsening health and the known toxicity of TDA 2,4 and 2,6, since August 1994 I was told by all the doctors I had seen (with the exception of Dr. Rea) that "my memory loss was permanent and I should just go on with my life." I was also told to "eat right and move on"—whatever that means. I was also told that my neurological problems are "psychiatrically based" and are not implant related. "You have no life-threatening illness, so just relax." Three doctors told me to return for a checkup in six months, with no suggestions for my health problems other than "biofeedback and psychiatric counseling."

[When Patty went voluntarily for a neuropsychiatric exam, one psychologist actually said, "You're feeling as if you're being misunderstood, aren't you? There's this huge communication gap that is causing you to feel persecuted. Come back in six months." This exam was scheduled specifically in relation to the class-action law suit that Patty and thousands of other women have signed on to. The psychologist did not even discuss Patty's physical condition with her.]

TDA is a poison. All these idiot doctors were telling me I was nuts. Either they do not really have a clue, or they are pretending not to know of its devastating effects.

I am treated like a neurotic woman. I can't stand it another minute. I refuse to see these doctors in Austin, if I cannot be treated with respect and concern.

By September 1994, I flew to Dallas to seek help from Dr. Rea. [Patty had read his book.] He immediately knew and understood all the harmful effects. I had researched my own health problems. Dr. Rea is my medical answer. Without hesitation he declared I had neurotoxicity and chemical sensitivity. He recommended 4-6 weeks of a sauna detox, organic foods, proper nutrients, and filtered water only in a safe, nontoxic living environment. He would prescribe antigen therapy if such therapy was needed.

By October 1994, I moved to Dallas for full, intensive treatment at the Environmental Health Center. I have not regretted my move for one minute. Dr. Rea has not only stopped my downhill spiral of health, but he has restored my memory and my energy level with his program. I thank God I found him before my memory and neuro problems were permanent. I'm not 100 percent well, but I know there is hope of a full recovery in time, with the correct treatment.

The answers are out there but the denial of anything associated with implants has grown too large for me to tolerate. I have not taken this sitting down. I have read and fought until I am blue in the face. I no longer have to fight for my life; I've found it. My life is back. I want other women to know that there is hope for them too.

Yes, the answers—actually, the warnings—were out there well *before* Patty had implants put into her body. Here are but a few of the many scientific studies and reports that have been published on the toxicity of silicone in the human body.

- A 1982 FDA paper by Nirmal K. Mishra, Ph.D., "Silicone Migration in Biologic Systems," discusses the deterioration and degradation of silicone devices. "Some recent studies indicate that solid silicone devices do indeed undergo a physicochemical decay inside the body and the microscopic fragments formed are engulfed . . . and are then transported to distal organs. . . . Examination of relevant necropsy materials revealed presence of silicone-like material in the liver, spleen, lung, and lymph nodes of the patient."

- The EPA report "Summary Narratives of Chemical Dispositions" includes this comment: "Toluene diamine is an existing chemical identified as carcinogen."

- OSHA's Material Safety Data Sheet states, "Toluene-2,4-diamine creates central system effects. Symptoms may include headache, nausea, vomiting, chest or abdominal pain, confusion, irritability, vertigo, faintness, weakness, disorientation, lethargy, numbness of extremities, pain in joints, drowsiness, weakness of vision and sluggish pupillary reaction, tachycardia, stimulation of the bone marrow and attempts at regeneration, liver tumors, and lymphomas. . . ."

- Dr. Frank Vasey, professor of medicine at the University of South Florida corroborates Patty's experience:"Two million women have undergone silicone breast augmentation mammoplasty. Perioperative short-term complications including infection, hemorrhage, tissue infarction (local tissue death), have been frequently noted. Multiple single case reports of women who underwent silicone breast implantation and later developed connective tissue diseases have been published, but most physicians have interpreted these observations as a meaningless coincidence."

No, Patty. You're not crazy. You've been poisoned.

"First Do No Harm" is one of the precepts of the Hippocratic Oath, taught to all prospective physicians in medical school. It is a valuable principle, and most doctors take it to heart.

Unfortunately, it seems that the principle was ignored by a number of physicians—especially plastic surgeons—when it came to silicone implants. Despite a growing body of information on their potential harm, a 1982 petition to the FDA by the American Society of Plastic and Reconstructive Surgeons (ASPRS) urged the deregulation of breast implants:

> There is a common misconception that the enlargement of the female breast is not necessary for maintenance of health or treatment of disease. There is a substantial and enlarging body (no pun intended) of medical information and opinion, however, to the effect that these deformities are really a disease which in most patients result in feelings of inadequacy, lack of self-confidence, distortion of body image, and total lack of well-being due to a lack of self-perceived femininity. The enlargement of the underdeveloped female breast, is, therefore, often very necessary to insure an improved quality of life for the patient.

Note the term *deformities* used for *small breasts.* Thus is a normal variation in women's bodies mined for opportunities for exploitation and profit.

Just three years later, at a 1985 conference sponsored by implant manufacturers, a leading plastic surgeon cautioned that "foam could be a time bomb . . . [in view of its] carcinogenic potential. Surgeons should not go on implanting." Yet, many surgeons continued to aggressively promote implants, indifferent to the dangers and whirling controversy.

And in 1992, no less an authority than the president of the AMA, Dr. James Todd, questioned the use of informed consent with breast implants in a letter to FDA Commissioner Kessler. Todd stated that the forms "may raise unnecessary concerns to a woman whose decision has already been made. . . ."

It's only too easy to understand. You've been diagnosed with breast cancer; your lymph nodes are affected. You've been advised to undergo radical surgery—a mastectomy of both breasts. You do it and you feel rotten. Why in the world would you not want something that might make you feel and look a bit like you used to, something that may keep a husband or a lover looking at you with desirous eyes? When your doctor recommends an implant, you jump at the possibility of being made whole again.

For more than three decades, plastic surgeons around the country have been given powerful and slick sales pitches, samples in hand, about the marvels of breast augmentation after radical surgery. Major scientific papers have been written touting the benefits of implants. And since breasts are such a powerful symbol of femininity, many women seek augmentation simply to enhance their figures. An extremely strong, emotional market for implants was created and nurtured in the United States: more than 1.3 million women have had implants since they were introduced by Dow Corning in 1962.

However, in the 1980s, more and more women started pressing lawsuits against the implant manufacturers. A large number of the implants leaked, releasing silicone into the hosts' bodies. By 1993, there were more than 10,000 individual lawsuits filed by women claiming their breast implants had poisoned them, and another 10,000 cases were on hold while a global settlement was worked out in federal court in Alabama.

In the fall of 1993, U.S. implant manufacturers agreed to pay $4.25 billion to settle present and future claims of women who have been harmed by implants. (That sum may jump to $4.7 billion during the 30 years women have to make claims.)

The settlement is open to any women who has had implants, whether or not she is involved in a lawsuit or has health problems at the moment. It is anticipated that at least 200,000 women will come out of their individual closets and join the class-action suit, which lists Baxter Healthcare, Dow Corning, and Bristol-Myers Squibb and its subsidiary Medical Engineering (manufacturer of the Meme implant) among the defendant companies that will pay the lion's share of the damages to the women—$3.7 billion. Union Carbide, 3M, and other smaller companies that manufactured implants will pay an additional $496 million, and $1.02 billion is earmarked for administrative costs and legal fees.

Hundreds of thousands of American women are presently sorry they ever heard of silicone implants because of the anxiety, pain, and suffering they have experienced from the implants. In some cases, silicone has invaded the implant's surrounding tissues or implant capsules. Implants cause acknowledged physical harm and possibly death. Reactions include autoimmune disorders such as lupus, rheumatoid arthritis, and chronic fatigue. Additional problems include mental depression, cancer, and scleroderma, a thickening of the connective tissue of the esophagus that makes it hard for the victim to swallow.

In an article by G. L. Troutwine in the August 1993 issue of *Trial* magazine, one attorney commented on information available to the FDA that was revealed during the course of implant litigation: "These are the beastly truths of the beauty fraud of breast implants. It was a fraud practiced on women susceptible to the ads and high-pressure sales tactics of manufacturers and cosmetic surgeons. It was a fraud practiced while the FDA stood by, deaf, blind, and mute."

Britta Austermeyer Shoaib is a doctor who has seen up close the ravages of the implants. She had gone to work for neurologist Bernard Patten at Baylor University College of Medicine in Houston in 1986. Dr. Patten had about 20 patients with a puzzling collection of symptoms affecting their nervous systems. Each women also had a silicone breast implant. Patten assigned Shoaib to study the connection. As their efforts became known, other doctors, who didn't know what to make of the complaints, referred women with these symptoms to the study. By 1994, the Patten-Shoaib patient list was 2,000 women and growing.

Interviewed by Linda Cornett for an article in the May 22, 1994 *Chicago Tribune,* Shoaib said, "Physically, silicone poisoning is compatible with AIDS in some ways. Because the immune system is very busy fighting the silicone, it neglects other corners of the body, the viruses and bacteria. It can't protect itself against everyday symptoms. We believe over the long run, every patient carries the risk of getting sick."

Besides making their hosts sick, the implants were blocking early diagnosis of new breast cancer. Data about the potential for undiagnosed breast cancer was published in June 1988 in the *Archives of Surgery* by Dr. Melvin Silverstein and colleagues, who had conducted a major study on the issue. Their conclusions were "More than one million American women have undergone augmentation mammoplasty. Ten percent (100,000) will develop or already have developed breast cancer. . . . Augmentation mammoplasty with silicone-gel-filled implants reduces the ability of mammography, our best diagnostic tool, to visualize breast parenchyma. When compared with our own non-augmented breast cancer population, augmented patients with breast cancer presented with more advanced disease; they had a higher percentage of invasive lesions and positive auxiliary nodes, resulting in a worsened prognosis."

A strongly worded editorial comment by Dr. LaSalle Leffall appeared directly after the Silverstein article:

> There have been numerous articles in the surgical literature stating that breast reconstruction following mastectomy does not interfere with early detection of local recurrence in the operative site. However, there has been little information concerning . . . breast cancer in patients following augmentation mammoplasty. With the fairly common use of [these techniques] the medical and surgical community should be aware of the authors' findings: these patients when compared with the non-augmented group with breast cancer present with cancers that are advanced and more invasive. . . . In this era of more detailed informed consent, surgeons should notify patients of this potential occurrence. Further, it seems prudent not to recommend augmentation mammoplasty in high-risk patients.

In 1991, Dr. N. Cruz of the University of Puerto Rico School of Medicine, San Juan, added to the information pool with an arti-

cle in the *Bulletin of the Medical Association of Puerto Rico:*
"The possible risks of silicone breast implants include capsular
contracture, interference with early tumor detection by routine
mammography, development of sarcomas in laboratory animals
(no human cases reported), silicone gel leakage, and connective
tissue disease. . . ."

Let's examine exactly what is an implantable silicone material. Is
this substance—silicone polymers—appropriate material to be
put inside of a woman's body, to remain perhaps for decades
without any system for monitoring its effects?

Silica, like carbon, is a reactive element, combining with other
chemicals to make various compounds. It comes in many forms,
both organic and inorganic. Inorganic silica compounds make
up a large proportion of the earth's surface—hard sand and rock.
Exposure to inorganic silica in its various forms, including
asbestos, can result in a variety of immunological diseases (J. D.
Sherman, *Chemical Exposure and Disease,* 1994).

Immune system responses were noted early. In 1974, Dow
Corning researchers William Boley and Robert Le Vier tested 49
silicones in rabbits to determine if the silicones would augment
immune responses to vaccines such as those administered in
immunization programs. While most of the silicones tested were
different from those in breast implants, the tests showed greater
antibody boosting by up to a hundredfold. The researchers stated, "We have data concluding that organo-silicone compounds
can stimulate the immune response" (B. Rensberger, *Washington
Post,* January 18, 1992). Apparently, this information was to be
kept private.

In the 1990s, Dr. Alan Broughton conducted immunological
studies that demonstrated marked differences between over 300
women who had silicone breast implants and women without
implants (Broughton and Thrasher, *Clinical Chemistry,* 1993).
The findings showed antibody elevations against the normal
components of a woman's body. The results reflect that, in the

presence of silicone, the body gears up to fight an invader.

Another chemical compound that has been put inside hundreds of thousands of women's bodies is polyurethane, which is manufactured from urethane and toluene diisocyanate. Polyurethane, of course, is the substance used in seat cushions, rug padding, and the like, and the name does not arouse much concern. But urethane is also called ethyl carbamate, a powerful carcinogen which has induced tumors in mice, rats, and hamsters, producing a variety of malignancies including leukemia, lymphoma, melanoma, and tumors of the lung and liver. Following World War II, Monsanto and DuPont began production of TDI, a key component in polyurethane. TDI causes serious and often irreversible immunological reactions. These components went into the production of polyurethane, which was inserted into women's bodies as a plastic film.

According to Sam Epstein, "Over 350,000 women with silicone implants wrapped in industrial polyurethane foam to reduce scarring are at higher risk of cancer. Polyurethane foam is manufactured from the carcinogenic TDI which breaks down into another carcinogen TDA. It should be further noted that TDA was removed from hair dyes by the cosmetic industry in 1971 following discovery of its carcinogenicity" (Cancer Prevention Coalition press release, September, 13, 1994).

Despite a lack of comprehensive tests on implanted women, however, a great deal was known to the regulatory agencies about silicone dangers. NCI has its own files on the silicone implants. The Cancer Prevention Coalition lists just a tip of the NCI findings on cancer:

"Carcinogenicity has been a widely discussed topic related to the injection of silicone in augmentation mammoplasty since the early 1950s. . . . Although relatively purer medical grade silicone is now produced, long-term complications related to silicone migration including calcification, lymphadenopathy, granulomas, and cancer remain as significant risks associated with the implantation of silicone gel-filled breast implants. . . . These case reports all have in common a long latency period and carcinomas are associated with complications related to silicone migration."

NCI based some of these statements on studies by its leading authority on carcinogenesis in the 1960s, the late Dr. Wilhelm Hueper. Heuper's studies showed that foam gradually degrades and induces malignant tumors in rats. He warned, "since the polyurethane plastics have been used in cosmetic surgery, . . . these observations are of practical importance . . . [and] should caution against indiscriminate use."

Clearly, enough information about the implants was emerging to make a compelling case for FDA intervention. However, it appears that the FDA refused to act for many years.

Take implants like Meme, an "improved" implant manufactured by Bristol-Myers Squibb's subsidiary Surgitek. Meme was supposed to prevent breast hardening, and Surgitek made a polyurethane foam for its cover. This foam leaked and probably accounted for some adverse clinical reactions, acting as a time-release system for additional TDAs. That same material, originally manufactured for use in such things as furniture upholstery, oil filters, and carburetors, went almost completely unmonitored for eight years until the FDA suspended sales of the polyurethane-covered implant in 1991 (N. Regush, *Mother Jones,* January 1992). About 10 percent of women with silicone implants received the polyurethane type.

As for Dow Corning, they knew about the effects of their silicone implants, too. When the FDA investigated Dow Corning's implants in 1987, its inspectors uncovered some important studies—and were punished for their work. Dow's own corporate studies showed that silicone-gel injection induced malignant tumors in rats. FDA inspectors stated in their report that the "Sarcomas in the rat study are . . . highly metatastic, lethal, and show no variation between sexes."

Internal memoranda written by the FDA scientists about Dow's two-year rat carcinogenicity study—which was initiated to see if silicone gel caused cancer—concluded that, "while there is no direct proof that silicone causes cancer in humans, there is considerable reason to suspect that it can do so." The doctors urged that "a medical alert be issued to warn the public of the possibility of malignancy following long term-implant(ation)." What did the FDA do? It reassigned the writers of the report.

By 1989, another FDA internal report surveying scientific literature remarked numerous case reports of cancer long after implantation and warned of the possibility of worsened diagnosis and prognosis when implanted women developed breast cancer. The report stressed the population studies which were claimed by the manufacturers and plastic surgeons as proof of safety were too short-term and flawed to negate the potential risk of cancer.

Despite the seriousness of these findings, FDA didn't move against the manufacturers. Nor did it demand the kind of independent tests that would conclusively deal with the issues. This from an agency that can demand $200 million in testing before it allows a company to bring a new drug to the market.

Growing public pressure (at least 14,000 women complained to the FDA about a mounting list of implant problems) finally forced the FDA to act in 1992. The relationship of the implants to cancer, to connective tissue disease including rheumatoid arthritis, and to systemic lupus disease was too hard to ignore. The agency placed a moratorium on the use of implants except for medical reasons.

It would be wonderful to say that, with the court settlement and the FDA suspension, women are now being compensated fairly for their illness and pain, and that fewer women will be convinced to even consider any kind of implants. But, the matter is not closed.

There were compelling reasons for the multibillion-dollar settlement that the media has not presented to the public. Chief among them was that the manufacturers knew in the 1970s that they were creating defective products that would leak their toxic contents into women's bodies. In fact, these companies had extensive private communications with each other discussing the broad range of implant defects. The memos reveal that the companies were putting profits before public health.

General Electric was involved early on with the manufacture of the silicone. And early on, those involved in producing and selling the product were nervous about it. One 1973 GE memo states, "Inasmuch as there are indeed risks involved with this market, we should endeavor to insure that we are adequately covered legally by the transmittal of this letter with all samples." Here is the letter:

It is recognized that silicone rubber and other forms of silicone material have been used in prosthesis and other medical devices, but no recommendation is made by General Electric for any non-industrial use of any of its silicone materials and no claim is made by General Electric Company for acceptability of its silicone products in applications pertinent to the human body or other medical applications or devices. . . . It is the responsibility of the purchaser to establish the acceptability of the use of any General Electric silicone products for any such application.

GE made the product, but would not accept responsibility for it. Especially telling was a handwritten letter from GE actually stating, "Do you want that bleeding into your patient's body? We say they all do it."

What GE wanted to avoid was publicizing the truth about its implants. The company's own internal memos tell a chilling story about PCBs, which were also part of GE's implant product. One August 25, 1975 memo from J. E. Nair, Regulatory Affairs Specialist, stated the following: "We have some concern for the potential migration of a polychlorinated biphenyl from one of our silicone polymers which is used as an implant material. . . ." The testing proposed by GE was apparently set up to find little migration of PCBs, if any. (This is a frequently used ploy by manufacturers to create results that will hide defects and put their products in a better light.) The study proposed to extract the PCBs into "simulated body fluids" using lactated Ringers solution. However, PCBs are fat-soluble and so are unlikely to be extracted by the water-based Ringers solution.

Apparently, GE recognized that there was trouble brewing, and it shut down its implant section. Between 1972 and 1976, GE had supplied silicone materials to Heyer-Schulte, McGhan Medical, and Medical Engineering, all of which produced implants. By November 1976, GE stopped its silicone manufacturing efforts and ceased supplying silicone materials to those customers who where using them to manufacture breast implants. It was a wise decision: legally, GE was not involved in the class action settlement in 1993. Ethically, however, GE was deeply involved for having supplied PCB-laced implants that were placed into the bodies of thousands of women. Clearly this will remain a long-lived, tragic, and very preventable legacy.

Two other examples show the manufacturers' culpability. A Heyer Schulte memo of January 22, 1973 identifies various defects the company had already identified in its implants. The memo was prominently stamped TRADE SECRET. After identifying that the silicone material came from General Electric, the memo identified the following defects:

1. Foreign objects, such as fibers or particles imbedded in the shell.
2. Bubble, entrapped air or void.
3. Gel, a small raised spot in the shell that is silicone of the same color and elastomer as the surrounding shell.
4. Thin Spot, a small area that is below minimum dimension.
5. Thick Spot, a small area above maximum dimension.
6. Soft Spot, an area that has a lower state of cure than surrounding material.
7. Undervulcanization, material that returns less than 90 per-

cent after 100 percent elongation.
8. Lines, marks, and fingerprints, any defect that is visible in the shell not covered above.

Here is how Heyer Schulte proposed to deal with some of these defects:

1. There were to be no visible foreign objects imbedded in the shell.
2. There shall be no visible bubbles allowed in the shell except in the patch area where it will be completely covered by the patch (where it will not be visible). Bubbles allowed in the patch area must be less than 1 mm in diameter.
3. There shall be no soft spots or undervulcanized areas in the shell.
4. No other defects shall be allowed that in the judgment of the inspector could affect the physical strength of the finished product.

No mention was made of the safety of this product, its potential health effects in the human body, or whether or not the product should ever have been put on the market.

On October 17, 1975, Jim Rudy, an employee of Heyer Schulte, described a few other problems he found in that company's silicone product. Rudy wrote of an experiment that allowed a steel ball to fall through the silicone mass of three different implant products from three different manufacturers. Rudy found that the implants varied significantly in thickness and tensile strength, indicating that there were absolutely no standards of uniformity or quality within the producers themselves. (There were no federal standards, either.)

Another Rudy interoffice memo on October 30, 1975 discussed a study describing problems relating to the physical migration of silicone, liver disfunction, and foreign body granuloma in four victims of the silicone injection. "It is my understanding," he added, "that similar non-nuclear and giant cell reaction results in some patients wherein silicone gel has escaped from the shell."

What had been anticipated finally happened. Rudy wrote a letter to the sales department in November 1975 admitting that "Heyer Schulte now has 15 active lawsuits involving leaking mammary implants. Of these 15, nine occurred in 1975 alone."

Now let's look at Dow Corning, the world's largest maker of implants up to 1992, when the company stopped production. Selling a defective product was definitely not a problem for this company for almost two decades, as indicated by this May 16, 1975 memo from one Tom Salisbury to 45 members of the medical products division sales team:

> It has been observed that the new mammaries with responsive gel have a tendency to appear oily after being manipulated. [It was leaking.] This could prove to be a problem with your daily detailing activity where mammary manipulation is a must.
>
> Keep in mind that this is not a product problem; our technical people assure us that the doctor in the O.R. will not see any appreciable oiling on product removed from the package. The oily phenomenon seems to appear the day following manipulation.
>
> You should make plans to change demonstration samples often. Also, be sure samples are clean and dry before customer detailing. Two easy ways to clean demonstration samples while traveling: (1) wash with soap and water in nearest washroom, dry with hand towels; (2) carry a small bottle of IPA and rag. I have used both methods and the first is my choice. I will be interested to hear if any of you are seeing the oiling.

In short, the implants had been leaking from the start. The message to the salespeople was lie, hide, and deceive.

Another example of Dow Corning's arrogance was an internal memo from Tom Talcott to a number of fellow employees on

January 15, 1976:

> During our task force assignment to get the new products to the market, a large number of people spent a lot of time discussing envelope quality. We ended up saying the envelopes were "good enough" while looking at gross thin spots and flaws in the form of significant bubbles. The allowable flaws are written into the current specifications. When will we learn at Dow Corning that making a product "just good enough" almost always leads to products that are "not quite good enough?"...Plant engineering or other effort to make uniform and flaw-free envelopes would still be useful.

Another Dow Corning memo written on June 8, 1976 by A. H. Rathjen, a company administrator, gave a stronger warning:

> I have proposed again and again that we must begin an in-depth study of our gel, envelope, and bleed phenomenon. Capsule contracture isn't the only problem. Time is going to run out for us if we don't get underway....Believe me when I tell you that the ASPRS is also going to begin their own investigation. A committee will be organized and they will come to the manufacturers asking questions. I would certainly be to our advantage to be ready for them.

Dow wasn't ready, and the proof was in the growing numbers of dissatisfied plastic surgeons. In 1976, Dr. John Wolfe of the Detroit Medical Center wrote a letter to Dow Corning: "We have the situation where implants are being put into breasts which are at high risk for developing breast carcinoma and we are seriously impairing our ability to recognize the carcinoma in its early and curable stage....If someone asked for my recommendation, I would say that anybody who would not use a saline-filled implant will be making a mistake."

Another year went by. A March 31, 1977 confidential memo from C. Leach to his fellow workers discussed the fact that the implants leaked regularly and often.

The contracture issue remains primary in the plastic

surgery community with many plastic surgeons shifting their prosthesis purchasing patterns based on often poorly founded irrational beliefs as to what role silicone-gel plays in capsule formation. Significant numbers of these changes are costing us business—i.e., shift to the inflatable by former gel users. I know of at least one loyal Dow Corning customer who believes that our prosthesis bleeds more than other gel prostheses and is considering shifting to a competitive gel product.

Notice the word *customer.* These products were promoted, advertised, and detailed to surgeons, not the women whose bodies were to bear the burden of the faulty products. Despite the fact that plastics-containing breast implant materials are complex, the failure to provide information directly to the real customer, the patient, was lacking. So too, was follow-up. It would have been simple enough to give each woman a form to send to the FDA, reporting her follow-up experience on a yearly basis. Nothing of the sort was done.

The memo continues:

Several customers, looking to us as leaders in the industry, asked me what we were doing. I assured them with crossed fingers, that Dow Corning too had an active "contracture/gel migration" study underway. This apparently satisfied them for the moment, but one of these days, they will be asking us for the results of our studies.

Beyond the mammaries and contracture, Dr. Swanson recently has been urging that appropriate studies be undertaken to determine the potential for migration of silicone elastomer particles throughout the body. Dr. Niebauer continues to publicly discuss the migration of such particles in his monkeys and it is very likely just a matter of time until the orthopedic community will be aggressively asking similar questions to those we are now hearing from the Plastic Surgeons.

I am not sure where this unrest is leading but suspect that our PMG [Products Management Group], as the steward of Dow Corning's implantable products, should not be too comfortable with our current lack of focus and coordinated leadership relating to this entire issue. I suggest that this question be addressed at our next PMG meeting and clear definition given as to what answers we can reasonably be expected to have as a manufacturer of implantable silicone materials, what answers we do have and what steps need to be taken to fill whatever gaps that may exist in our needed storeroom of knowledge. In my opinion, the black clouds are ominous and should be given more attention.

Apparently no one in final authority was listening and the black clouds grew. By 1977, "just good enough" went to bad. What emerges—through continuing scrutiny of Dow Corning memos—is that a key concern for the company was competition and sales, not quality or human health. No better case in point is the 1983 memo to territory managers and sales representatives on the subject of Natural Y, one of the trade names for Dow's implant:

> Speaking with plastic surgeons, the sentiment is unanimous; Natural Y claims are unfounded; product is not new and they don't appreciate a patient telling them what product to use.
>
> In the medical community, undocumented claims are just that, claims. Ask the doctor to produce support data! [Translation: Challenge the doctor who complains and demand he produce his own "study."]

Clearly, nothing—not even internal warnings from its product developers—was going to stop Dow Corning from continuing its sales.

Dow Corning deserves a special place in this story of questionable corporate behavior. The silicone implant product is not the first time the parent company Dow Chemical has knowingly sold a product that caused life-threatening damage to humans. During the Vietnam War, the company produced the herbicides known as Agent Orange. Dow officials had known of the dioxin contaminant in the product since the 1940s, and knew it had toxic properties. Dow's own studies showed extreme toxic reactions in animals and humans. (The company sponsored dioxin studies on humans in prisons in 1965.) Federal agencies eventually caught up with Dow's early research, and EPA and the National Academy of Science later classified dioxin as carcinogenic, fetotoxic, and immunotoxic. Yet, Dow deceived its customers and sold the defoliant as aggressively as possible to the military and, after the war, for home and farm use. In fact, in 1965, the company called a secret meeting of the various Agent Orange manufacturers for one purpose: to warn them to lower the dioxin content in their various herbicide products to avoid government regulation of the whole industry (Clorfene-Casten, *The Nation,* November 30, 1992).

At the war contractors' meeting, Dow's medical director listed the extensive human health effects which the company had already identified—including liver damage, nervous system disorders, peripheral neuropathy, and so on. And the medical director, along with major administrators, admitted that if chloracne (the nasty, tell-tale body and face skin eruptions) shows up, the damage to the body was systemic.

However, when challenged in public about the effects of Agent Orange, Dow's public relations engine revved up. Spokespersons went on record stating that, "Beyond a case of chloracne, there are no other reported health effects due to the exposure of Agent Orange." And the company began to attack the veterans who had come home with the predicted Agent Orange exposure symptoms, calling them unstable drugheads. Thus, Dow did three things as part of its corporate policy on herbicides: discussed the problems of their very toxic product internally and secretly; allowed a contaminated and faulty product to be used on innocent victims; and attacked the victims for the very problems the company knew would occur.

Dow's corporate behavior was the same for silicone implants. That Dow Corning was aware of problems with the implants is shown by their secret internal memos. Yet, the company sold the products anyway. And when the media started to get wind of what was happening in 1991, Dow's first public relations tactic was to insist that, "any connection between the implants and health problems in women was coincidental. . . . Company officials acknowledge that there may be some link to disease in . . . hypersensitive women."

Then Dow aggressively attacked the victims, dismissing those who complained about the implants. According to a 1992 report by Anna Quindlen in the *New York Times,* "They treated their consumers like crybabies. They didn't take them seriously. . . . Officials at Dow Corning, treating the pain of women whose implants had gone haywire, [called them] Hysterics, Complainers, Crybabies."

Dow aggressively impugned the motives of its various critics and dismissed allegations of problems as "junk science," according to an editorial in the *Washington Post Weekly* of February 24, 1992. That's the same ploy many polluting companies use to confuse the public.

By 1992, Dow's "attack the victim" approach had backfired, resulting in a series of angry responses from women throughout the mainstream press. A new chairman and CEO, Keith McKennon, was appointed to lead the company. Considering the company's corporate ethic, McKennon was an appropriate choice. He had "dealt with public relations fights over dioxin and Agent Orange and . . . this background is very pertinent to a meaningful resolution of the mammary issue" (*Washington Post Weekly,* February 24, 1992). This chairman was to adopt another stance: show concern and sympathy for the women wearing Dow's implants.

McKennon came on to the job running. In a series of public interviews, he gave a succession of highly suspect statements. He promised to establish a women's council to advise the company after consulting with women on both sides of the implant debate. A great public relations ploy—there is no true debate save for the one initiated by those profiting from the sales. Then he promised to investigate the effects of implants—as if more studies were really necessary. He addressed the 300 articles connecting autoimmune disease to silicone implants by stating that, "A lot of the research we rely on is done on animals. That in itself bothers some people," suggesting that animal research is not truly valid, although all major drug research is based on animal studies. And he stated, "In all of our studies, immune responses don't exist. It does not trigger the immune system." The key words here were *our studies,* meaning those funded and directed by the company.

Finally, McKennon discussed for public consumption the issue of "rupture rate," avoiding the more compelling fact that the implants began to bleed through their covering from the very moment they were placed in a woman's body. McKennon also promised a whole batch of new studies, conducted in reputable universities, to get at the "truth."

The reasons for all these evasions, half-truths, and obfuscations? McKennon's real motives for public consumption were summarized in the first corporate memo he addressed to his "Fellow Dow Corning Colleagues" on February 11, 1992:

> I am personally convinced these devices fill an important medical need, and do not pose an unreasonable risk to users. More importantly, thoughtful and able physicians and surgeons all across America agree. But it must be said that there are some thoughtful and able physicians who disagree. Again, I believe Dow Corning has a responsibility to play a key role in resolving those differences. . . . Dow Corning has built a tremendous reputation over the past 50 years; we're not going to lose it in 50 days.

In a nutshell, (1) keep positive the public perception of Dow; and (2) control the dialogue; confuse the public, keep involved, and persuade or co-opt the naysayers.

There are two postscripts to this story. The first might prove quite dangerous for women who have not had implants yet. The chemical companies are not taking their legal defeat lightly, and are, if nothing else, gearing up for both a public relations war and a "scientific" battle.

In 1995, Dow Corning published a full-page ad in various national newspapers stating that silicone implants are safe, and declaring that new studies conducted in prestigious research centers have found no harm.

But a small *Chicago Tribune* headline—"Breast-Implant Expert Faces Ethics Question"—on December 15, 1994 pointed to the deeper story beneath this ad:

> Dr. Peter H. Schur is a nationally known rheumatologist, a full professor at Harvard Medical School and the editor of a prestigious medical journal. But when he helped write an article defending breast implants, then had it published in that journal [Arthritis and Rheumatism] last February, he failed to mention another credit: He is a $300-an-hour consultant to the lawyers who work for implant makers.
>
> This year's service to the lawyers has included critiques of medical reports, reviews of patient records and trial testimony. Schur estimates he has put in about 100 hours worth roughly $30,000 for four law firms.
>
> Ethical standards for medical journals state that authors of articles should disclose conflicts of interest and editors should never pass judgement on work involving areas of personal financial gain.
>
> Some attorneys who represent women with implants contend the manufacturers' law firms have tried to stifle unfavorable articles by hiring Schur and other journal editors. In my view, the evidence suggests that the manufacturers have attempted to control science by hiring experts who are key players in the decision-making about what gets published.
>
> . . . In 1992 and 1993, doctors who believe implants cause disease submitted at least two articles to Arthritis and Rheumatism. One article concluded the silicone evidence "is compatible with the hypothesis" that the implants are harmful.

Schur rejected both papers. [While] Schur rarely treats implant patients, [he] has become a widely quoted defender of the devices.

Another rheumatologist, Dr. Matthew Lang, on staff of Brigham and Women's Hospital (affiliated with Harvard Medical School) worked on a Dow Corning-sponsored Women's Health Cohort study. He is vocal implant advocate. (Schur also worked on the study.) He too, eventually disclosed that he had been a consultant to the law firms representing the manufacturers in lawsuits brought by women who claim they were harmed by the implants.

*EXTRA!*, the magazine of Fairness and Accuracy in Reporting (FAIR), reported in January 1996 that Dow Corning contributed $5-$7 million to the implant research. "Three of the Harvard study's six authors were either paid by implant manufacturers for other research or had agreed to act as experts in litigation on the company's behalf. Dow Corning was given a chance to review at least some of the Harvard study questionnaires before they were mailed to participants. And according to Dow Corning's general counsel, 'Each external scientific study that Dow Corning funded was only after consulting with legal counsel to determine its impact on the breast implant litigation.' Harvard claimed, impossibly, to have included women with 40-year-old implants (silicone implants were not marketed before 1962) and the statistics were skewed by the inclusion of women whose implants have been in place for as little as 30 days." So much for the studies Dow Corning refers to in their infamous ad.

Other studies, like those at Emory University and at the University of Michigan were directly funded by Dow Corning. But, the study generating the largest press is the one conducted at the prestigious Mayo Clinic, which showed "no link between breast implants and disease." *EXTRA!* adds, the "Mayo clinic studies were made possible by grants from a foundation whose chair has admitted that it acted as a 'facilitator' delivering the manufacturers' funds."

Apparently, the Mayo studies were poorly designed and executed. *EXTRA!* revealed that the Harvard and Mayo studies failed to assess whether women with silicone implants were healthy. *Ms.* magazine reported in March 1996 that the women were not examined; researchers relied on medical charts where symptoms like skin rashes are less likely to have been noted; the women were not interviewed by the researchers, and no attempt was made to inquire about symptoms that weren't on the charts.

The Mayo Clinic instead looked at groups of women with and without implants and compared the incidence of certain connective tissue diseases, like rheumatoid arthritis and lupus, because connective tissue-type symptoms kept cropping up in court. *EXTRA!* stated:

> The ballyhooed Mayo results amounted to no more than that, of 749 women with breast implants and 1,498 without, a "specified connective tissue disease was diagnosed" in five implanted women and ten controls—an identical rate. During the research period, Mayo changed their "specifications" to include an extremely rare inherited disease that had shown up on the control group only. Without those three cases, women with implants would have had a 43 percent higher rate of the specified diseases.
>
> NIH finds that it takes up to 15 years or more for silicone-related diseases to show up. Mayo's subject sample had implants for a mean of seven years.

The researchers at Mayo concluded, "We had limited power to detect an increased risk of rare connective tissue diseases. . . . Our results cannot be considered definitive proof of the absence of an association between breast implants and connective tissue disease."

Hardly the stuff to base an entire public relations campaign on. Eventually, however, the claims, repeated and repeated, caught on and a compliant mainstream press reprinted Dow's "new truth."

And Dow Corning found one more way to fight back. Since Dow Chemical Company, the parent, was absolved from liability (the implants were a joint venture of Dow Chemical and Corning, Inc.), on May 16, 1995 Dow Corning declared bankruptcy. Back in 1994, Dow Corning had agreed to pay $2 billion as part of the compensation package. As a result, all Dow Corning compensation was suspended—a dreadful event for women who are truly hurting.

In the meantime, parent Dow Chemical started buying back 25 million shares of its common stock valued at almost $1.9 billion. The repurchase program was considered "a good use of its surplus cash." Dow Chemical's stock continued to rise during 1995.

Because of all this, women suffering from the effects of silicone breast implants are organizing a national boycott of Dow Chemical. The United Silicone Victims is a coalition of over 150 breast implant support groups around the country. Their rallying cry is "Silicone Implant Makers Are Life Takers. Boycott Dow."

To all women—do not wait for another corporate-funded study. Do not be confused by doctors for hire. Let caution and skepticism be your guide. If you have silicone implants in your bodies, get them out fast. Your figure may be less shapely, but you will be far healthier. Doctors state most women can return to normal activity in about a week after surgery. And if you've never had an implant, avoid them if you can. The size of your breasts are not as important as the condition of your health.

# 9

# GOVERNMENT REGULATORS OR CORPORATE SHILLS?

On February 17, 1993, senior EPA management met for an informational briefing on "Breast Cancer and Pesticides in the Human Environment: What's Next?" Ruth Allen, Ph.D., environmental epidemiologist for the agency, addressed the group. Allen went over the latest publications connecting breast cancer to environmental toxins.

She discussed the 1993 New York study that strongly correlated levels of DDE in women's blood with increased risk of breast cancer in New York. She spoke of the Israeli breast cancer study linking a decline in pesticide contamination of Israeli cow's milk to a drop in breast cancer mortality rates. She spoke of the Long Island breast cancer studies, and added that Congress mandated a multimillion dollar NCI study on the role of pesticides, electromagnetic fields, radiation, and air pollutants as possible factors in the excess breast cancer in the area.

She noted breast cancer is a major medical problem and the most common cancer in women in the industrial world and increasing in the developing world, while acknowledging the experimental evidence identifying certain chlorinated organic poisons with estrogenic properties. And she urged that the issues be seen in terms of prevention: develop less-toxic alternatives to organochlorine pesticides.

Allen gave EPA senior management a thorough analysis of the breast cancer/environment connection. Given this strong linkage, did the EPA attempt to implement plans for prevention? No.

Here's how EPA really works.

## EPA Conflicts of Interest

The EPA—the government agency charged with protecting American citizens from toxins in the environment—has not followed its own mandates. Although its administrators may cry that they do not possess the power to make major polluters follow their orders, or that the agency does not have sufficient resources for testing and enforcement, there are other reasons, too. One of the most insidious is that high-level regulatory work can lead directly to a plum job with a company that had been the object of oversight. Because of this potential, top executives in the regulatory field rarely take action that might alienate the very industries that they are supposed to regulate.

The incineration industry seems to be an especially attractive avenue for former EPA administrators. The CEO of Browning Ferris Industries, a leading incinerator operator, is William Ruckelshaus, head of EPA from 1970 to 1973 and again from 1983 to 1985. (Between his two EPA terms, Ruckelshaus was a director of Monsanto, and after 1985 he was a paid consultant to that firm.) Waste Management, fined many millions of dollars for its heavy EPA violations, has over 25 former EPA employees on its payroll. These men and women were once charged with administering environmental regulations; now they're guiding polluting companies in opposition to or around the same regulations.

Russell Train, EPA administrator from 1973 to 1977, sits on the board of Union Carbide. Lee Thomas, EPA administrator from 1985 to 1989, is executive vice president of Georgia-Pacific, a paper manufacturer that bleaches with hydrogen chloride, which releases dioxin. William Reilly, EPA administrator between 1989 and 1993, sits on the board of directors of DuPont.

This revolving door between regulatory agencies and industry partially explains why oversight of giant polluters such as Dow, Monsanto, and DuPont is so tenuous, and why EPA's most vigorous enforcement efforts are directed at smaller companies that offer little in the way of future employment. (Corner gas stations, with their potential for leaks from underground gasoline tanks, are ripe for EPA action.)

The history of how EPA has dealt with dioxin is a perfect example of how deeply compromised the agency is in regulating industries. Three stories tell the tale.

### *The Cate Jenkins Story*

The sordid story of what happened to Cate Jenkins, Ph.D., conscientious EPA chemist turned whistleblower, is one of fraud, coverup, and disgrace. Jenkins's treatment by her fellow EPA officials after she discovered the possibly fraudulent studies conducted by Monsanto on its workers exposed to dioxin reveals two elements of EPA's strategies: the entanglement of EPA with industry, and the agency's effort to disgrace Jenkins while avoiding any follow-up on her recommendations.

In 1980, Francis Kemner and others filed suit against Monsanto after being exposed to a spill of 19,000 gallons of Monsanto's chlorophenol intermediate—a dioxin-contaminated chemical used in making wood preservatives—from a train derailment in Sturgeon, Missouri. The jury found for the plaintiffs with nominal awards—as low as one dollar for actual damages— because it did not believe the plaintiffs had proven they had suffered harm. However, it awarded more then $16 million based on their outrage at Monsanto's behavior. The following are some of the allegations made by the plaintiffs' attorneys about Monsanto:

- Monsanto lied to its workers about the presence and danger of dioxin in its chlorophenol plant so that it would not have to bear the expense of changing its manufacturing process.

- Monsanto knew how to make chlorophenol with significantly less dioxin content but did not do so until after the Sturgeon spill.
- The company knowingly dumped 30-40 pounds of dioxin a day into the Mississippi River between 1970 and 1977.
- It lied to EPA that it had no knowledge that its plant effluent contained dioxin.
- Monsanto secretly tested the corpses of people killed in accidents in St. Louis for the presence of dioxin and found it in every case.
- Lysol, a popular household cleaner made from Monsanto's Santophen, was contaminated with dioxin with Monsanto's knowledge.
- Shortly after a spill in the chlorophenol plant, Monsanto and OSHA both measured dioxin on the plant walls. Monsanto's measurements were higher than OSHA's, but the company issued a press release saying they had failed to confirm OSHA's findings.
- Exposed workers were not told of the presence of dioxin and were not given protective clothing even though the company was aware of the dangers of dioxin.
- Even though the Toxic Substances Control Act requires chemical companies to report the presence of hazardous substances in their products to EPA, Monsanto never gave notice and lied to EPA in reports.

When Jenkins analyzed the test data discovered during the Kemner trial, she concluded that Monsanto's methodology in its studies on dioxin dating back to the 1940s was flawed and wrote to her superiors about it on February 23, 1990. She requested that the Scientific Advisory Board or the Office of Research and Development audit the records of these studies.

The Monsanto studies had concluded there was no increase

in cancer as a result of high levels of dioxin exposure after a major explosion at Monsanto's plant in Nitro, West Virginia in 1947. These studies were critical to the EPA, which had classified dioxin as a Group B2 compound—"inadequate human evidence but sufficient animal evidence for carcinogenicity." Had dioxin been classified in Group B1, EPA would acknowledge "limited human evidence of carcinogenicity," a significant difference from regulatory and legal points of view. The effects of the less-onerous rating were felt far beyond Nitro. It meant denial of Veterans Administration benefits to thousands of Vietnam War veterans, who had been exposed to dioxin-contaminated Agent Orange, and their children.

EPA policy analyst William Sanjour wrote an in-depth report on the whole matter in July 20, 1994, and much of the following is based on that report.

Two weeks after Jenkins sent her memo to the Science Advisory Board, Monsanto Vice President James Senger wrote to the chairman of that group complaining about Jenkins's memo. How Monsanto had obtained a copy of the memo was not mentioned. The board had beaten him to the punch, however; the day before, it had rejected Jenkins's request. The board forwarded her memo, without comment, to the National Institute for Occupational Safety and Health (NIOSH) and the EPA Office of Toxic Substances.

Typically, the EPA was moving quickly on behalf of a polluting company while dragging its feet in enforcement.

A few weeks later, the national press picked up the story, and Monsanto's CEO wrote a letter to EPA Administrator William Reilly, calling for the agency to announce that Jenkins did not speak for the EPA. EPA complied.

Sanjour made a number of Freedom of Information requests for documents. He stated, "It is clear from the FOIA record that Monsanto had access and communications with EPA that were not available to the general public." Sanjour's FOIA requests were for several letters from former EPA employee John Moore—then working as an attorney for Monsanto. In April 1991, Moore had complained about the investigation of Monsanto to EPA Assistant Administrator of Enforcement Raymond Ludwiszewski—who later left the agency for a partnership in a law firm that represents many corporate clients before regulatory agencies.

Another Moore letter, on March 12, 1992 to EPA criminal attorney Howard Berman, reveals something of the relationship between Monsanto and EPA:

> For all the reasons I have previously discussed with you, there is no basis for a conclusion that fraud was perpetrated. The inquiry by EPA's criminal unit should be concluded expeditiously so that Monsanto can clear its good name and such references to the alleged criminal nature of the studies will cease. In our last conversation, you indicated that you would get back to me quickly on the status of the scientific review of the studies and, if possible, what body is doing the review.

Besides giving special access to Monsanto, the EPA was also expending considerable time and money trying to find ways to discipline Jenkins for speaking out. They learned that they had no legal grounds for this, but reassigned her away from any work that was Monsanto-related and made her life at the office miserable. Because of this treatment, Dr. Jenkins filed a complaint in April 1992 with the Labor Department claiming that she was being harassed for carrying out legal activities. Jenkins's legal complaints and petitions were eventually successful—she was awarded back pay and an opportunity to continue doing the kind of work she is most qualified to do.

Sanjour summed up the sorry affair: "Our top government officials were silent, or even worse; they let it be known that they despised the messenger and had nothing but friendly feelings for the accused. The U.S. government gave no support or encouragement to a scientific, civil, or criminal investigation of Monsanto. No mere office director in EPA is big enough or strong enough to take on an influential giant like Monsanto with that support and encouragement."

### PVC Policy

When it comes to PVCs, EPA is clearly in the business of protecting industry. More dioxin is produced by PVC manufacture than by any other process. According to the 1995 Greenpeace report "PVC: A Primary Contributor to the U.S. Dioxin Burden," PVC is the largest and fastest-growing segment of the chlorine chemistry industry and a major contributor to dioxin contamination from medical waste incinerators. The EPA has identified PVC plastic as the dominant chlorine donor in the environment.

In 1988, the EPA drafted rules regulating the waste created during one stage of PVC production. Those rules required producers to monitor and treat a list of contaminants, including dioxin, in the waste. However, according to a 1995 *In These Times* report by Joel Bleifuss, "In 1990, at the request of the Vinyl Institute and PVC producers like Dow Chemical, the EPA deleted dioxin from that list, thus allowing the industry to produce waste without any concern for its dioxin content."

In another EPA-granted exemption for a different stage of production, the agency told PVC makers they didn't have to worry about dioxin. A 1990 EPA document written by R. Kinch and J. Vorbach explained: "The agency is not regulating all of the constituents considered for regulation in order to reduce the analytical cost burdens associated with compliance with this rule on the [waste] treater."

### Incinerator Policy

No more flagrant example of the EPA closing its eyes to pollution is its active support of the incinerator industry—a source of some of the most egregious chemical and dioxin pollution in the country. Despite the thrust to burn, ample evidence indicates that incineration may very well be the *worst* way to dispose of toxic material.

The agency has a long record of backing the waste management industry in legal battles over industry permits and the enforcement of environmental laws. The agency either looks the other way or actively breaks the law. Ellen and Paul Connett, editors of *Waste Not, The Weekly Reporter for Rational Resource Management,* report ongoing cases where EPA is standing side-by-side with incinerator companies against citizen action in the courts as well as in the board rooms.

A chummy connection exists between incinerator owners—who stand to make many millions—and the politically powerful. This relationship factors into decisions on the placement and building of incinerators, their operation, and the disposal of toxic residues. Monitoring records are unavailable to the public, as are records concerning the waste materials fed into incinerators.

Politics dominates the science. Influenced by former Vice President Quayle's Council on Competitiveness, the EPA retrenched on a number of positions. For instance, in the early 1990s, intense public pressure was brought to bear in an effort to keep the Waste Technologies Industries incinerator in East Liverpool, Ohio from operating. Sited just a few hundred yards from homes and a school that would be blanketed by tons of toxic emissions every year, the plant owed its existence to illegal manipulations of EPA's permit-granting process. The plant even failed its trial burn. Blake Marshall, president of Von Roll America (the builder of WTI) wrote to Quayle asking for help. WTI representatives met with the Council on Competitiveness, along with a deputy assistant EPA administrator, after which EPA authorized a "shakedown," in which a facility gets up and burning for 180 days. Toxicology experts and East Liverpool activists met with officials from the EPA and the Bush White House, to absolutely no avail. And although vice-presidential candidate Al Gore came out strongly against the plant, after the election he said that the federal government had "incurred certain legal obligations . . . toward the company that had invested tens of millions of dollars." President Clinton, who has major ties to the original owner of the plant, has been silent on the matter. WTI continues its operation today.

Around the country, the story is the same. The Government Accountability Project's publication *Bridging the Gap* reports that ThermalKEM, a hazardous waste incinerator in Rock Hills, South Carolina has a troubled past with staggering abuses. In 1987, the incinerator exploded. In 1990, state and federal regulators found scores of violations, including overfeeding and the storage of damaged waste drums on site.

The incinerator in the heart of Jacksonville, Arkansas had been burning 2,4-D, part of the Agent Orange herbicide left in 55-gallon drums after the Vietnam War. It finally stopped at the end of 1994. Prior to that, however, malfunctions interrupted the burning regularly and often, exposing workers and townspeople to enormous quantities of dioxin. "Injuries and illness to workers at the Vertac incinerator were not reported," said Kim Stille, assistant area director of the OSHA's Little Rock office in an article in the December 22, 1994 *Arkansas Democrat Gazette*. "It was willful because management knew about it and was deterring people from reporting injuries and illnesses. In fact, employees were intimidated by the management into not reporting them." News reports and citizen testimony indicate EPA Region VI knew of the violations and accidents, yet refused to stop the burning.

In general, incinerator operations are flawed: records are incomplete at best and violations are repeatedly ignored; emissions are far greater and more toxic than EPA regulations are supposed to allow. Yet a September 22, 1992 internal EPA memo from Sylvia Lowrance, Director of Solid Waste, to all ten regional offices details ways to evade the requirements of the law. It instructs the offices on how to issue permits to hazardous waste incinerators that do not meet EPA performance standards. In fact, the letter confirms that hazardous waste incinerators cannot meet EPA's requirements for near-total destruction of hazardous wastes. It states that as early as 1984, the agency possessed scientific information showing that hazardous waste incinerators could not destroy some of the most dangerous wastes as completely as regulations required.

Present EPA head Carol Browner announced that she was suspending construction of all hazardous waste incinerators until research was done on their safety. Her action was empty public relations, since the EPA had already ceded licensing powers to 44 of the states. District EPA offices across the country are aggressively promoting more burning machines despite their knowledge of the failure of this technology.

Thus, the question of community health and safety continues to take a back seat to the accumulating force of political and industrial power. The public sector bears the risks while the private sector reaps the rewards.

## Failures of the USDA

Regulatory failure is not limited to the EPA. In spring 1994, the Government Accounting Office (GAO) released two reports— "USDA's Role Under the National Residue Program Should Be Reevaluated" and "Changes Needed to Minimize Unsafe Chemicals in Food"—that called for restructuring the federal food safety system. The GAO report cited extensive problems with the current system of monitoring unsafe chemical residues and contaminants in the nation's food. In this case, the USDA shares responsibility for the failures with the EPA and the FDA.

These agencies are responsible for approving food-use chemicals before they are employed. They are supposed to sample and test food products to ensure their safety, and take regulatory action when violations occur.

However, the agencies do not assess risks in the same way. The USDA's National Residue Program, which supposedly ensures that drugs, pesticides, and other industrial chemicals do not contaminate meat and poultry, is inadequate because testing is not comprehensive and methodology is flawed, states an article in the February 1995 issue of *Environmental Health Perspectives*.

The same article mentions that the GAO also found that USDA's Food Safety and Inspections Service (FSIS) does not test imported meat and poultry for heavy metal residues or drugs and pesticides not allowed in the United States but used by exporting nations. In addition, FSIS does not have complete information on chemicals not used in the United States or on newly created chemicals.

Neither the EPA nor the FDA is able to provide all the information and assistance the FSIS needs for the program. While the EPA had previously evaluated some of the pesticides, the agency does not know their health and environmental effects today and is reevaluating them—in the eventual hope of re-registering most of the products. The re-registration process will not be complete until 2006.

## Nuclear Coverup

So invested is the nuclear industry in energy and weapons, rather than admit the potential dangers, the industry has consistently ignored or covered up the possible dangers. The Department of Energy has tried to suggest that there is a threshold below which nuclear radiation is safe and has done so by skewing science, creating false public relations, and offering up "propagandistic claims that we should simply forget about low doses of radiation—they just don't matter," says Dr. John Gofman. "This is not science, it is just rhetorical edict."

Adverse effects became more apparent with each bomb test and each radiation leak. Extensive research has been carried out on animals exposed to radiation. However, as complaints of human illness and harm to livestock exposed to fallout came in, the reports were "investigated" and later suppressed (R. J. Smith, "Scientist Implicated in Atom Test Deception," *Science*, 1982).

According to Gofman, the agencies charged with regulating nuclear energy—the Atomic Energy Commission (AEC) and its successors, the Nuclear Regulatory Commission (NRC) and the Department of Energy (DOE)—have an unalterable primary mission— "to promote and preserve the nuclear empire, no matter what reckless projects it might undertake. All other considerations are simply out the window, unpatriotic, indecent—and above all, not to be tolerated. So, whenever public health considerations appear to thwart or to be moving toward thwarting the major mission, there must always be one loser, the public health."

Moscow, June 1994. An international symposium, "Women, Politics, Environmental Action." Two hundred women from 20 countries gathered to talk, give papers, and share their pain and fears about Russia, this most polluted country. Woefully neglected by decades of government indifference, Russia is now devastated by the ravages of nuclear radiation left essentially forever by the 1986 Chernobyl explosion.

I moderated a panel on "The State of the Environment: The Health of the Nation." Throughout the three-day symposium, the stories people told illustrated their unrelieved anxiety and anguish. Svetlana, a vital 28-year-old from Kiev, told me she is terrified of having children because Kiev is "far more contaminated than the government will admit and we know how hard it is for children to survive into adulthood." Alexei Yablokov, the Russian equivalent of our EPA administrator, spoke of a drop in average Russian lifespan from 71 to 59 years. Krystyna of Poland spoke of children whose immune systems were so compromised they had constant colds, flus, bronchitis, asthma, and pneumonia and were failing to thrive. Nina spoke of increasing numbers of tumors and cancers in the adult population. Young children's teeth are rotting and falling out—mysteriously.

Every single Russian who spoke conceded her rage and fear, and criticized the government for keeping a lid on the truth. They urged their American counterparts to go home and tell the truth about Chernobyl. I took back with me a video about Vladimir Chernousenko, the physicist in charge of the early cleanup, now considered a pariah by his government. Exiled from his own country and dying from cancer, Chernousenko is spending the rest of his diminished life in an effort to warn the world. He estimates that 65 million people will eventually be affected by eating the hot food, by the long-term effects of cancer, and by the changes in DNA which will show up as birth defects in the next and subsequent generations.

Fast forward to 1996, the tenth anniversary of Chernobyl. But the official and media analysis of the catastrophe is not what you'd think it would be. The World Health Organization announced that some of the Russian people's problems are psychosomatic—supposedly brought on by the stress of anticipating the effects of nuclear radiation. *Sixty Minutes* reported this as a serious scientific theory.

The mainstream American media has yet to evaluate the extent of the human damage of Chernobyl. Their fixation on the matter seems to be to show that such accidents could not happen here. Reports generally parrot official statistics that no more than 33 people have died as a result of Chernobyl.

The real story factors in the long-term effects of the radioactivity: the cancers that will show up years later, the stillborn and aborted children, the weakened immune systems and consequent death from other diseases. Greenpeace Ukraine has estimated 32,000 deaths directly related to the blast. Dr. Gofman estimates 475,000 fatal cancers plus about an equal number of additional nonfatal cases occurring over time both inside and outside Russia.

This miscoverage of Chernobyl has left Americans with the impression that we are safe here. We are not. We have witnessed the disaster at Three Mile Island. However, a major blast does not seem to be the American way of endangering the populace. Low-level nuclear emissions can and do cause just as much havoc, silently—a fact withheld from the public. The reason this knowledge is treated like classified information is that the U.S. Nuclear Regulatory Commission (NRC) and the International Atomic Energy Commission (IAEC) are committed to protecting the nuclear industry—in all its permutations: continued military enterprises, nuclear power plants, nuclear medicine, mammography, and others. Billions of dollars are at stake.

The nuclear coverup did not begin with Chernobyl, nor with Three Mile Island. It began decades ago, during the cold war when U.S. workers were making atomic bombs and missiles and when these workers became exposed to low-level nuclear emissions.

Dr. Thomas Mancuso's story is just one of many. In June 1965, Mancuso (of the University of Pittsburgh) became the principal researcher in a major project to determine the biological effects of low-level ionizing radiation among atomic energy workers. After 12 years of funding by the Atomic Energy Commission, and $5.2 million in grants, the Department of Energy ordered Dr. Mancuso removed from the study. Why? His findings were not compatible with industry's or the government's agenda.

Mancuso's project showed that very small amounts of ionizing radiation—amounts below approved levels for workers— had caused cancers and deaths in workers at the Hanford, Washington plant and other nuclear facilities. At first, the Energy Department urged Mancuso to publish his research early, before the latency period for cancer expired. Unwilling to be responsible for a misleading report, Mancuso steadfastly refused. Twelve years later, in the final year of the study, his courage was vindicated—positive findings began to appear. As he reported in his paper, there is a "positive relationship between low levels of ionizing radiation and the development of . . . cancers." Other researchers also studied the workers and came to the same conclusion.

In a clear attempt to scuttle this research effort, the Energy Department had Mancuso's funding cut, and then transferred the entire project to Oak Ridge Associated Universities and Batelle Pacific Northwest Lab. Oak Ridge was owned and operated by Union Carbide, a major participant in nuclear weapons building, creating an immediate conflict of interest. In a final irony, the workers in Mancuso's study were told that the amounts of radiation they were exposed to would have no effect.

John Gofman's story is a parallel. What saves this distinguished 77-year-old scientist from the bitterness of witnessing what he calls 50 years of "corruption all the way" is his basic optimism and sharp humor. "Every time I put out something true, the garbage will increase," he says. "But the truth must be on the record, and someday, when I'm gone, there will be a critical mass. People will say, 'You bastards. You've been killing us off all along and we're not going to take it any more.'"

In 1963, Gofman was appointed head of the Lawrence Livermore Laboratories in California. AEC Chairman Glenn Seaborg asked Gofman to study the health effects on humans of nuclear radiation released during the agency's atomic tests and "Atoms for Peace" programs. Gofman told me this story in a 1996 interview:

> We were asked by the AEC to undertake long-range studies of the potential dangers for man and other species from a variety of so-called "peaceful uses of the atom." Naturally, we presumed that the AEC seriously wanted to know the truth concerning the magnitude of possible hazards. In fact, in assigning this study mission to us, Chairman Seaborg assured us that he wanted favorable or unfavorable findings made available to the public. "All we want is the truth," Seaborg said, and he gave the scientists an annual $3.5 million budget.
>
> We have learned, to our great dismay, that these assurances were illusory. It is now clear that the AEC had not contemplated seriously that the studies might reveal serious flaws and dangers in the "peaceful atom" programs. This kind of "truth" proved to be quite unwelcome.

By October 1969, Gofman found that radiation was more harmful than anyone had suspected. The AEC's radiation-protection standards were publicly revealed to be so high as to be the cause of thousands of cases of infant mortality and cancer. Gofman and his partner, Dr. Arthur Tamplin, demanded a tenfold reduction in the AEC's maximum permissible-radiation dose to the general public. They calculated the cancer and leukemia hazards to the generations of exposed Americans to be *20 times* as great as had been thought previously. And they claimed that the hazard to future generations in the form of genetic damage and deaths had been underestimated even more seriously.

The Gofman-Tamplin findings were heresy to the AEC, and the agency completely rejected their conclusions, suddenly claiming that Gofman was "incompetent." Gofman's staff was reassigned, and funding for trips to conferences—where he might testify about AEC laxity—dried up, although others with the right party line got plenty of money. Gofman's office, once the hub of great activity, became a silent tomb. "No one would come into my office, no one," he remembered. Fellow scientists, younger and with little job security, would come to him secretly and say, "John, I've looked over your calculations; you're right, but I can't help you. They'll slit my throat."

Gofman summarizes, "This whole business is so corrupt, from the bottom to the top. There's a massive campaign to lie about low-dose radiation, to downplay the whole thing and denigrate the health effects. Then, when you compound the lies, it becomes the knowledge of the period. So these days, we have 'biomedical unknowledge.' Radiation is going to be the vitamin of the twenty-first century. We won't be able to live without it! Anyone with a deviant opinion will be pressured because of jobs." (Gofman says the only "safe" nuclear scientists are those who have retired and have nothing to lose by speaking out. Change comes only when people have nothing to lose.)

What emerged early was the phrase "as low as practicable" (ALAP) to calm the public. According to Ralph Nader, "The AEC was to determine not the safest level of emissions, but the lowest level of emissions that could be attained without causing excessive economic penalties for nuclear power producers."

That was only the start of an accommodation to industry. By 1996, perhaps in response to the growing concern about nuclear radiation, the nuclear industry supporters moved into high gear. The Eagle Alliance, whose founding members are a who's who of CEOs from the nuclear power industry (ComEd, Westinghouse, Yankee Atomic Electric, Duke Power, Los Alamos National Labs, Washington Public Power, Argonne National Labs, Northern States Power, TVA Nuclear, Edison Electric Institute, etc.) along with a few Nobel laureates, has begun to glorify the values of all the nuclear industries.

These are heavy players, and they carry a great deal of weight in the public eye. It's easy for them to capture the minds of unaware citizens: two of the major nuclear players (GE and Westinghouse) already own TV networks and many more media outlets.

On the other hand, those radiation scientists with no financial interest in the nuclear industry—and there is a small but struggling number—all agree: there is no safe dose of radiation—no proven threshold below which biological damage does not occur. These few brave voices may not be politically correct, but their studies continue to demonstrate the true health effects of radiation: Cancer, leukemia, infant mortality, and genetic damage.

## FDA: Priorities and Policies

The priorities of various administrators and policy-makers at FDA appear to be focused on the protection and support of drug companies. As with EPA, one reason may be the revolving door between the agency and industry. In the premiere issue of *Alternative Medicine Digest* in August 1994, the editor stated, "Over the years I have periodically gone to the public library to research the backgrounds of top FDA executives and those of large companies in the food and drug business. The 'revolving door' pattern is obvious. Congress itself revealed in 1969 that 37 of 49 top officials of the FDA who left the agency moved into high corporate positions with the large companies that it had regulated. A 1965 GAO study found that 150 FDA officials owned stock in the companies they were supposed to regulate." In addition, 203 FDA employees simply had not filed financial disclosure statements, while several had ignored FDA requests that they divest themselves of their personal investments in drug companies, establishing a conflict of interest that makes impossible unbiased regulatory judgment.

Back in 1970, Commissioner Charles C. Edwards, in testimony before the House Subcommittee on Intergovernmental Relations admitted what appears to be the true mandate of the FDA when he said,"[It is] not our policy to jeopardize the financial interests of the pharmaceutical companies." Little appears to have changed over the years.

### Deeds and Misdeeds

The history of FDA deeds and misdeeds, omissions and commissions, reveals an agency with seriously skewed priorities. The following examples each reveal a different way that public health takes a back seat to power and profits:

*Illegal Pesticides.* According to the Environmental Working Group (EWG), the FDA is failing in its job to monitor pesticides in the American food supply.

In its publication *Forbidden Fruit*, EWG states that domestic as well as foreign fruit and vegetable growers are using pesticides that are banned by U.S. law on crops that end up on America's grocery shelves. Some of the pesticides that are showing up—like the cancer-causing fungicide Captan, the neurotoxin Dursban, and the estrogen mimicker Endosulfan—were banned by the EPA because they pose a significant health risk. And the FDA doesn't really have a clue how much of our food supply is contaminated.

Analyzing 14,923 records from the FDA's routine pesticide monitoring program for 1992 and 1993, EWG found a substantial variance between the illegal pesticides identified by FDA chemists and those reported as violations by FDA enforcement personnel.

The EWG report stated that "one-third to one-half of all pesticide residues detected on some crops were illegal. This includes 51.7 percent of the detected residues on apple juice, 50.6 percent on green peas, 28.4 percent on pineapples, 26.4 percent on pears, and 22.6 percent on carrots. These high rates point toward a potentially high level of illegal pesticide use on these crops that is likely escaping detection by the state enforcement authorities and the FDA." It concludes, "It is clear from this analysis that illegal pesticide use is widespread. Domestic and foreign growers routinely use popular pesticides on crops for which they are not registered."

And according to an Associated Press report in the October 30, 1995 *Chicago Tribune,* the FDA's new computer program, developed to better protect Americans from tainted foods and medicines imported by foreign companies, doesn't work. And the FDA doesn't know how to fix the problem, although it had spent $13 million trying. FDA will have to spend an additional $8 million to have the computer system running nationally by 2001.

*Antibiotic Abuse in Livestock.* Antibiotic use is out of control. In some cases, the antibiotics no longer work in humans because we have been randomly over-exposed to them in our diets. Peter Montague wrote in the August 11, 1994 *Environment & Health Weekly:*

> Someone discovered in the 1950s that feeding low levels of antibiotics to livestock will increase weight gain. Even today no one understands how this works, but for 40 years farmers, urged on by drug and chemical companies, have fed antibiotics to healthy animals to speed growth. An estimated 15 million pounds, about half of all antibiotics, are fed to farm animals.

> Ironically, the FDA recognized the public health implications of this problem in 1977, and published a Federal Register notice announcing its intention to curb the routine feeding of antibiotics to livestock. Drug and livestock corporations responded by bringing intense pressure on Congress, which promptly ordered FDA to back off. Everyone agreed that using

antibiotics in livestock was creating disease organisms resistant to antibiotics. But corporate lobbyists argued then that no one knew for sure that such organisms could infect humans. Since that time, definitive evidence has come to light, but FDA still has not acted. . . . FDA remains paralyzed and antibiotics remain freely available without prescription.

*Aspartame.* Despite a string of failed and fraudulent studies, NutraSweet is the staple of diet products around the world, and a major dietary choice for children and adults. It also causes brain lesions, headaches, mood swings, skin polyps, blindness, brain tumors, insomnia, and depression. It can erode intelligence and short-term memory. In 1991, the NIH published a bibliography entitled *Adverse Effects of Aspartame* listing 167 reasons to avoid it. However, thanks to some brilliant political maneuvering aided by public relations experts at Burson-Marsteller, manufacturer G. D. Searle won a long struggle to transform this questionable, even dangerous product into a cash cow.

Under the direction of Commissioner Arthur Hull Hayes, FDA closed its eyes to the problems of aspartame. Hayes, who was appointed by President Reagan in April 1981, came to his job with the goal, according to the *New York Times,* of being more sympathetic to industry officials than past holders of the office. In approving aspartame for commercial sales, Hayes ignored the negative recommendations of the FDA's board of inquiry and the final report of the task force that noted "faulty and fraudulent product testing, knowingly misrepresented findings and instances of irrelevant or unproductive animal research where experiments have been poorly conceived, carelessly executed, or inaccurately analyzed."

*Bovine Growth Hormone.* In supporting Monsanto's marketing of rBGH, FDA not only opposed labeling milk from rBGH-injected cows, but went one step further: it opposed labeling products free of rBGH and threatened legal action against milk suppliers and grocers who so labeled their milk.

FDA's position on labeling was developed under the direction of Michael R. Taylor, an attorney who joined FDA in 1991 after almost a decade as a partner in the law firm that Monsanto hired to gain FDA approval of the hormone. He was also the point man in bringing Monsanto's lawsuits against milk producers who labeled their products "rBGH-free."

*Generic Drugs.* The FDA had been in no hurry to rush these cost-saving copycats to the marketplace. With exploding health-care costs, pushing generics through as fast as possible would make good sense—for the consumer. However, Joshua Shenk wrote in a January 1996 *Washington Monthly* article, "For years the drug industry pressured the FDA to preserve the industry's competitive edge by holding up generics. The agency obliged, insisting that a generic undergo the same testing as a new drug, even though it might be identical to a drug already on the market. That practice was changed in 1985, when generics accounted for only 14 percent of prescriptions written. Today, they account for 45 percent and the FDA now allows generics on the market the day a patent expires. But, since Congress has refused to grant the agency the authority to charge user fees to test generic drugs, it has insufficient resources to review them; that means useful and more affordable generics aren't making it onto the market."

*Silicone Breast Implants.* FDA's foot-dragging on removing this product, of course, has come back to haunt the agency. Women with the leaking implants across the country are successfully suing for damages done to them, damages that did not necessarily have to be—had FDA acted in a timely manner on the information it had.

In August 1987, FDA was presented with the results of a two-year study conducted by Dow Corning on the effects of silicone gel implanted in rats (as reported in the *Federal Register* of May 17, 1990). The data from the study indicated that the silicone induced increased incidence of fibrosarcoma at the implant site. Metastasis was recorded in a number of these animals.

Four FDA staff scientists—Drs. Lorentzen, Luu, Sheridan, and

Stratmeyer—commented on these findings in an internal memo: "While there is no direct proof that silicone causes cancers in humans, there is considerable reason to suspect that it can do so." And, "Silicone gel-filled breast implants all allow slow diffusion of gel through the silicone elastomer shell into surrounding tissues." They suggested that FDA issue a medical alert to warn the public of the possibility of malignancy that might occur following long-term implant of silicone breast implants.

Instead of accepting their recommendation, the FDA transferred the scientists out of that section.

*Conflicts of Interest in Research.* According to an investigative report by Robert Sherrill published in the January 9, 1995 *Nation:*

> To get FDA approval, drugs are supposed to be subjected to rigorous and objective testing by independent laboratories to determine their safety and therapeutic value. Much of this testing is done by doctors at academic medical centers and paid for by pharmaceutical companies, which are often the medical centers' main source of research funds.
>
> . . . If a researcher at the state's flagship university were bothered by a colleague's close ties to a drug company, chances are he wouldn't be too comfortable bringing his concerns to the top. Up there, financial links to drug companies abound. The medical school dean at the University of North Carolina at Chapel Hill sits on the board of a Durham pharmaceutical company. The chancellor has significant stock holdings in a drug company that sponsors research at UNC.
>
> The FDA finally publicly acknowledged the danger in the cozy relationship between drug companies and campus docs. [In September 1994] it proposed that from now on scientists testing a drug for government approval will have to say whether they have financial ties to the company that produced the drug. But the FDA, being the marshmallow that it is, assured the docs the new rule was not intended to keep them from making a fast buck on the side but merely to let the FDA know about possible bias.

What are the consequences of the kind of "oversight" practiced by FDA? Major health risks. According to Julian Whitaker, writing in *Health and Healing Newsletter* in October 1994, "In 1988, the General Accounting Office did a report on the 'post-approval risk' of all the drugs the FDA has approved since 1976. They found that 51 percent of drugs in common usage by physicians since 1976 had risks that were not uncovered in the exhaustive, expensive, preliminary trials the FDA demands of all drugs." Whitaker quoted a 1991 *JAMA* article indicating that 2 million people are hospitalized each year and 60,000-140,000 die each year from drug reactions, meaning that far more people die from prescription drugs than from illegal drugs. Whitaker updated this report in January 1996, noting that an article in the October 9, 1995 *Archives of Internal Medicine* estimated that preventable prescription drug-related diseases and deaths cost the nation $77 billion a year.

The FDA is compiling a "watch list" of approved drugs reported to create potential problems. Three chemotherapeutic drugs, including tamoxifen, used in breast cancer treatment have already been listed. But FDA's solution to the problem is to have the drug company revise the label, not to ban the drug.

### Actions Against Nonpatentable Substances

However, when it comes to harmless nutritional supplements that are not patentable, FDA's policy has been to try to get them banned. One of the best examples of this was FDA's attempt to gain control over natural vitamins and herbs. (The agency was roundly defeated in Congress because of intense public pressure.)

The Nutrition Labeling and Education Act (NLEA), passed in 1990, had authorized the FDA, starting in December 1993, to prohibit supplement producers from making health claims not endorsed by "significant scientific agreement," a more stringent standard than had been applied before. The FDA saw this as an opportunity to exercise its control over a very large market.

The FDA claimed it wanted to subject products to basic truth-in-labeling regulations. However, the supplement industry and millions of consumers saw the agency's actions as an effort to destroy the supplement business. That would allow pharmaceutical companies to take what were mainly natural products and convert them into far more expensive drugs, at far greater cost to consumers, with far more restrictive doses.

Under the proposed regulations, FDA would centralize information, thereby acting as a final arbiter of what health information the public would receive. The agency would have had the power to pull megadose vitamins off the shelves and require that they be administered only by prescription. It also wanted to prevent supplement companies from distributing research papers from medical journals about the value of their products, claiming that supplements used for therapeutic reasons are "unapproved drugs."

The agency also suggested that Americans would be threatened with disease and death if they continued to have unrestricted access to some nutritional supplements. This allegation was debunked by an Association of American Poison Control Centers study that reported "not a single death was attributed to overdoses of vitamins or minerals" between 1983 and 1990.

Despite its loss in Congress, FDA kept firing at supplement manufacturers. In 1993, Commissioner Kessler presented an FDA report entitled "Unsubstantiated Claims and Documented Health Hazards in the Dietary Supplement Industry" to a Senate committee chaired by Orrin Hatch. The report listed over 500 vitamin claims which the agency said were unsubstantiated. On October 21, 1993, Hatch's staff reported on their review of the FDA documents. Here's what they found:

- Of the 528 products listed, 142 were not manufactured, sold, or distributed by the company to which they were attributed.
- Thirty-four of the listed products did not exist.

- Six products did not carry the claim the FDA had alleged.
- Seventeen products were no longer being sold when the FDA's report was released. Duplications and mistakes accounted for another 25 products.
- More than half of the 528 products were attributed to three small companies. The FDA never contacted the first company. It inspected the second, but never sent the company a report. It sent two warnings to the third company, and the company changed its promotional material for 19 products, forwarding this new material to the FDA. Even so, all 19 of the products were included in the FDA report.

"Unapproved" natural remedies in general get short shrift by the FDA and practitioners of alternative medicine can come under extreme pressure.

Developing a new drug in the United States is very expensive—costing about $200-$300 million. But once a patented drug is approved, a company stands to make hundreds of millions each year. In a phone interview, Dr. Ralph Moss, formerly associated with the Memorial Sloan-Kettering Cancer Center, said, "I believe the FDA actually serves the interests of the drug industry by erecting a very high regulatory barrier that no small or medium-sized company can ever hope to jump over. It's a fact that few, if any drugs have ever been approved for the treatment of cancer that were not patented by a major pharmaceutical company or monopolized in some other way."

### Treatment of Nonconventional Practitioners

Historically, FDA has not supported new drug trials for so-called "alternative" therapies. These included Vitamin C and laetrile. Vitamin C, of course, is sold over the counter, and a number of studies affirm its healing properties, despite establishment attacks on Dr. Linus Pauling, the vitamin's most vigorous proponent.

Laetrile (also known as amygdalin) is a controversial substance that, according to alternative practitioners, has shown some benefit in cancer therapy. It occurs naturally in approximately 1,200 different plants, making it impossible for anyone to gain a monopoly on it. Perhaps because of this economic consideration, the substance—extracted from apricot kernels and bitter almonds in small foreign factories—has gotten a very bad rap, being called a poison by manufacturers of chemotherapeutic drugs—some of the most poisonous drugs which humans create.

Laetrile's healing potential was identified in early research by a number of scientists. One of those scientists was well-respected cancer researcher Dr. Kanematsu Sugiura, who for decades was on the staff at Memorial Sloan-Kettering Cancer Center (MSKCC). His work consistently showed that laetrile reduced cancerous tumors in animals. Laetrile proponents say, that when used as part of an overall nutritional program, it is one of the most promising and effective treatments for cancer.

But almost from the beginning, the substance has been surrounded by fierce controversy. In 1975, FDA stated "there is no sound scientific evidence that it is either effective or safe"; ACS, ever industry's friend, called it "goddamned quackery." Even MSKCC attacked the substance virulently.

During the 1970s, each time Sugiura's experiments yielded positive results, officials at MSKCC would find ways to diminish them in public. His studies were deliberately misrepresented or called "spurious," an adjective eagerly picked up by the press. MSKCC also found ways to abort laetrile studies by other doctors.

This coverup enraged a number of MSKCC staff members, including Dr. Moss, who banded together to counter the negative campaign by hospital officials. Moss and his fellows tried to get the truth out by sending copies of Sugiura's laboratory notes to a number of writers. They also wrote their own 48-page report about laetrile, and released it at a press conference on November 18, 1977. The next day, Moss was fired from MSKCC.

The reputation of laetrile deteriorated; by 1979, the elderly Sugiura told reporters, "I am not allowed to talk about laetrile." But he died believing in and defending his work to other scientists.

Despite establishment efforts to denigrate alternative therapies and their advocates, the *New England Journal of Medicine* reported a Harvard Medical School study that Americans spent $13.7 billion on these therapies in 1990. Fewer than a third of Americans who used alternative health care admitted this to their regular doctors.

The reason for this reticence is clear: In commentary accompanying the study, Dr. Edward Campion epitomized establishment opinion by scoffing at alternative remedies as "patently unscientific" and "in direct competition with conventional medicine." The "public's expensive romance with unconventional medicine is reason for our profession to worry," Campion wrote. But as Dr. Alan Gaby, president of the American Holistic Medical Association says, "Alternative medicine is anything the people in power don't like."

Dr. Adriane Fugh-Berman, herself a practitioner of alternative medicine at the Taoist Health Institute in Washington, D.C., listed a number of reasons for the hostility in a September 6, 1993 *Nation* article entitled "The Case for 'Natural' Medicine":

> The medical establishment . . . is largely satisfied with our current disease care, or crisis management system and which likes to pretend that a true health care system that emphasizes prevention and the most benign therapies is not possible.
>
> Pharmaceutical companies, the mother lode of research money, are not about to fund studies of herbs and vitamins, which are unpatentable, inexpensive, and potentially competitive with profitable drugs. . . .
>
> Peer-reviewed medical journals in the U.S. rarely see fit to publish studies that call standard medical practices into question.
>
> The medical profession is almost religious in adhering to its

own traditions and is deeply suspicious of change. "We receive as much training as a Jesuit priest," notes Dr. Henry Altenberg, author of Holistic Medicine: A Meeting of East and West. "Practicing alternative medicine is heresy against our training as well as a betrayal of the guild."

The price for betrayal can be high. Historically, FDA has not supported medical practitioners who chose to practice outside the mainstream. Its personnel can act like gestapo-type officers, and not necessarily because certain medical practitioners were quacks and charlatans. Rather, it appears they sometimes crack down because a doctor's alternative methods are getting stunning results in treating cancer without radiation or chemotherapy. These healing practitioners became a threat to the medical establishment.

The stories of Dr. Ray Evers and Dr. Stanislaw Burzynski are but two of many. Evers was harassed and persecuted by the FDA in the 1960s. Burzynski is having his troubles today.

My name is Ray Evers, M.D. I am a practicing medical physician in a rural community in South Alabama near Florida. I was born and raised on a farm not too far from here. My lifelong dream has been to help the chronically ill, the suffering, those poor souls to whom many medical doctors have said, "There is no hope." I have treated thousands of patients throughout the U.S. and from several foreign countries who have come to me for treatment. My files are filled with letters and case histories of those who came to me without hope and left with new hope for life. Hundreds of them have testified in my behalf in my court cases.

I admit my therapy differs from that of many other medical doctors in that I attempt to return the body to its natural state by using nature's own means rather than resorting to surgery or drugs. I believe in treatment by the nutritional, nontoxic metabolic method rather than the symptomatic method which is not the standard modus operandi of the ordinary medical doctor. . . .

Because I believe in freedom of choice among patients and

medical doctors, I have been hounded by agents of the federal government, agents of state and local government and by medical associations in what can only be described as a vicious and insidious attempt to destroy me personally, my work and freedom of choice.

Why? My only crime has been to advocate an unshaken belief in holistic medicine. If I treated symptoms rather than the whole body, I would be a part of the regular medical crowd. I could have a huge, lucrative practice treating people and ordering pills and lab tests. But I would be deserting the very people who need me most. I treat the whole body. When you treat only symptoms, you are really playing games with patients. They accuse me of playing games; in truth, they are the game players.

Needle stabbing, exposure to constant radiation, powerful drugs, and a lack of proper vitamins and minerals weaken many patients. . . . You cannot treat chronic conditions in a few minutes and help a patient to live. You cannot treat a symptom when the whole body is sick.

The fight has been long and costly, seven long years of persecution, prosecution, and attempted destruction. It has drained me of my last resources. I have taken personal bankruptcy. My home and furniture have been auctioned off. I have been the target of lawsuits; investigated, bugged, harassed by agents, and raided by agents of the state and federal governments.

I was subjected to Nazi-like treatment by agents of the federal government. I even attempted to flee from the horrors of their action by moving to a foreign country. But there is no place to escape. These agents reached out their long arm to the Bahamas in an ongoing conspiracy.

Our results [with laetrile and other alternative treatments] were far superior to that of conventional methods. The use of any and all of these unconventional methods held promise and actually enabled us to get better results in our unconventional therapies than we were getting with the conventional medicine. These results were not published because they were from individual practices. We were all on the private level; we had no funds or grants to really investigate or document our results.

The conventional forces claim (and rightly so) that we do not have any documented evidence, only anecdotal. Give us $10 billion as was done by President Nixon to rid America of cancer and let's see what we can do toward doing and documenting research work. The conventional bureaucracy has money from NCI, various drug companies, etc., while we have to finance our own research with only monies obtained from our patients. Is this a fair comparison? . . .

Basically, . . . cancer research is bought and paid for by the major drug companies. . . . Financial desires are so great that today, we do not have the great health system of which we boast in America; we only have a health sickness system.

Evers finally went to Juarez, Mexico, to work, establishing an alternative medical care center. However, the stress of his struggles contributed to his illness, and he tragically died of cancer but two years after the center's opening. The struggle with the government had literally killed him.

The FDA has not changed its practices over the years. Alternative therapy literature is full of stories of physicians who have been equally harassed. One of the most chilling is that of Stanislaw Burzynski, M.D., which has been reported by Julian Whitaker in *Health and Healing.*

For years, Burzynski has been treating cancer patients with a nontoxic therapy called "antineoplastons" that he originated. Hundreds of his patients who previously had terminal cancers are now in complete remission. Yet the FDA has been trying to put Burzynski out of business for more than a dozen years, culminating in 75 criminal charges filed on November 20, 1995 that could put Burzynski in jail for 229 years.

This persecution began in 1983 when the ACS put Burzynski's therapy on their unproven methods blacklist. A few months later, the FDA tried to shut his practice by filing a civil suit in federal court. Judge Gabrielle McDonald ruled that Burzynski could continue his work, but could not ship antineoplastons across state lines.

Robert Spiller, the FDA lawyer assigned to this case, seemingly infuriated that the judge did not stop Burzynski's practice, told the doctor's lawyer, "We did not get him that way, but we can use the criminal justice system." (Spiller was later promoted to Associate Chief Counsel for Enforcement.) And since 1983, Spiller and other U.S. attorneys have terrorized Burzynski and his staff with four grand jury investigations. Despite continued raids on his Houston clinic and the seizure of almost 1 million documents, the FDA failed time after time to convince grand juries to indict Burzynski.

There are solid medical reasons for FDA's failure. In 1991, NCI experts reviewed the charts of seven patients with "incurable" brain cancer being treated with antineoplastons, noting antitumor action in all seven and complete remission in five. The experts called for long-term trials of the therapy to more accurately assess benefit. Burzynski sought permission for the trials from FDA.

The FDA sat on Burzynski's proposal until 1994, all the while trying to prove that he was sending his therapy across state lines. Joining the FDA was the Texas State Board of Medical Examiners, which tried to put Burzynski on indefinite probation even though no patient had ever complained to the board about the doctor. At the board's hearings, seven physicians, including the NIH's chief of neuroradiology, testified that without antineoplastons many patients would die, but the board was not impressed. Instead, the board's president wrote that "the efficacy of antineoplastons in the treatment of human cancers is not of issue in these proceedings." This case, too, was thrown out in court and a judge chastised the board for being arbitrary and capricious and for abusing its discretionary powers.

In 1994, the FDA granted Burzynski permission to do clinical trials on antineoplastons, and at his own expense, he began four separate trials. However, the agency still has not stopped its harassment. After Burzynski and three of his patients who were diagnosed as terminal but are now free of cancer appeared on CBS's *This Morning Show,* the FDA seemed to go into a frenzy. The agency again raided Burzynski's clinic, herding employees into a closed room for interrogation while ransacking the office. Then the FDA began its fourth grand jury investigation: eight months of subpoenas, witnesses being forced to appear without counsel, and abusive questioning. One clinic receptionist actually collapsed of a heart attack. And in a subsequent raid on the clinic, the FDA seized the x-rays and MRIs of Burzynski's most responsive patients, including those evaluated by the NCI, in an effort to prevent the doctor from showing this evidence of the therapy's success. The FDA finally convinced a grand jury to indict Dr. Burzynski, and his trial is scheduled to begin in late 1996.

Dr. Whitaker closed his report of the FDA's vendetta with this warning: "If the FDA wins its unholy war with Dr. Burzynski they will not only destroy one of the most promising cancer therapies we have, they will also reinforce the message that any physician or scientist with the talent, energy, and courage to make a positive difference in the health field had best move to another country."

# 10

# THE CANCER
# ESTABLISHMENT

President Nixon proclaimed war on cancer in the early 1970s. We have spent more than $22 billion in public funds on this war since then, and hundreds of millions of private funds. What have we to show for this immense expense of time, money, and expertise?

Incidence of some major cancers—including breast cancer—are rising rapidly. Rates of cancer mortality are holding steady. And the cancer establishment—the organizations that are supposedly dedicated to fighting this scourge—have turned into cash cows for pharmaceutical companies, politically correct researchers, and bureaucrats.

The members of the well-funded cancer establishment include the National Cancer Institute, the American Cancer Society, some 20 comprehensive cancer centers such as Memorial Sloan-Kettering Cancer Center and Boston's Dana-Farber Cancer Institute, which receive many millions from the NCI and ACS. We can also add researchers at universities and medical centers who accept NCI funding, leading chemotherapy and radiation manufacturing firms, and the FDA.

This establishment protects the status quo of cancer. Not only has it been reluctant to accept the environment as a causal factor in cancer, but it has at times actively campaigned against such an idea. Well-placed political leaders of both parties use their vast powers to protect polluting industries. Government regulators block information about or access to alternative therapies that are often natural and unpatentable. This plays into the hands of drug companies selling expensive therapeutic drugs and those powerful, polluting business interests whose ties to the government run deep. Together, they control the national dialogue on cancer.

The cancer establishment is an interconnected, socially homogeneous (mostly older white males) bastion. In his book *The Cancer Industry,* Dr. Ralph Moss says, "The top leaders [of the cancer organizations] generally see eye-to-eye on the major questions concerning cancer. They favor cure over prevention. They emphasize the use of patentable and/or synthetic chemicals over readily available or natural methods. They set the trends in research and are careful to stay within the bounds of what is acceptable and fashionable at the moment."

Financial considerations dominate because cancer means big profits. According to the Cancer Prevention Coalition, as of 1992, the costs of cancer were estimated at more than $110 billion annually.

Cancer drug sales are soaring—over $1 billion annually, despite a 1987 GAO finding that, "For the majority of the cancers we examined the actual improvements (in survival) have been small or have been overestimated by the published rates." Most authorities acknowledge that, since 1987, cancer rates have remained steady.

## The Genesis of Power

Sharon Batt, author of *Patient No More: The Politics of Breast Cancer,* discussed the early years of the cancer establishment:

Cancer fundraising was first owned by the American

Society for the Control of Cancer (ASCC). The first cancer fundraising turf war took place in the mid-1940s when Mary Lasker took over ASCC and transformed it into the American Cancer Society. Lasker was the wife of advertising tycoon Albert Lasker who pioneered a campaign urging women to smoke, using the slogan, "Reach for a Lucky Instead of a Sweet." She added leading businessmen to the board and applied corporate advertising and fundraising techniques to cancer charity work. Lasker also cultivated links with influential federal politicians and drove the lobby to expand the National Cancer Institute into a major research institute.

... When the tax-funded NCI began to boom in the late 1940s, the ACS worried that the American public would let their donations flag. "We're going to be skunked," said the scientific director of the ACS. "People are going to say, `If we're giving all this money in taxes, why do we give it out of our philanthropy?'" The two agencies agreed to divide the turf; the NCI would use its funds, raised from taxes, for research; the donations-dependent ACS would have jurisdiction over services and education. The ACS lobbied the government for NCI appropriations and in return the NCI let ACS bask in the spotlight. ... In the postwar years, the budgets of both NCI and the ACS expanded exponentially.

In *Crusade: The Official History of the American Cancer Society,* historian Walter Ross wrote, "Spurred by the effective lobbying of the ACS, the NCI budget began growing rapidly. In 1950 it totaled nearly $19 million; in 1960 it had risen to $91 million; and by 1970 to $190 million."

And according to *Unhealthy Charities,* the 1990s NIH budget exceeds $7 billion, with about $2 billion going to NCI.

## National Cancer Institute

NCI is a powerful government agency. With its vast resources—an annual budget of over $2 billion a year—it funds a large portion of the major cancer research in this country. Along with this monetary clout comes the ability to set the priorities for this research.

The priorities and policies of NCI are determined by a 15-member board of directors and a three-member Cancer Panel, all of whom are appointed by the President. The first Cancer Panel chair was Benno C. Schmidt: investment banker, drug company official, MSKCC board member (now honorary co-chair). The late Armand Hammer, chair of Occidental Petroleum, served as the next head of the Cancer Panel, and was also the chair of the President's Cancer Panel. Occidental is a major manufacturer of carcinogenic materials; a subsidiary is Hooker Chemical Company, implicated in the environmental disaster at Love Canal.

Those board members are in no rush to push pollution as a causal factor in cancer. NCI has other priorities. For starters, NCI's answer to prevention is "early detection"—a well-funded emphasis on mammography. But according to Sam Epstein, "NCI and ACS have failed to investigate the relation between increasing breast cancer rates and their high-dose mammography administered without warning to some 300,000 women in the 1970s. NCI has also failed to aggressively explore safe alternatives to mammography, especially for premenopausal women."

In 1986, NCI launched the Cancer Prevention Awareness Program as part of its effort to reduce the rate of cancer mortality to 84 per 100,000 people, or one-half the 1980 rate. Five years later, the goal had changed significantly: NCI announced that its new goal was to reduce cancer mortality to 130 per 100,000. Save for a small window of new research into environmental causes, NCI seems stuck.

Until the 1990s, when a few individual scientists were beginning to discuss the issues, NCI had been obdurate in admitting there may be a connection to breast cancer and the environment. In fact, one NCI scientist, Forrest Pommerenke, admitted in the early 1990s that he considers studying poisons "speculation," adding, "While there may be some plausibility, the evidence is small." He acknowledged that toxins are stored in the body fat, and that breasts are fatty, but claims there is no relation to the growing epidemic.

Sam Epstein of the Cancer Prevention Coalition criticizes these priorities. In an article in a 1993 issue of the *American Journal of Industrial Medicine,* he wrote:

> NCI discounts the role of avoidable involuntary exposures to industrial carcinogens . . . and has also failed to provide scientific guidance to Congress and regulatory agencies on fundamental principles of carcinogenesis and epidemiology, and on the critical need to reduce avoidable exposures to environmental and occupational carcinogens. [An] analysis of their $2 billion budget reveals very limited allocations for research on primary cancer prevention, and for occupational cancer which receives only $19 million annually, 1 percent of NCI's total budget.
>
> Problems of professional mindsets in NCI leadership—fixation on diagnosis, treatment, and basic research (some of questionable relevance), and the neglect of cancer prevention—are exemplified by the composition of the Executive President's Cancer Panel and the National Cancer Advisory Board. Contrary to the explicit mandate of the National Cancer Act, the Board is virtually devoid of recognized authorities in occupational and environmental carcinogenesis.

NCI not only avoids prevention, spokespersons for NCI and MSKCC (NCI's prototype comprehensive cancer center) have publicly attacked a breakthrough study showing a correlation between toxic chemicals and breast cancer: the 1992 Falck/Wolff study linking organochlorine—PCBs, DDT, and Dieldrin—with breast cancer. (See chapter 3.) After the study's publication, the establishment closed ranks. EPA ignored the study, stating, "There is no plan to require the removal of electrical transformers and the like containing PCBs because there is no determination of an unusual health risk to the public." Dr. Walter Rogan, an epidemiologist at the National Institute for Environmental Health Sciences, said, "This is an issue that has arisen periodically since PCBs were first [found] in breast milk a number of years ago. . . . The question of a link between environmental contaminants and breast cancer is a live issue, but it's very difficult to study so widely dispersed a contaminant as PCBs and even more difficult to study the whole class of dispersed persistent polyhalogenated pesticides and industrial chemicals which persist in a world now polluted with hundreds of unregulated chemicals."

However, while NCI attacks the research of others, NCI-supported research at MSKCC and other centers is sometimes tragically misdirected.

Just one instance of an outlandish waste of resources: in June 1993, NCI committed to a five-year cancer project to use computer-geographers at Brookhaven National Laboratory, a nuclear laboratory in Long Island. Brookhaven is profoundly contaminated; pesticides, heavy metals, electrical power lines, air pollution, and, by its own admission a 40-year cesspool of radioactive emissions and toxic waste make up a lethal soup for surrounding communities. Breast cancer rates are at an all-time high in the area surrounding the laboratory, and according to a *Primetime Live* telecast, are 59 percent higher than in Islip, less than 20 miles away. The purpose of the study was to examine the overlap between various local environmental hazards. But in the original plan for the study, low-level radiation was not even included.

An expose of the situation was reported by Laura Flanders in the Winter 1994-1995 issue of *Covert Action*.

> It has a part-time staff, a budget, and even its own customized stationery that says Long Island Breast Cancer Study. But 11 months after the NCI created the multimillion-dollar environmental research project under heavy pressure from local activists and Congress, something is still missing: research. No Long Island women have been interviewed about their breast cancer histories, or have had their blood tested for toxic chemicals. No air, water, dust, or soil samples have been collected, and no electromagnetic fields measured.

Because the issue of low-level nuclear radiation is so political, because the nuclear industry has so much invested in the "safety" of its product and processes, NCI did what had to be done—design a study with the appearance of authenticity, but which would actually find very little. There is every possibility that the cancer establishment does not want to find real answers on the breast cancer-radiation connection. According to John Gofman, "There is massive speculation throughout the medical literature about possible causes of breast cancer such as diet, pesticide residues, and environmental estrogens. But the one proven cause of breast cancer—nuclear radiation—is almost never mentioned."

The reasons for this selective blindness are power and self-serving interconnections. The cancer establishment comprises a power group that decides how to spend billions of dollars of taxpayers' money each year. Research is fiercely competitive, and the cancer establishment—even the public sector of it—must be considered a business in which vast profits are to be made.

For instance, NCI granted Bristol-Myers Squibb exclusive rights to use the data from government-funded human use clinical trials, as well as an exclusive "first right of refusal" to harvest the bark of the Pacific yew tree from federal lands.

According to an article by Jamie Love in the Fall 1994 *Public Citizen,* a publication of Taxpayer Assets Project:

> When Taxol entered the U.S. market, its wholesale price was $4.87 per milligram, or more than $9,000 for a completed treatment for some types of cancer. Taxpayer Assets Project investigated the pricing of Taxol and found that Bristol-Myers Squibb was acquiring clinical grade taxol from Hauser Chemical, one of the government's contractors, for less than 25 cents per milligram. Bristol-Myers Squibb was charging U.S. consumers about 20 times its cost of production for the drug. . . . Several congressional hearings were held on Taxol and on many other high-priced drugs which benefited from government funding. Taxpayer Assets Project initiated new studies

and found that of the 37 cancer drugs invented after 1955, the beginning of the modern NCI drug-screening program, 34 were developed with significant government funding.

. . . Findings revealed that the drugs developed with government funds were . . . about three times more expensive than drugs developed with private funding. Clearly, the drug companies were not "passing" on the benefits of government funding to U.S. consumers, who pay for the research."

Love also stated that the NIH routinely fails to collect and disseminate information about the government's role in the development of new drugs. It's not an accident. "Rather, it is just one more example of NIH's efforts to accommodate industry," he stated, adding that NCI officials demonstrated surprising hostility "over a number of routine questions about the extent of the Bristol-Myers Squibb role in development of Taxol and of the government's actual costs of producing Taxol."

Protecting their friends, the establishment's main focus continues to be on "management" or "cures." The highly toxic and disfiguring treatments remain hopelessly similar for all cancer victims. "They discourage other kinds of research," said Jessie Gruman, executive director of the nonprofit Center for the Advancement of Health in Washington, D.C., stated in an article by Michelle Slatalla in the October 10, 1993 *Chicago Sun-Times*.

Any other cancer therapy is derided, ignored, or blacklisted. In 1990, the Office of Technology Assessment found at least 180 studies published in peer-reviewed journals supporting alternative methods, and the NCI refused to investigate them, according to an editorial by Sam Epstein in the December 23, 1991 *USA Today*.

A symbiosis dominates the cancer industry. Big business has a long history of supporting the cancer establishment. And the one industry that stands to gain the most is the drug industry. Thus, the leaders of drug companies take an unseemly interest in the NCI and its research centers.

MSKCC's 1988 annual report showed that Richard Gelb, chair

of Bristol-Myers Squibb, was also vice-chair of MSKCC. Richard Furlaud, former president of Bristol-Myers Squibb, was also serving on the MSKCC board. James Robinson III, formerly chair of American Express, is a director of both Bristol-Myers Squibb and MSKCC.

Ralph Moss identified the industrial ties of 17 members of MSKCC's board in 1988. "Of nine people who serve on MSKCC's policy committee, seven have direct links to drug companies (Merck, Pfizer, and Squibb). MSKCC owned large blocks of shares, from 1,000 to as much as 14,000, in major or multinational drug companies that manufacture cancer drugs. MSKCC's 1987 annual report lists the fact it owns securities in the following drug companies: American Home Products, Bristol-Myers Squibb, ICI, Eli Lilly, Merck & Co., and Schering Plough Corp.

And according to a 1991 report, Bristol-Myers Squibb still controlled key positions on the boards of overseers and managers of MSKCC. The company is the nation's largest chemotherapy drug producer, and in 1993 it raised the hopes of the afflicted with its announcement of the "magic bullet" of monoclonal antibodies, which will need clinical trials at—where else?—MSKCC.

The Center's 1988 and 1991 annual reports list additional overseers from such industrial giants as Exxon, RJR Nabisco, Philip Morris, Texaco, General Motors, Bethlehem Steel, Owens-Corning, Pennzoil, Olin, and the Rockefeller Family Associates. The 1991 report states that Bristol-Myers Squibb offers awards to leading doctors at MSKCC.

Other members of MSKCC boards of overseers and managers or President's Council come from top levels of the media (Roone Arledge, Barbara Walters, *Reader's Digest* CEO George V. Grune), where information can be distilled and controlled.

Finance, insurance, and scientific technology leaders are also represented. Barbara Gimbel, a past president of the Society of MSKCC, was appointed by President Bush to serve on the National Cancer Advisory Board, a principal policy adjunct to NCI. Evelyn Lauder of the Estee Lauder cosmetics family was a prime contributor to the new MSKCC-Evelyn H. Lauder Breast Center, a $20 million unit offering one-day diagnosis and counseling, a wig consultant, and a boutique for special items that patients might need.

And there are other avenues of interconnection. In 1993, President Clinton appointed Dr. Harold Varmus as head of the NIH. From 1991 to 1993, Varmus was a member of the MSKCC Board of Scientific Consultants.

The corporate connections help explain why NCI has a long history of failing to support and at times even actively opposing legislation to reduce exposure to environmental carcinogens. NCI remained silent when President Bush compromised the Delaney Clause—the part of the Food, Drug and Cosmetics Act designed to prohibit carcinogenic additives, including pesticides in processed foods—and when President Clinton's EPA head Carol Browner announced her goal to abolish it. (In July 1996, Congress voted to abolish the clause.) It refuses to undertake epidemiological studies on the great majority of pesticides which are common dietary contaminants and are known to induce cancer in animals. Nor will NCI study the large number of people living in contaminated homes in spite of repeated recommendations of the National Academy of Science.

According to Sam Epstein, NCI claims that 17 percent of its $2 billion annual budget is allocated to "primary care prevention," but he maintains that this claim is grossly inflated since it includes a wide range of programs that are irrelevant to prevention. At best, Epstein says, cancer prevention receives less than 5 percent of NCI's budget. NCI remains visible on mammography, which the agency aggressively though erroneously promotes as "prevention" through a well-funded program.

There are some indications that NCI's policies are changing, slowly. For instance, as a founding director of the International Breast Cancer Prevention Collaborative Research Group, Devra Lee Davis was pleased to see representatives from NCI at the group's 1992 conference on Breast Cancer and Environmental Factors.

In what may be a significant NCI breakthrough, by 1995 Dr. Louise Brinton, Chief of the Environmental Studies Section was supervising two environment-based studies focusing on DDT, PCBs, and PBB. "Pesticides have hormonal activities," Brinton admitted.

One study is an ongoing 20-year program being conducted in Michigan on 2,000 women exposed to the PBBs that contaminated animal feed. NCI is working in conjunction with the Michigan Department of Public Health. The other study is being conducted on a population in Triana, Alabama exposed to the DDT toxic runoff of an industrial plant.

Other environment-based studies include a breast cancer study of Native Alaskan women who have been exposed to organochlorines through the food chain. So far, NCI has included 85 percent of Native Alaskan women. They are beginning to identify a breast cancer trend. Another one is studying Asian immigrants living on the West Coast. Because their breast cancer rates go up after they arrive here, NCI is interested in why, which generation of emigrees are affected, what is in their diet, when do the hormonal levels go up, and how high do they go. And because Dr. Brinton admits that "radiation can effect breast cancer risks," another NCI study is being funded and conducted on women exposed to nuclear radiation—in Russia.

Despite these apparent thaws in NCI's stand against environmental causes of cancer, other parts of NCI have gone in the other direction. A report by Kate Cahow in the November 1995 issue of *Environmental Health Perspectives,* the publication of the U.S. Department of Health and Human Services, tells of a study led by Susan Devesa "to identify cancers accounting for rising incidence rates, quantify changes that have occurred regarding incidences from the mid-1970s to early 1990s and contrast incidence and mortality trends to provide clues to the determinants of temporal patterns." While researchers put forth a variety of theories for the increased incidence of some cancers, Devesa stated unequivocally, "With respect to the concern that we might be having large increases in cancer incidence due to environmental influences, I think our studies show that is not the case."

Philip Cole, professor of epidemiology at the University of Alabama, Birmingham, agreed with Devesa: "What is not correct is that those airborne or waterborne levels of carcinogens have been shown to cause cancer in human beings." And in the same article, David Rall, retired assistant surgeon general with the Public Health Service and former director of NIESH, added, "There is no such thing as proof when it comes to assessing the impact of potential environmental and occupational carcinogens on human health. Nobody knows how much environmental and occupational chemicals affect the overall cancer rate.... It's very difficult to prove anything."

Perhaps most indicative of NCI's focus was the search for a successor to Dr. Samuel Broder, the head of the agency, in December 1994. Health and Human Services Secretary Donna Shalala announced the names of the search committee, which included Dr. Paul Marks, president and CEO of MSKCC; Dr. Christopher Walsh, president of the Dana Farber Cancer Institute; Dr. Joseph Goldstein, chair of the Department of Molecular Genetics at the University of Texas and a director of Regeneron Pharmaceuticals; and Dr. Maxine Singer, President of the Carnegie Institute. Shalala said, "We are looking for an individual with an understanding of excellence in cancer research, who has vision to explore new directions." Here is Sam Epstein's take on the committee, which he wrote to President Clinton on February 21, 1995:

> The search committee represents a predominant emphasis on research in treatment and basic molecular biology. There is no representation of scientific expertise in innovative directions of cancer prevention, particularly avoidable environmental and occupational causes of cancer. Nor is there representation of citizen groups with such concerns. The commit-

tee also reflects interlocking conflicts of interest with NCI, which funds committee members and their institutions, and with pharmaceutical and biotechnology companies, which are major beneficiaries of taxpayer-funded NCI cancer drug research.

## American Cancer Society

A conference sponsored by the Massachusetts Breast Cancer Coalition in October 1994 brought together over 400 men and women to explore the issues surrounding the breast cancer epidemic. Prominent testimony came from experts in science and the environment who made compelling connections between environmental toxins and breast cancer. The testimony was presented to a distinguished panel of legislators and government leaders in public health, and representatives from EPA, NCI, and ACS.

Testimony began on the first morning of the two-day conference, and was scheduled to continue through the afternoon of the second day. By the lunch break of the first day, the representative from ACS had left.

The American Cancer Society was founded by the Rockefellers in 1913. By 1944 Elmer Bobst, president of the American branch of the Hoffmann-LaRoche pharmaceutical company; Albert Lasker, advertiser of Lucky Strike cigarettes; and James Adams, former official of the Johns Manville asbestos company, were among its board members.

The society's ability to capture media attention with its agenda is legend, turning the ACS into a money machine. According to *Unhealthy Charities* by James Bennett and Thomas DiLorenzo, ACS leads the list of the 20 largest health charities, and it is the country's largest private philanthropic institution. In fact, ACS enjoys the status as the premier charity in the cancer field. In 1995, *U.S. News & World Report* listed the organization as having a total income of $391.8 million; $373.1 million of that came from private support. The magazine stated, "The ACS's top funding priorities are cancer research ($98 million), public education ($69 million), and direct help to patients, such as transportation to treatment and rehabilitation services ($54 million)."

The reasons for its success are many. Its personally addressed, computerized fundraising letter, emanating from local ACS offices across the country, goes to millions of Americans like clockwork. The letter that I receive periodically makes the following astonishing statements:

> Your gift to the American Cancer Society will help save lives all across Illinois. Today, half of all cancer patients are cured. But cancer is still the second leading cause of death in the U.S. So we must all help in the fight against cancer by generously supporting vital research efforts. In the last decade alone, we've made tremendous gains in our understanding of cancer and treatments for it. Our studies have linked smoking, overexposure to the sun, and some diets to cancer. . . . Please give generously today.

Yet whether ACS is truly working for the public health is questionable. Bennett and DiLorenzo argue that ACS actually hinders disease research because it controls the direction of almost all cancer research through its close ties to NIH. Thus, most cancer research occurs at a small number of institutions that are members of a tightly knit group. This noncompetitive environment does not promote the kind of experimentation needed to challenge the status quo and make scientific breakthroughs.

A review of ACS activities indicates that issues of control and profit are important to the organization. ACS is not working to prevent cancer or reduce the awesome costs of conventional treatment; it is part of the money machine that services politically correct (and connected) research and that maintains the status quo. Sam Epstein states, "Cancer's overall cost is more than $100 billion a year. Direct costs of cancer include more than 50 million visits to physicians, a million operations, at least 750,000 radiation treatments, and uncountable diagnostic tests. Indirect costs include research—in possibly nonproductive areas. . . . And contrary to the constant hype coming from the offices of the cancer establishment, our ability to treat and cure cancer has not materially improved over decades. The mortality for nonlocalized breast cancer alone has remained a static 18 percent over the last 40 years."

The close links between ACS and NCI create an interdependent cancer establishment that feeds off itself. A 1977 hearing on the National Cancer Program before the House Subcommittee on Intergovernmental Relations and Human Resources revealed the close ties among the two groups: for instance, high NCI officials are invited to attend ACS banquets and scientific meetings. In addition, the hearings revealed that NCI priorities are dictated by ACS policies.

In *The Cancer Industry,* Ralph Moss explains that ACS and NCI personnel interlock on many committees. He quotes journalist Ruth Rosenbaum, who claims that an "ACS-controlled clique . . . dominates NCI policy and funding decisions. They've turned [NCI] into a funding pump."

If this is the case, then the important question is what priorities dictate the funding? ACS funds basically go in two directions: (1) to established treatments that are promoted by large drug companies, whether or not the treatments have shown real progress in helping cancer patients; and (2) to those researchers at various institutions who are connected to ACS's board of directors.

Let's take funding for established therapy first.

Bennett and DiLorenzo state, "Social pressure to conform to group norms and prevailing wisdom about what constitutes good research are powerful forces shaping the disease-research agenda. Those who deviate from the norm are viewed as radicals and are ostracized, feared, loathed, and denied access to research funds. Thus, even without reference to the mundane notions of profit, self-interest, or greed, a scenario can be developed in which innovative disease research is stifled and impeded by the best of intentions. When the roles of profit and self-interest are also taken into account, additional evidence arises that health charities discourage directions in research."

ACS actually has a publication titled *Unproven Methods of Cancer Management,* which title, according to Moss, is a euphemism for quackery. The list is an index of possible cancer treatments and their advocates. Once the practitioner and the treatments are put on the list, further research funding for the doctor and his efforts—positive or not—usually dries up. When inquiries are received concerning a particular therapy, the answer is, "If no one has heard of it, they [the ACS] put it on the Unproven List." Wise doctors tread not at all in these areas, for the establishment can bring tremendous pressure on doctors who attempt to treat cancer in ways not sanctioned by the major agencies.

Who are the advocates of these unorthodox therapies? The ACS primer states that "a few hold M.D. or Ph.D. degrees," but this is a gross misrepresentation. Moss checked the list and found that "over 77 percent . . . are medical doctors or doctors of philosophy in scientific areas. In most cases, they hold medical degrees, they have spent their working lives treating and/or researching cancer; the doctors of science have usually attempted to apply their knowledge of a particular area of research to the cancer problem." And most of these doctors were educated in the finest institutions in the United States and England.

"Of the sixty-three unproven methods included in the ASC book in the 1970s and 1980s, twenty-eight or 44.4 percent had not been investigated at all. In seven cases, or 11.1 percent, it appears that the results were not negative at all, but actually positive" states Moss. There is every possibility chemotherapy would not be so lucrative if nontoxic nutrients and drugs were found to be truly effective in the cancer fight.

The logical question is, what research therapies is the ACS willing to support? The answer: Despite the fact ACS has no laboratories for testing and no general system for making medical judgments, its constant refrain is that the only legitimate cancer treatments are radiation, chemotherapy, surgery, and hormones. The companies that produce the materials for these treatments, such as Bristol-Myers Squibb, Merck, ICI, Hoffmann LaRoche, Schering Plough, Lederle, and Lilly, all have close ties to ACS and NCI.

A search on Lexus/Nexus reveals ACS board members who include top executives of the insurance, advertising, communications, pharmaceutical, and chemical industries, and directors of banks and large investment firms. Representatives from labor and public interest groups are absent.

ACS's official policy on conflict of interest for its board of directors reads like a model of ethics:

> All Directors, Officers, and Executives of the American Cancer Society shall scrupulously avoid any conflict between their own respective individual interests and the interest of the American Cancer Society, Inc. in any and all actions taken by them on behalf of the ACS, Inc. in their respective capacities.

Reference to this conflict of interest was made in the ACS's 1992 annual report, so the policy is quite clear. Yet, this commitment, and the requisite signature of each board member apparently guarantees little. In an attempt to determine whether ACS research funds go to institutions with which ACS board members were affiliated, Bennett and DiLorenzo went digging. They checked out board memberships that were on the ACS's IRS Form 990 and they checked out the number of grants and grant amounts from the 1990 issue of *Cancer Facts and Figures*.

Matching the names of ACS board members with institutions receiving awards in ACS's fiscal years 1988 and 1989, Bennett and DiLorenzo found that "287 awards worth $29.9 million went to institutions with representation on the ACS board. These figures represent 34.2 percent of the 383 grants and 35.2 percent of the $84.9 million in total 1988 research dollars. In 1989, a total of 769 grants worth $83.3 million were awarded; 295 (38.4 percent) of those grants and 32.9 million (39.5 percent) of those dollars went to institutions represented on the ACS Board. . . . What we have shown is that there are close, direct links between the institutions that receive ACS research funding and the individuals who control the ACS itself. . . . The same institutions are regularly funded year after year."

At the back of the 1995 issue of ACS's publication *Cancer Facts and Figures* is this fine mission statement: "The American Cancer Society is the nationwide, community-based, voluntary health organization dedicated to eliminating cancer as a major health problem by preventing cancer, saving lives and diminishing suffering from cancer through research, education, advocacy, and service."

However, reading the booklet for what it leaves out shows what ACS's true priorities are. It consistently omits critical information about cancer prevention, although it has several pages on the hazards of tobacco. It ignores the environment-cancer connection, and answers the question "Can cancer be prevented?" this way: "About 170,000 lives will be lost to cancer because of tobacco use. About 18,000 cancer deaths will be related to excessive alcohol use, frequently in combination with cigarette smoking. Diets high in fruits, vegetables, and fiber may reduce the incidence of some types of cancers. . . . Regular screening and self-exams can detect cancers of the breast. . . ." In other words, the victim is at fault.

When discussing breast cancer risk factors, the booklet identifies the usual suspects: factors over which women have no control. However, mammograms play an important role in ACS strategy. "Since adult women may not be able to alter their personal risk factors in any practical sense, the best current opportunity for reducing mortality is through early detection."

Under the section heading "Unproven Risks," the 1995 booklet actually states, "Public concern about environmental cancer risks often focuses on risks for which no carcinogenicity has been proven or on situations where known carcinogen exposures are negligible." Ignoring the cumulative and synergistic aspects of pesticide exposure, the booklet adds, "Many kinds of pesticides are widely used in producing and marketing our food supply. While some of these chemicals cause cancer at high doses in experimental animals, the very low concentrations found in some foods are generally within established safety levels."

The authors of this section do mention DDT as persisting in the body fat, but add that the concentrations in tissue are low, and the evidence is not conclusive. As for nuclear power plants, those risks are dismissed because the "nuclear facilities are closely controlled and involve negligible levels of exposure for communities near such plants." As for radiation in general, the society identifies only ionizing radiation (x-rays, radon, cosmic rays, and ultraviolet radiation) as proven to cause human cancer.

With 26.8 percent of ACS monies (1992-1993) going to research, one wonders just what programs or technologies the ACS is supporting. ACS had allocated a total of $98,417,198 to established treatment centers across the country during the fiscal year ending August 31, 1994. In Illinois alone, "ACS granted $500,000 to seven Illinois researchers pioneering prevention projects in the nutrition and anti-tobacco arenas." It also hosted "innovative, fun-filled events for the Great American Smokeout and the Great American Lowfat Pigout, . . . and boasted of the fact it had "created a cutting-edge public service campaign targeted to youth for the Great American Smokeout." (Thirteen hundred Chicago schoolchildren gathered in Grant Park on November 17, 1994 to "Jail Joe Camel" for the eighteenth annual "Great American Smokeout." There was a mock trial and Loyola University cheerleaders also performed for the crowd.)

In the meantime, while the numbers of breast cancer victims continue to grow and ACS fundraising continues on, here's what the Cambridge Women's Community Cancer Project says about ACS.

For decades, the public relations office of the ACS has told us that the American Cancer Society is "leading the fight against cancer," yet they have consistently downplayed the environmental links to cancer such as DDT and other pesticides, PCBs, low-level radiation exposure, and electromagnetic fields. The word carcinogen is rarely found in ACS literature, except as it relates to smoking.

The ACS has failed to support publicly important environmental legislation such as the Clean Air Act. The ACS did not fight for the Toxic Substances Control Act. The ACS did not fight for recent clean water legislation. The ACS has never publicly supported occupational safety standards or efforts to reduce radiation exposure.

The ACS's mission statement says they are "dedicated to eliminating cancer as a major health problem by preventing cancer . . . ," yet their National Conference on Breast Cancer in Boston did not address the causes of breast cancer or environmental links to breast cancer in any of the 40 conference workshops. Instead, the conference focused on treatment and detection, methods that have been used for over 50 years which have failed to lower mortality rates for breast cancer.

The American Public Health Association, the nation's premier public health organization, has called for a broad phaseout of chlorine-containing organic compounds known as organochlorines, because of their probable link to breast cancer and other health-related problems. The Clinton administration has also called for a phaseout of chlorine through a comprehensive plan to overhaul the Clean Water Act. Despite this, the ACS has failed to support publicly the proposed phaseout of chlorine. . . . ACS does not support the Delaney Clause.

Sheila Kaplan, in the quarterly *PR Watch* (1994), gives further evidence of ACS's true priorities:

While produce growers and distributors got word last spring that the Public Broadcasting Service was about to broadcast a "Frontline" documentary on the cancer risk that pesticides pose to children, the industry alerted its public-relations firm, New York-based Porter/Novelli.

The firm's image-control specialists quickly crafted a rebuttal to help the industry's Center for Produce Quality quell public fears about the chemicals.

Next, Porter/Novelli, a lobby and public-relations shop, called another client, the American Cancer Society. The PR experts, whose Washington office is led by Steve Rabin, rushed their rebuttal over to the headquarters of the cancer society, for which they have done pro bono work for almost 20 years.

In response, the cancer society sent guidelines to its branch offices for answering public inquiries about the issue—guidelines that included points Porter/Novelli had drafted for the industry group and that downplayed the risk of cancer from pesticides.

The public relations machine went into full gear again in October 1995 when ACS wrote to its regional directors to be careful during Breast Cancer Awareness Month. "Certain environmental activist groups may be picketing ACS offices during October to voice their concerns about the perceived inattention to the environmental causes of breast cancer by ACS and the cancer research community." The directive stated, "Volunteers and staff should be on call to be able to respond to demonstrators at anytime during October. October 27 has been designated by these groups as 'National Cancer Industry Awareness Day' and may be the day with the highest likelihood of a protest."

In the event of a demonstration, local ACS officials were to use a model Q-and-A prepared by national headquarters. If asked about the society's interest in environmental causes of breast cancer, ACS volunteers were to respond, "We support many investigators working in this area. In March 1995, the Society had $10.7 million in grants in effect that pertain to environmental carcinogenesis and cancer." That $10.7 million represents approximately 2.5 percent of the approximately $400 million that ACS raises annually—hardly a deep commitment.

As for why the ACS does not support the Clean Indoor Air Act and the Toxic Substances Act, the official line is that these acts "provide too little protection." And going on the offensive, volunteers were supposed to bring up this wondrous bit of illogic: "Because of better and more widely practiced early detection methods, breast cancer incidence rates have gone up, because more cancers are being detected. However, death rates from breast cancer have held steady in recent years. This indicates there has been improvement in survival." Actually, this obscures environmental toxins, the real reason for the increase in breast cancer in industrial countries. And considering all the ACS money going to conventional treatment research, that death rates are steady is hardly a recommendation for present therapies.

As for implants, the ACS gives a mixed and very dangerous message. In a position paper on silicone gel breast implants, the ACS commends the FDA for "its continued concern for the well-being of cancer patients and other users of silicone implants and for its diligence in exploring the safety issues still in question."

Well and good. But the position paper adds, "For implant patients who are not experiencing any difficulties, there is no need to consider removing the implants. . . . The American Cancer Society does not believe that it would be in the best interest of cancer patients if silicone breast implants were totally removed from the market, based on current evidence. The Society calls on the Food and Drug Administration to base its final decision about . . . implants on substantive scientific evidence." These final words echo Dow Corning's call for substantive scientific evidence, meaning more delay.

Lillian Lovitt is a Connecticut-based art director who designs children's books and magazines. In October 1993, when she was 47, she was diagnosed with breast cancer. After undergoing surgery, chemotherapy, and radiation, she was told by her friends to "get active." One of her friends gave her the Cambridge

Women's Community Cancer Project pamphlet about ACS.

Lovitt did two things. She first wrote a letter to ACS asking them to direct its energies to real prevention and environmental protection, to confront polluting corporations, and to appoint women and activists to its board. She also asked them to stop exaggerating cure rates, and to please spend wisely any monies she might help to raise.

Then she took 500 copies of her letter and joined what she calls a carefully staged ACS breast cancer march on a Connecticut parkway, with hundreds of women and men: breast cancer survivors (many in wheelchairs), their families and supporters, ACS "volunteers," and the media. The goal of ACS was to raise money. Lovitt's goal was to hand out copies of her letter along with the pledge cards.

"Within minutes after I started, I was surrounded by screaming ACS volunteers and a state trooper who demanded to know if I had a permit to do what I was doing," she said in an interview. "He threatened me with arrest if I didn't stop handing out my leaflets. I was surprised at the volunteers' hostility. They followed me, harassed me, and shouted names at me."

Lovitt went to the local state police headquarters, found that she was doing nothing wrong, and went back to the parking lot to put copies of her letter on the windshields of cars.

Lovitt remembers her disgust at what happened next. "When the press left, suddenly the organizers—those wearing the T-shirts with *ACS* on them—left too. Their job was done. Taking their pledge cards and money with them, they had gagged us, abandoned the patients and their families—who were still pushing wheelchairs along the sand on the beach. They got what they wanted." Lovitt had given copies of her letter to members of the press, but no mention of it was made in any reports of the march.

While ACS touts its many accomplishments and claims it is on the winning side in the war on cancer, it's clear that the real winners are the pharmaceutical companies and polluting industries whose actions ACS covers up. The result is an out-and-out war on real cancer prevention and the delaying of better, less-invasive treatment.

Think twice before you respond to ACS's next fundraising appeal.

## Drug Companies

If NCI is the research arm of the cancer establishment and ACS is the fundraising and public relations arm, then the drug companies are the manufacturing and marketing arm. Chemotherapeutic drugs dominate the American approach to cancer treatment. And through advertising and public relations, the drug companies are trying to make sure that they maintain that dominance.

"Drug companies reach into deep pockets to fund their marketing campaigns—after all, drug manufacturing is the most profitable industry in the country," states an article by Cynthia Cott in the August 31, 1992 issue of *The Nation.* "In 1990, the top ten pharmaceutical companies had a profit margin three times that of the average Fortune 500 company. . . . The pill czars have been pouring money into marketing. . . . Their methods of directly pitching products are well known. At meetings sponsored by drug companies, doctors are wined, dined, and dazzled by promoters of the host's drug du jour. Magazine ads . . . make heady promises, then list the side effects in fine print."

Present pharmaceutical agents employed to combat cancer are in a category all their own. They are enormously expensive; ACS admits the average cost of treating cancer amounts to about $160,000. Most of these drugs are manmade substances, often developed at taxpayers' expense, sometimes extracted from plants found in nature and then patented by large pharmaceutical companies. They are then aggressively and elegantly advertised in major peer-reviewed oncology journals throughout the country as "the newest breakthroughs."

Pharmaceutical companies that sell drugs that heal also sell products that kill. At least four of the drug corporations—Lederle Division of American Cyanamid, ICI-Zeneca, Eli Lilly, and Upjohn—produce nonpharmaceutical chemicals in their other divisions that have been linked to cancer as well as other adverse effects. ICI alone produces four fungicides, 27 herbicide preparations, ten insecticidal preparations, and one soil fumigant. American Cyanamid makes a whole host of pesticides and insecticides.

A woman with breast cancer may be treated with Eli Lilly's chemotherapeutic agent, Oncovin, its antibiotic Ceclor, and its pain reliever Darvon. For her distress, she may be prescribed Prozac, recently linked to cancer. Lilly's Animal Health division produces bovine growth hormones—with their possible link to breast cancer—other growth promoters, and unregulated antibiotics which are fed to cattle, swine, and poultry and then passed on to the consumers.

The leading drug companies affect our economy because they are major players on the financial markets. They affect our government's deficit because they enjoy lucrative research grants, patent rights, and tax subsidies for developing new drugs. They affect our government itself because their hefty PAC donations influence legislators who write the rules and because their corporate directors have a close relationship with government regulators. They affect our medical system because they play major roles at significant cancer centers across the country.

Dr. Peter Greenwald, director of cancer prevention and control for NCI, has admitted, "You cannot do research on pharmaceuticals without having some partnership with industry" (Morris, *Houston Chronicle,* February 5, 1992).

The interrelationship with government and the drug companies' power to create and control markets may make an investor in the stock markets dream of dividends. The tight connection between government and drug/chemical companies forms a nearly unbreakable spiral of contamination, illness, need for treatment, more contamination, and profits.

Controlling the public dialogue about cancer also helps ensure continued sales. Bristol-Myers Oncology Division was a major sponsor (along with Revlon, Lifetime Television, and Rhone-Poulenc Rorer, a drug and pesticide-manufacturing company) of the National Breast Cancer Coalition conference held in Washington, D.C., in May 1994. Over 500 women convened for two days to learn about the disease and then to storm the steps of the Capitol to advocate greater national attention to breast cancer and more funding for research. Any mention of alternative therapies was rapidly shot down.

Or take the medical company Amgen. It makes millions of dollars selling Neupogen (Filgrastim), which is used to decrease the side effects of chemotherapy. The cost of the medication is between $6,000 and $10,000 per patient. The company boasts: "We are excited about the possibility for future growth in bone marrow and other cell support treatment and believe that Amgen, with Neupogen . . . is squarely positioned to take advantage of opportunities in this area."

What would happen to Amgen if doctors stopped administering chemotherapy to cancer patients? What would happen if unpatentable drugs and alternative therapies were promoted? Hundreds of millions of dollars would be lost to the drug companies—money that secures the power of the drug companies, the regulating agencies, and the research facilities. It is no wonder that the cancer establishment fights for the status quo.

# 11

# INDUSTRY'S RESPONSE TO THE EPIDEMIC

**D**o the officers and decision-makers of polluting industries know they are poisoning us? Of course. Their own research scientists have provided plenty of data on that. But since the focus of big business in general extends only to next quarter's profits, it makes more sense for them to endorse shortsighted policies in order to delay finding alternatives to polluting processes and deleterious products. Thus, business will pay public relations firms and lobbyists millions of dollars a year in what amounts to hush money to mislead the public about the issues. They will subvert the regulatory process, protest environmental laws, denigrate independent research, and fight continued rearguard action against the idea that health-friendly production processes can be implemented in our economy.

## Corporate Manipulation and Control

In the *Rachel's Environment and Health Weekly* of July 22, 1993, Peter Montague identified strategies that polluting industries consciously employ to mislead the public:

- Deny that environmental and health problems are real.

- Delay the inevitable. Give heavily to the arts, sports events, and local schools; crush your adversaries in court; fund irrelevant scientific research; demand more studies; sow the seeds of doubt, especially about the economic effects of about environmental programs.
- Dissemble or lie to the media.
- Divide the adversaries. Keep them quibbling, and destroy their credibility, cohesiveness, and confidence.
- Create complex paper trails—contracts, subcontracts, leases, and subsidiaries.
- Defeat legislative proposals that are not in your best interests.
- Demand the government use risk assessment whenever possible. "A well-written risk assessment can prove anything is safe."
- Control the public dialogue. Demand hearings where the public gets limited time slots to state its case. Make sure the public can only ask questions.
- Deflect attention away from corporate behavior. Individuals within the corporation are not to be held responsible for anything the corporation does.
- Make the public guilty for its personal choices.
- Control the pace of change, and make necessary conversions on the corporation's timeline.
- Support the big ten environmental groups when they work to pass unenforceable legislation. Such legislation undermines confidence in government, splits the environmental movement, wastes taxpayer money, bloats the bureaucracy, and convinces the public that real change is impossible.
- Focus on controlling chemicals one at a time.
- Convince the public that change is hopeless.

Two other strategies are also popular with polluting industries:

*Political Action Committees (PACs).* Dow Chemical, the

largest manufacturer of chlorine in the world, is one of many companies that give money to political candidates. Dow put up nearly $2 million from 1981 through 1994 to guard its turf with PACs, according to an *Audubon Magazine* report in the November 1995 issue. The company spent more than $500,000 in congressional races between 1981 and 1988. From 1989 to 1994 Dow Chemical, along with its subsidiaries Destec and Dow-Elanco, and Dow Corning funded 14 affiliated PACs which gave $1,208,545 to congressional candidates. In addition, both Dow Chemical and Dow Corning are members of the Chemical Manufacturers Association, which contributed $83,835 to candidates between 1989 and 1994.

*Industry-Sponsored Research.* Industries fund studies at universities and medical centers with the expectation that the conclusions will dovetail with the best interests of industry. "Much of the science research in the U.S. is being done at universities that are funded by corporations, or in the corporation's own research labs," says Joe Belluck, staff attorney at Public Citizen's Congress Watch. A major mission of various industry-supported "scientific" public interest groups is to convince the media that environmentalists are single-issue hotheads motivated by politics, and that industry's science is rational.

Dioxin is part of the paid science syndrome. A 1995 *In These Times* story about the EPA's reassessment of dioxin notes that the agency's Science Advisory board was reviewing the 1994 reassessment. William Greenlee of the University of Massachusetts and John Graham of the Harvard Center for Risk Analysis were chosen by EPA to critique the section of risk assessment that dealt with the question of what quantity of dioxin is "safe." (To even debate this issue is a tragic waste, since so much independent evidence indicates that there is no safe level of dioxin.) Not only had both men "consistently challenged the validity of the dioxin health-risk conclusions contained in the EPA ... report," but both had received major grants from dioxin-creating industries. Greenlee admitted receiving several million dollars in research grants from the Chemical Manufacturers Association and Dow Chemical. Graham's Harvard Center is heavily dependent on Ciba-Geigy, GE, Georgia Pacific, ICI, Kodak, Monsanto, Olin, and Dow.

Although the idea that the companies that are the bedrock of our economy could be so cynical about their responsibilities to society seems outlandish, it is all too true. In case after case, involving all classes of pollutants, the strategies summarized above have been honed to perfection by industry and their paid representatives.

### Pollution of the Great Lakes

The Great Lakes are a significant repository of organochlorines—from pesticide and animal feed runoff from farms, from toxic incinerator emissions that can travel up to 1,200 miles. This contamination is so significant that Canada and the United States set up a treaty body called the International Joint Commission (IJC) to monitor that aquatic environment. In 1994, based on the reports of a number of scientific boards, committees, and task forces composed of distinguished experts, the IJC commissioners called for a sunsetting of chlorine—which they determined was a unified class of chemicals—as an industrial chemical. The commission's 1994 report stated, "The characteristics of persistent toxic substances make them much less amenable to traditional pollution control efforts. . . . The Great Lakes Water Quality Board supports this view, concluding that there is no acceptable assimilative capacity for persistent bioaccumulative toxic substances. . . . Therefore, the only appropriate water quality objective is zero."

The industries that were cited as the source of the Great Lakes pollution in the IJC report fought back savagely.

Gordon K. Durnil, an attorney from Indianapolis, is a long-time Republican party activist. President Bush appointed him to the IJC, on which he served as U.S. chairman from 1990 through 1994. Witnessing industry's hostile response to IJC's recommendations and seeing their attempts to confuse both the science and the public, he wrote *The Making of a Conservative Environmentalist:*

> I watched the chemical industry, through its lobbyists, fight any potential for change and then try to avoid responsibility for its action. . . . The lobbyists use tricky qualifying words to deflect the truth. Rather than join the dialogue regarding the responsibility we all have to future generations, their typical tactic was to disrupt such dialogue.
>
> . . . Successful environmental protection depends upon public pressure. But when the public hears one side say everything is bad, and the other side say nothing is bad, the thought is mentally excused from their concerns. It is easier to believe that nothing is bad, rather than to believe that everything is bad. The news media add to the confusion with their concern about "balanced stories." Quite often, a group of scientists will issue various papers setting out a suspected linkage between the discharge of some substance at the local factory and adverse health effects in a community. . . . To balance the story, the reporter calls the local factory for their side. Technical people are normally not available, but Fred, the P.R. guy always is. Fred says, "those people have bad science and are premature in their findings." The story then reflects those two views, with a headline that probably mentions bad science. The reader has a choice when absorbing such a balanced story. Change her habits or just go on doing what she had been doing. And of course, it's easiest to keep on doing what we have been doing.

The polluters' strategies are blatantly applied at biennial IJC meetings. Representatives of chlorine-related industries attend every IJC meeting and attack environmental groups and independent scientists who present their own research. Especially vulnerable are those who offer personal testimony about their breast cancer or their developmentally delayed child. Industry attacks these presenters as "emotional" and not scientific.

Durnil remembers seeing lobbyists organize employees from

large companies, spreading them around the room so there was one of their own in each discussion group to make sure that none of the groups came to any conclusions adverse to industry's position. They confuse the issues in various ways: by making spurious attacks on the scientific methods and conclusions of anti-industry studies; by trying to change the ground rules for accepted research methods; by attacking the independent scientists themselves; and by having hired guns make reassuring statements about the safety of individual chemicals while cynically avoiding the deeper truth about bioaccumulation.

For the 1994 meeting, the chlorine industry hired spokespeople, including a number of university professors from the United States and Europe, who in panel discussions either denied that health problems are linked to continuing pollution or claimed that the link between the two is not really very strong. It also hired the consulting group CanTox to rebut the findings of IJC scientists.

Linda Locke, program manager for CanTox, laid out the assumptions underlying the chlorine industry's "scientific" efforts, which of course were at odds with the IJC's work. Included were such misleading statements as chemicals do not show adverse effects below certain threshold concentrations and metabolic processes allow organisms to accommodate low doses of chemicals.

"Applying these principles," Locke said, "it can be concluded that chlorinated chemicals span a wide range of molecular structures and cannot be considered as a single group. . . . The application of sound scientific principles is necessary to identify chemicals of concern and to design effective environmental protection strategies to control their possible impact." In other words, test each individual chemical by itself, don't be concerned with affects of ongoing exposure, and call for more studies.

The chlorine industry also likes to make claims about the millions of employees who could lose their jobs if chlorine is phased out. This threatened (but not completely valid) loss always scares people, especially those in localities that depend on these industries. But Durnil challenges those estimates, stating, "It is the lobbyist tactic of fear and paranoia in denouncing all efforts to prevent adverse effects to human and ecosystem health by claiming that every action of pollution prevention or remediation will cost 'zillions' of jobs. The reasonable position would seem to be one that would provide environmental protection and economic growth, yet not take away job opportunities or health options from citizens." (See Appendix A.)

And industry demands for "certainty" in all scientific conclusions before they will reduce their pollution are more delaying tactics. Gordon Durnil put this argument in perspective, too:

> Whenever a suggestion is made to protect health, especially human health, we hear about bad science and the lack of scientific certainty. We heard those claims in the breast implant discussions, and we heard it again . . . as the tobacco industry testified before Congress. Still, governments demand absolute scientific certainty of the cause/harm linkage before changing a standard. And industry denies responsibility because absolute certainty of the causal relationship to the harm has not yet been found. Think about that. What other aspect of our lives demands such certainty before exercising caution?
>
> Not the law—we convict people on the subjective judgment of twelve individuals. Not education—where 70 percent can be a passing grade. Not religion—where there is always room for forgiveness and atonement. Not health care—take two aspirins and call me tomorrow. Certainly not the news media—who never seem to be accountable for what they said yesterday. Accounting? Engineering? Architecture? All have room for error, with miscellaneous accounts, sway factors, etc. But in the governmental regulations of the manufacture, use, and disposal of persistent toxic substances, we demand scientific certainty. We demand absolute proof of the causal relationship to harm. And the certainty we demand is that the

onerous substance causes harm, not that the substance does not cause the harm.

...The U.S. and Canadian governments estimated that somewhere between 60,000 and 200,000 chemicals are being discharged into the Great Lakes. A pretty wide range, wouldn't you say? What it tells us is that we don't even know for sure what is being discharged. We do know however, that most of it has never been tested. The chemical manufacturing industry was upset with me over the recommendation to treat chlorine as a class. They say that each substance must be looked at one at a time to determine its potential for harm. Should we take them seriously and begin to look at 60,000 to 200,000 chemicals one at a time?

If so, we might get a good start by the year 3000 or so. So, as you enjoy the Great Lakes, or as you go about your daily business, what is being discharged into the environment might adversely affect you, your child, or your grandchild. But no real caution can be required of the discharger because there is no absolute certain proof. . . . Eighty percent certainty of such harm is not good enough. Ninety percent, so far, is not good enough. We need one hundred percent absolute proof of harm, or we keep on doing what we have been doing. Surely we need to change our way of thinking.

### *Industry Front Groups*

In the October 1995 issue of its quarterly publication, Greenpeace stated that "Dow and its corporate allies often work through trade organizations and front groups so that the fingerprint of the corporation is obscured. Dow writes the checks but the work is done by neutral-sounding groups like the Clean Industry Coalition, the Alliance for Reasonable Regulation, the American Council on Science & Health, the Council for Agricultural Science and Technology, and many more."

The Soil and Water Conservation Society is supported by government agencies, Zeneca Agricultural Products, Monsanto, and a number of "conservation and farm organizations." This group publishes the *Journal of Soil and Water Conservation* and holds national conferences. The January/February 1995 conference discussed the conservation provisions of the 1995 farm bill. Considering that both Zeneca and Monsanto manufacture products that have already been identified as harmful, it is impossible to believe that the conference did anything but create a lobby against stricter regulations on pesticide applications.

Industry positions are vigorously advocated by trade associations such as the Chemical Manufacturers Association. This group—with a membership of well over 100 chemical manufacturers—has already mounted its own primetime TV ads, extolling its members' ability to control pollution.

The American Council on Science and Health (ACSH) is involved in the debate over herbicides. It is supported by over 100 chemical and food companies. Its executive director, Elizabeth Whelan, has a record of attacking environmentalists and their campaigns. Whelan participated in the attack on David Steinman's *Diet for a Poisoned Planet.* And according to an article in the March 1990 *Columbia Journalism Review,* she called the attack on the pesticide Alar (applied to apples) "an absolute travesty" fomented by "rather irresponsible" journalists. The same article stated that the ACSH has received a grant of at least $25,000 from Uniroyal Chemical Company, the maker of Alar.

Whelan's 1990 budget of $1.1 million came from donations from Exxon, Union Carbide, Dow Chemical, Con Edison, Coca-Cola, and other corporations. In addition, her defense of hormones in cows was backed by the National Dairy Council and the American Meat Institute.

The *CJR* article concludes, "Perhaps it would be best to say that she enthusiastically embraces the chemicals-are-safe philosophy of those who happen to support her financially. People ought to know that so they can digest her views with whatever grains of salt they deem necessary."

And then there are the "grassroots" organizations that are funded by major polluters. These "astroturf" groups, as Laura

Flanders calls them in an article in the July 1996 issue of *EXTRA!*, purport to be speaking for women, but the words are coming straight from corporate public relations. In the guise of being concerned about breast cancer, they are reliable spokespeople for industry's positions.

One of the most oft-cited spokeswomen in the breast implant debate is Sharon Green, executive director of the national breast cancer organization Y-ME. In August 1995, Green testified before Congress that women should have the option of choosing silicone gel implants—a false choice if there ever was one. Green repeated her pro-silicone pitch in subsequent months on *Oprah,* in *Ms.* magazine, and in a segment on WBBM-TV in Chicago. None of these media outlets saw fit to mention that Green's organization is the beneficiary of many thousands of dollars from Dow Corning, Bristol-Myers Squibb, and Plastic Surgeons Associated.

### President Clinton's Council on Sustainable Development

The President's Council on Sustainable Development (PCSD) was established in June 1993. The PCSD took shape during talks between Vice President Gore, World Resources Institute President Jonathan Lash, and Dow Chemical executive David Buzelli. Lash and Buzelli co-chair the council. Now, representatives from such industrial giants as Dow Chemical, Ciba-Geigy, Georgia Pacific, and Pacific Gas & Electric are sitting down with representatives of the Sierra Club, Environmental Defense Fund, and AFL-CIO.

While dialogue about creating economic growth that does not damage the environment goes on in the PCSD, business as usual reigns among the council's corporate members.

In response to a November 1994 EPA special review—and threat of cancellation—of 20 of the most widely used corn herbicides—Ciba-Geigy mounted a campaign to keep its own Atrazine and Atrazine-containing herbicides off EPA's hit list. Seeking to enlist the support of farmers who used Atrazine, the company sent a scare letter to its customers, telling them to stock up on their favorite pesticide before it was removed from the market. Farmers were also asked to join a massive letter-writing protest to keep the 35-year-old carcinogenic pesticide on the market.

In a brochure attached to the campaign letter, Ciba-Geigy praised the attributes of Atrazine. It also claimed, "If Atrazine is cancelled, more than 20 herbicides will no longer be available; Atrazine alternatives are more expensive and less effective; growers should have a choice to use Atrazine." The brochure urged farmers to "Tell Your EPA What You Think."

Considering the serious public health consequences of the continued use of such products, it is hypocritical that this occurred while the Ciba-Geigy CEO and his fellow polluters were talking with representatives of the environmental community about a democratic agreement to help save the planet.

## Public Relations and Industry Priorities

If there is any issue as toxic as the poisons themselves, it is the mean-spirited battle for the minds and souls of the general public on health and environmental issues. We are being lied to, misguided, misinformed, and deliberately confused because of the power of large drug and chemical companies to buy high-priced public relations campaigns and unethical activities.

A number of giant PR firms have been hired by private industry and public agencies to promote products or an agenda decidedly *not* in the public interest. Let's start with E. Bruce Harrison, author of the book *Going Green: How to Communicate Your Company's Environmental Commitment* and founder of the international PR firm that bears his name and that brings in more than $6 million in billings a year.

John Stauber told Harrison's story in a 1994 issue of the quarterly *PR Watch:*

> Harrison's "commitment" began when, at age 30, he was appointed "Manager of Environmental Information" for the

manufacturers of agricultural pesticides and other poisons and was assigned to coordinate and conduct the industry's attack against Silent Spring. They hit back with the PR equivalent of a prolonged carpet bombing campaign. No expense was spared in defending the fledgling agrichemical industry and its $300 million/year in sales of DDT and other toxins. The national Agricultural Chemical Association doubled its PR budget and distributed thousands of book reviews trashing Silent Spring. Along the way, they pioneered environmental PR "crisis management" techniques that have become standard industry tactics. They used emotional appeals, scientific misinformation, front groups, extensive mailings to the media and opinion leaders, and the recruitment of doctors and scientists as "objective" third-party defenders of agrichemicals.

 . . . Due in part to Harrison's PR work, the warnings of Silent Spring have never been adequately understood or heeded. Today, agrichemical contamination of soil, air, water, animals, and people is one of the most ubiquitous and difficult environmental health disasters we face.

 Harrison . . . is alive and thriving. In 1973, he and his wife established their own PR company, drawing in clients such as Monsanto and Dow Chemical, who were among the sponsors of the campaign against Silent Spring. The PR trade publication, Inside PR, named him as its 1993 "PR All Star," stating that by writing Going Green he had "confirmed his status as the leading [PR] thinker on environmental issues" and as a continuing "pioneer in the field."

Stauber also featured the work of another giant PR firm, Hill & Knowlton, which is leading the fight for Monsanto and bovine growth hormone. The company's lobbyists have helped defeat state legislative attempts in Wisconsin, Minnesota, California, and Vermont to require labeling of milk with rBGH. FDA Commissioner David Kessler approved the hormones while H & K's Howard Paster served as Clinton's chief lobbyist. Paster returned to Hill & Knowlton as its CEO just weeks after FDA's approval.

Other organizations are working hard to promote rBGH. Monsanto itself underwrote a 1993 television program—"BST and Milk"—touting the benefits of growth hormones. The program aired nationally on CNBC as part of American Medical Television's "Health Styles" series right after FDA approved rBGH.

The AMA and the American Dietetic Association were both active in promoting the hormone. The AMA has a long-term history of involvement with Monsanto on rBGH. As early as June 30, 1989, Dr. Roy Schwarz, Assistant Executive Vice President of AMA, had put himself in the Monsanto camp with this letter to Dr. Virginia Weldon, Monsanto's vice president of scientific affairs:

> The amount of advance communicating Monsanto and the other BST companies have been doing on this product is impressive and certainly will help create an informed marketplace once FDA approval has been obtained. As you know, the AMA is open to the possibility of reviewing studies on BST safety after the FDA has completed its work. . . . I see no reason for the medical community to be anything but comfortable with the safety of this product for people and milk. . . . Continued good luck at Monsanto.

As for chlorine, the best example of PR ingenuity and activity is that of international firm Ketchum Public Relations, ranked seventh in billings in the 1993 *O'Dwyer's Directory of Public Relations Firms* with net fees of $45.6 million. This firm can pay for the talent, creativity, and know-how to distort or question science, threaten the opposition, pressure the media for "balance," and hire well-paid experts to offer bogus studies to debunk work that is not compatible with the industry agenda.

Among Ketchum's clients are pharmaceutical firms including Merck and Bristol-Myers Squibb, and the Chemical Manufacturers Association, whose membership includes some of the biggest polluters in the country. (Dow Chemical is the largest producer of dioxin in the United States. Yet thanks to a brilliant public relations campaign, the public sees it as deeply concerned about the environment. Consumers rank it among the 10 U.S. firms with the best environmental reputations, according to the magazine *American Demographics.*)

Ketchum serves its clients with a host of imaginative tactics. The company's environment section chair, John Paluszek, announced at the 1994 gathering of the Public Relations Society of America, "When the dioxin-chlorine controversy broke last week, [September 1994] we saw an opportunity to make our already topical, jam-packed program even more current. The dioxin issue is about to become one of the hottest issues to face the nation, and the world. It is a paradigm case for the 'Smart Environmental' conference where we will discuss the hard choices, the prioritizations, that must now be based on sound science and sound economics."

"Sound science" are those studies, usually paid for by industry, that find conclusions compatible with industry's agenda. All others are attacked as "unsound."

"Sound economics" are those policies that bring profits for the corporation—cancer prevention and social responsibility for disease be damned.

Ketchum's work is not only ingenious, but heavy-handed. The company leaves no stone unturned in helping its clients obscure their role in the cancer epidemic.

Back in 1991, Clorox needed to counteract the fears of consumers about the environmental impact of its household cleaners. The company hired Ketchum. The PR firm outlined various ways to deal with worst-case scenarios should Clorox products become the target of protest or criticism. In a memo leaked to Greenpeace, the firm recommended labeling environmentalists as "terrorists" and then suing "unalterably green" journalists for slander.

And according to a news story in the August 14, 1991 Oakland *Guardian Bureau,* that was not all. Among the PR tactics recommended by Ketchum were portraying Greenpeace as a violent organization whose scientific research is suspect, launching a "Stop Environmental Terrorism" campaign urging Greenpeace to be less irrational, enlisting the support of national union leadership to defend Clorox in the name of saving jobs, dispatching teams of "independent" scientists to serve as ambassadors to the media and government officials, and conducting daily opinion surveys to measure the impact of the crisis and public reaction to the counter-measures.

Ketchum and its clients haven't stopped with crisis intervention. Take the October 1994 conference on "Breast Cancer and the Environment: Women's Action on Prevention" held in Dayton, Ohio and sponsored by WEDO and Greenpeace. (This conference was the third in a series of four that year which took place across the country on the same subject.) Over 200 attendees—breast cancer victims and activists—heard environmental and cancer experts discuss the xenoestrogen connections to breast cancer. The speakers included nationally recognized cancer experts such as Devra Lee Davis, Sam Epstein, and Ernest Sternglass.

Paige McMahon, a long-time employee of Ketchum who was at that time serving the Chlorine Chemistry Council (CCC) as communications director, sent this letter on October 17, 1994 to Dr. Paulette Olson, Director of Wright State University Women's Center, one of the supporters of the Dayton conference.

> I am writing to you on behalf of the Chlorine Chemistry Council (CCC) to express our concern about the conference on "Breast Cancer & the Environment," at your campus on October 22, 1994. . . .
>
> The Chlorine Chemistry Council is committed to researching and understanding risk factors associated with breast cancer. Based on the conference schedule, it appears as though this event will focus almost exclusively on the alleged association between breast cancer and environmental factors at the expense of known scientific fact. We are concerned about the overwhelming number of speakers who are neither

scientifically nor medically qualified to discuss known and alleged risks. The roster does not include any representatives of such nationally recognized research organizations as the American Cancer Society, National Cancer Institute, Susan Komen Foundation, the National Alliance of Breast Cancer Organizations, or the American Health Foundation. The staffs of these organizations are research pioneers and the best-informed breast cancer experts in the country. In addition, medical staff from leading clinics such as the Dana Farber Institute have not been included in this program.

I would like to speak with you about your interest in breast cancer and the environment. I would like to offer you the opportunity to listen to some experts who view the issue and the science differently than the speakers on the program. I feel it would be beneficial for you and your students to see and understand the scientific aspect of this issue as distinct from the advocacy perspective.

This letter was a classic of polluting industry public relations. McMahon attacked the validity of the conference speakers, implying that they were "advocates" without scientific credentials, and that CCC's people were "scientific." She claimed that representatives of organizations who were not invited—all of which have refused to research the environmental connection or that have closed the door on alternative therapies—are the real experts. There are those out there who really know—who have a level of credibility that the conference speakers do not. She called for balance on the program, and imputed a cynical "concern for the environment" to the CCC.

Of course, she did not mention that ACS had pulled out of co-sponsoring the 1994 Albuquerque breast cancer conference at the last minute, claiming it was "too controversial." Why would they then send speakers to a conference that had essentially the same agenda? And NCI actually tried to pressure Dr. Davis to not appear at Albuquerque, citing the Hatch Act, which prohibits federal employees from participating in political activities. (Davis ignored the pressure and did appear, offering important testimony.) And ironically, although McMahon was demanding that the WEDO conference willingly accept industry-related speakers, no outsiders are allowed in the CCC's meetings.

Keith Ashdown, director of communications of the Cancer Prevention Coalition (CPC), wrote a response to McMahon's letter:

> Her statements are meant only to confuse and distort the reputations of the speakers. . . . Ms. McMahon has worked for the Ketchum Public Relations firm for many years. Ketchum . . . has made millions of dollars trying to discredit scientists and citizen activists who have targeted corporate polluters, namely many of their clients [and] some of the most infamous polluters on the planet.
>
> In fact, Ketchum is one of the most unethical PR firms in existence. They have tried to label environmental groups as "terrorists" and "communists."
>
> . . . Ketchum spent hundreds of thousands of dollars to personally discredit an award-winning journalist, David Steinman, who writes on pesticides in food. Commenting on Ketchum's attack, Mr. Steinman stated, "They went after me personally because there was no way to discredit my data. They sent out personally defamatory materials to talk shows that had scheduled me for upcoming shows. Many cancelled after receiving materials from Ketchum." Clearly, Ketchum is not a reputable firm.

Apparently, McMahon and other professionals connected to the chlorine industry did reveal themselves to some participants of the Dayton conference; there was a nasty shouting match in the halls between McMahon and Stephanie Slowinski, a volunteer with Ohio's Green Environmental Coalition. Slowinski reported that McMahon accused the conference of being "one-sided" and accused the local organizing group of being a front for Greenpeace—an attempt, Slowinski believes, to make Greenpeace appear to be extremist and contemptible. Slowinski angrily responded, "I spent nine months organizing this conference and I'm not paid; you people have a multimillion-dollar budget to do your work."

She was on target about the budget. The explosion of anti-chlorine sentiment that followed the IJC's recommendation activated the chemical and related industries to create a strategy for survival. The CCC is spearheading the campaign.

According to a report in the November 21, 1994 *Chemical and Engineering News*:

> CCC members boosted the council's budget, unleashing about $12 million in 1994 to combat calls for a chlorine phaseout. That's up from 1993's $2 million budget. Likewise, the CCC payroll has increased from two to 20 full- and part-time employees. And these figures are just "the tip of the iceberg," says J. Roger Hirl [Occidental Chemical CEO officer and chair of CCC's board]—industry contributes people and resources equal to at least ten times that amount.
>
> And CCC's budget could rise to $15 million in 1995, says Dow Chemical vice president for environment, health and safety David T. Buzzelli. The extra money would be used to expand the council's research program. Currently, 33 percent of the budget goes to scientific research. For example, CCC is sponsoring an evaluation of the dioxin reassessment done by EPA. . . . The new question about whether some chlorinated organics in the environment behave like hormones and disrupt the human endocrine system also warrants more study. . . .
>
> To help fine-tune its strategy, CCC has enlisted the aid of two public relation agencies. Ogilvy, Adams and Rinehart of New York City helps CCC with "in-reach" activities—developing programs and materials for use by industry. The other agency, Ketchum Communications, Pittsburgh, advises on media relations. It was Ketchum that helped CCC brief the media before the release of EPA's dioxin reassessment. Three scientists met with more than 400 media sources.

The effect of this kind of influence was that the EPA's

Reassessment of Dioxin was given far less play in national media than were the media's earlier headline efforts to detoxify the chemical.

Clearly, the chlorine industry does not take criticism lightly. The plans developed by the Chlorine Chemistry Champions Workshop, sponsored by the CCC in Williamsburg, Virginia on September 28, 1994, could well be the role model for the whole anti-environmental movement.

The workshop's title was, "Chlorine Chemistry: The Future Is in Our Hands." Those attending included outgoing CCC managing director Brad Lienhart, former Dow Chemical employee, and his replacement Kip Howlett, formerly an executive with Georgia Pacific, one of the companies that produces paper bleached with chlorine. Jace Hassett of Occidental Chemical, Ed Murphy, grassroots director of the CMA, and the ubiquitous Paige McMahon also spoke. Leading two "interactive sessions" was Roger Lindberg, senior vice president of Olgivy Adams & Rinehart.

According to an anonymous observer who gave notes on the workshop to an environmental group, "The tone of the entire meeting had the familiar ring of a pep rally for industry attendees to learn how to defend chlorine in the media and sell their ideas to state and federal policy makers. The strategies have the earmarks of a well-planned political campaign." The following is a summary of the report compiled by the observer. Readers beware: neither truth nor social good are issues here.

Charles River Associates ballyhooed their claim that 40 percent of the gross domestic product and 1.3 million jobs are dependent on chlorine. (These figures are hotly contested by Greenpeace. See Appendix A.) They assured attendees that the "chlorine champions" program would use the public distrust of government and regulations to their advantage. The program would also emphasize how little the public truly cares about the environment.

Paige McMahon stated that environmental issues are not on

the public's radar screen (although surveys consistently rank the environment as one of the top five issues). She said that people are more concerned with health, crime and jobs. She also cited the "generally balanced" media coverage of EPA's dioxin reassessment. (She did not mention that the same compliant media had played a role in industry's effort to "detoxify" dioxin in the early 1990s.)

The group discussed outreach to other groups that might be sympathetic. Ranchers were seen as allies, since they spray beef carcasses with chlorine. A conference sponsored by the Society of Environmental Journalists would be ripe for networking.

As for the dioxin reassessment, time was their ally. They looked forward to the 120-day comment period established by the EPA's reassessment guidelines, and knew that the EPA would finalize the report only after a Scientific Advisory Board review in the fall of 1995. The advice there: Let the process play itself out. Tell the government not to rush into any action. (They did acknowledge, that "the dioxin situation can go in any direction." The IJC report urging a ban on chlorine "gives Greens weight and credibility.")

They vilified environmental groups in general and Greenpeace in particular. They said Americans believe environmental groups are "on the run" and Americans are sick of being scared to death.

Understanding all this, especially the powerful truth that "all environmental issues are local," and in response to both federal and state actions, the group created a campaign plan which included both proactive and reactive strategies: the use of scientific and economic expertise; educating industry stakeholders; a 50-state monitoring of environmental activity, with assigned coordinators working in 20 states identified as "priority."

More time would be spent with grassroots groups in the 20 key states. They would assemble a database of 35,000 "downstream" users of chlorine—divided by both users and legislators, and then make phone calls to identify chlorine "champion" activists. Assigned people would serve as spokespersons, media reps, and plant tour guides.

What works in the chlorine industry's favor? Public ignorance and apathy. Because of these, it is cost-effective for industry to spend millions each year finding ways to recycle the same paid-for science, half-truths, myths, and scare tactics. They worked before, and absent public outcry, they may work again.

## Media Power and Complicity

Award-winning environmental journalist Eric Greenberg used to work for the *New York Daily News*. His astonishing series about the city-wide asbestos contamination in New York's public schools created a popular uproar resulting in an emergency clean-up that caused the schools to open three weeks late.

Greenberg's editor initially refused to even consider the story when the investigative journalist brought him the idea. "Who cares?" the editor said, dismissing Eric with a wave of his hand. It was only after Greenberg's intense and articulate argument that the editor allowed the first story—of one contaminated school—to be printed. The enormous public response convinced the editor to run the series.

"Environmental journalists have real trouble doing original and important stories that the public needs to know about, that affects them where they live," Greenberg said, "and it's been an uphill battle." Greenberg told me a few simple reasons why he feels journalists have to fight to get space on environmental issues:

- Environmental stories are too complex and a reporter may not be adequately trained or able to do the job.
- Editors believe such stories don't sell papers.
- Editors believe the public doesn't want to hear about the pollution.
- If we do a good story, and it gets the public interested, there's no guarantee there will be a follow-up.

- Environmental stories can't compete with the public hunger for the O.J.-Princess Di-sports frenzy that sells the dailies.
- You can't prove that the folks suffering from rare forms of cancer, asthma, and bronchitis downwind of an incinerator are really getting sick from the toxic ash.
- There's no sense of media social responsibility anymore. Compelling stories sell papers. No one sees our job as education.

In June 1994, Greenberg was laid off from his job. Since he left the *Daily News,* he has not seen one environmental story on its pages—not even buried deep in the second section. "They're just not interested."

With some striking exceptions, the mainstream media have been distressingly silent about key environmental issues. It appears it is not just reluctance to investigate because of complexity or lack of interest. More than likely, important environmental stories that confirm industry-related contamination and subsequent illness are blacklisted. Corporate offenders are protected.

Corporate policies dictate the actions of publishers, editors, and station managers. These people make decisions that support industry in various ways. Thus, the American public may be told that cancer rates are rising or falling, depending on which study has just been released, but there is precious little press attention to the reasons why the cancer rate is so high, or why cancer mortality rates have remained basically unchanged for decades. At the same time, the mainstream media also serves as eager cheerleaders whenever NCI, ACS, or some well-connected cancer hospital announces the latest "breakthrough" in treatment.

It's hard to find too many folks in the mainstream press willing to admit that the war on cancer has turned into a rout. There are a number of reasons for this silence, and they include a media that is no longer independent of corporate interests.

### *Corporate Media Holdings*

As of 1992, 14 large, expanding corporations dominate the daily newspaper industry, not to mention their influence in radio and TV. According to Ben Bagdikian, author of *The Media Monopoly,* "The number of daily papers in the country has continued to shrink, from 1,763 in 1960 to 1,643 in 1989." Bagdikian identified the 14 companies: Gannett, Knight-Ridder, Newhouse Newspapers, Tribune Company, Times Mirror, Dow Jones, International Tomson, New York Times, Scripps-Howard, Hearst, Cox, News Corp. (Murdoch), Media News Group (Singleton), and Ingersoll Newspapers.

The concentration in the magazine field is even greater according to Bagdikian; from 1981 to 1988, the number of dominant corporations dropped from 20 to three: Time Warner, News Corp., and Hearst. As for TV, despite takeovers, corporate turbulence, and declining viewership, the three television networks—Capital Cities/ABC, CBS, and NBC—"still dominate the field."

"General Electric, the tenth largest U.S. corporation and a major defense contractor bought RCA, owner of NBC. . . . GE brings a complication that distinguishes it from small, local companies: it has, through its board of directors, interlocks with still other major industrial and financial sectors of the American economy in wood products, textiles, automotive supplies, department store chains, and banking."

Under the law, a director of a company is obliged to act in the interests of the company. But when an officer of corporation A sits on the board of corporation B, on whose behalf does this director act?

For example, Bagdikian states, "The most influential paper in America, the *New York Times,* interlocked with Merck, Bristol-Myers, Morgan Guaranty Trust, Charter Oil, Johns Manville, American Express, Bethlehem Steel, IBM, Scott Paper, Sun Oil, and First Boston Corporation."

Bagdikian concludes:

As media conglomerates become larger, they have been integrated into the higher levels of American banking and industrial life. Half the dominant firms are members of the Fortune 500 largest corporations in the country. They are heavy investors in . . . agribusiness, airline, coal and oil, banking, insurance, defense contracts, automobile sales, rocket engineering, nuclear power, and nuclear weapons. Many have heavy foreign investments that are affected by American foreign policy.

It is normal for all large businesses to make serious effort to influence the news, to avoid embarrassing publicity, and to maximize sympathetic public opinion and government policies. Now they own most of the news media that they wish to influence.

In addition, the media is not about to distress its advertisers, some of whom may be doing the polluting. For example, Chicago-based Commonwealth Edison, listed by the Council on Economic Priorities as one of the ten worst polluters in 1993, is a major TV and print advertiser. Dow Chemical spends millions on its network TV messages, "Making a Difference in What Tomorrow Brings."

General Electric, the owner of NBC, is the corporation that for the two decades before 1964 was the principal operator of the Hanford nuclear facility in Washington, and has been identified as a potentially responsible party at 51 Superfund sites. The company was also among the Council on Economic Priorities' worst-ten list of polluters in 1993. How likely is it that NBC will do much investigative reporting on any of the environmental stories connected to GE?

GE controls the licenses for NBC's six owned-and-operated TV affiliates. These stations, located in key markets, are worth an estimated $2.5 billion. According to research done by the media watchdog group Fairness and Accuracy in Reporting (FAIR) and reported by Sam Husseini in the November 1994 issue of its publication *EXTRA!*, these assets could be threatened if the "FCC ruled that GE's criminal record—including a host of fraud, environmental, financial, and employment violations—made the corporation unfit to hold broadcasting licenses." No FCC sanctions against GE have yet been made.

GE's questionable activities, along with the immense scope of its nuclear pollution, goes essentially unreported by NBC News because of the control of the parent company. "Don't go over backwards to go after us just because we own you," GE chair Jack Welch once said to former NBC News president Lawrence Grossman. Husseini cited instances in which NBC News edited out or excluded negative reporting on GE. And the news department has also plugged subjects dear to its corporate parent's heart, as with a 14-minute series on a GE-manufactured breast cancer detector.

The situation at NBC is not unique. In the rush to consolidate media power, Westinghouse, another major polluter, bought CBS in 1995.

And over at ABC, *20/20,* the second most popular TV newsmagazine, didn't need its new Disney owners to define its priorities. Thanks to Victor Neufeld, who took over as executive producer in February 1987, "few environment segments have been aired" by *20/20,* according to the January 1994 *EXTRA!*

Lois Neufeld, Victor's wife, runs Media Access, a public relations outfit whose clients include the nuclear industry-financed U.S. Council for Energy Awareness. The group's board consists of top executives from virtually every major company involved in nuclear power, including General Electric, Westinghouse, and Bechtel. Neufeld has also had the Industry Coalition for the Environment as a client. This organization includes CMA, American Petroleum Institute, National Association of Manufacturers, Society of the Plastics Industry, DuPont, General Motors, and others.

"It's a big conflict," said Dan Goldfarb, formerly a producer with *20/20.* "Since Victor Neufeld took over *20/20,* there has never been a story in any way critical of the nuclear industry or the chemical industry as far as I know. I think it's pretty clear what's going on."

The number of *20/20* reporters and producers who, off the record, identify a pattern of ignoring significant environmental stories and putting a happier face on others is legion. In the 18 months after Neufeld took over *20/20,* there was a staff exodus. The one reporter who has stayed on is consumer reporter John Stossel, who according to the April 9, 1995 *Chicago Tribune* has "revealed an unabashed disdain of much government regulation." The *Tribune* identified Stossel as accepting $135,280 in fees for speeches he gave during 1994. He accepted thousands of dollars from such organizations as the Center for Market Processes, California Agricultural Production Consultants, American Feed Industry Association, Chemical Industry Council of New Jersey, American Farm Bureau, Soap and Detergent Association, and Southeastern Poultry and Egg Association. Clearly, it may be quite difficult for any reporter to maintain objectivity under these conditions.

### *The Media and Dioxin*

For years, the toxicity of dioxin has been downplayed in the media. Some newspapers, specifically the *New York Times* and the *Chicago Tribune,* have had financial interests in pulp and paper mills that bleach with chlorine—a process which spews out dioxin. (Casey Bukro, environmental reporter for the *Tribune,* admitted his paper's financial connection to the pulp mills, adding that he does most of his environmental reporting from a "business point of view.") Rather than address the toxicity of dioxin, both these papers have played a major role in a national effort to verbally detoxify the chemical. For a significant period in their history these two major dailies, along with most of the print media, played variations on a recurring theme: "Dioxin isn't as toxic as we thought." And the public, uneducated and unaware, bought the line.

On July 24, 1983, the *St. Louis Post Dispatch* reported that EPA scientists declared ". . . dioxin is the most potent substance they have ever studied, that it probably causes cancer in humans . . . that it presents an unacceptable cancer risk when found in water in parts per quintillion (ppq)."

The paper elaborated that the EPA report "contrasts sharply with industry claims that there is no proof that dioxin causes any serious long-term health problems in humans other than a serious skin rash called chloracne."This has remained industry's consistent position.

However, ever since 1983 industry and government regulators have been waging and winning the dioxin public relations battle. The revisionists took over the dioxin dialogue and the public became victims of a giant media turnaround. The May, 23, 1991, *St. Louis Post Dispatch* headline said it all: "Dioxin Scare Called Mistake." By September 1991, despite mounting international evidence of dioxin's toxic properties, 26 other newspapers in the United States and Canada had jumped on the bandwagon.

The change of heart of the media impacted greatly on America's Vietnam War veterans. The Department of Veterans Affairs (DVA) had for years found ways to deny compensation to veterans suffering from myriad problems including rare forms of cancer, nerve and liver disease, and severe psychological damage. This group of symptoms came to be called Agent Orange syndrome.

Until 1991, the DVA, under orders from the Reagan White House, had been steadfast in its refusal to grant benefits. While government leaders looked the other way, industry continued to manufacture dioxin-contaminated products or pollute through dioxin-contaminated processes.

Frustrated, the Vietnam Veterans of America went to court. They achieved a major breakthrough on May 3, 1989 in San Francisco when federal judge Theron Henderson threw out the DVA regulations that had been used to deny Agent Orange disability claims. He ruled that the DVA had been operating illegally: where there was a statistical correlation between exposure and a particular illness, a vet should get the benefit of the doubt.

Enter the Centers for Disease Control (CDC), mandated by Congress in 1982 to conduct the epidemiology study that DVA had never done. However, secret Reagan White House memos reveal that the CDC was directed *not* to find causation between exposure and the myriad health effects the veterans were experiencing. So the CDC "cooked the books." Dr. Vernon Houk (now dead of cancer) eagerly became the point man, and later the spokesperson for the fraudulent veterans study. The scientists actually revised the protocol in the middle of the study, diluting the scope. They limited the tests to a thin group of veterans, eliminating all officers and studying only those in service during a specific year. That move effectively erased many thousands who were known to be directly in the path of the spray missions. When the American Legion and Dick Christian, the former head of the Army's Environmental Study Group, offered the CDC the use of the Herbs Tapes, a complete computerized history of spray missions, showing exactly where the troops were at any time, the CDC leaders rejected the data. Then, the CDC brazenly announced that they could not find sufficient numbers of exposed veterans to conduct the study. It concluded that Vietnam veterans were no sicker than the control group, and the study was cancelled.

The American Legion tried to challenge the CDC. Representative Ted Weiss (now deceased) held hearings in 1990 on the Legion's allegations, and witnesses from CDC came forward with admissions of fraud and the acknowledgment that the White House Agent Orange Working Group (AOWG) had heavily pressured if not influenced the outcome.

On August 2, 1990, the American Legion and Weiss announced the committee's findings of fraud and the Legion's decision to sue Health and Human Services, the DVA, and the CDC. The only major newspaper willing to print anything was the *Washington Post.* CBS's *60 Minutes* spent weeks investigating the CDC study, yet never aired the story.

Yet CDC's fraudulent "findings" made headlines across the country. Dr. Houk became industry's darling as he promoted the new public relations lie. Through the fall of 1991, media cooperation allowed industry's lies to become accepted truths.

The *Chicago Tribune's* headline on September 1 read, "On 2nd Thought, Toxic Nightmares May Be Unpleasant Dreams." The story quoted Dr. Houk, "If dioxin is a human carcinogen, it is, in my view, a weak one. . . ."

The *Los Angeles Times* of August 19 stated, "Dioxin Joins List of Costly False Alarms," and reported that the CDC did not consider dioxin levels found in Times Beach to represent a significant health risk.

In the *New York Times* of August 15, former EPA administrator William Reilly was quoted as saying, "We are seeing new information on dioxin that suggests a lower risk assessment . . . should be applied." On August 19, the *Times* followed with this claim: "Once thought of as the most toxic chemical known, [dioxin] does not deserve that reputation." On September 1, the *Times* added, "the threat from dioxin has been downgraded from cataclysmic to slight or even nonexistent."

In an August 18 article headed "Dioxin: Not So Deadly After All?" the *Chicago Tribune* wrote: "Concerns about Agent Orange will have to be re-evaluated. . . . We do those who suffer from these disorders no favor by wasting millions of dollars and years of irreplaceable time in futilely blaming dioxin instead of hunting down the real causes. . . . There are fresh data to support the revised assessment of dioxin."

Where are those fresh data? The *Tribune* didn't reference any in the article. Conversely, between 1982 and 1991 such prestigious, peer-reviewed journals as the *American Journal of Industrial Medicine, Journal of the NCI, British Journal of Cancer, New England Journal of Medicine, Scandinavian Journal of Work, Environment and Health, JAMA, Occupational and Environmental Health, International*

*Journal of Epidemiology,* and *British Journal of Industrial Medicine* all published compelling data on the relationship between the components of Agent Orange and dioxin and the connection to rare forms of cancer, especially soft tissue sarcoma and non-Hodgkins lymphoma.

Lost in all the media distortion was the fact that Dow has known about dioxin's toxicity for decades. A June 24, 1965 letter from V. K. Rowe of Dow's Biochemical Research Laboratory to Ross Mulholland of Dow Chemical of Canada states, "This material is exceptionally toxic; it has a tremendous potential for producing chloracne and systemic injury." Others who have known about dioxin's toxicity are Monsanto scientists, the EPA, the CDC, and the National Institute for Environmental Health Sciences. It takes very little effort for a good reporter to uncover these documents (Clorfene-Casten, *The Nation,* November 30, 1992).

Finally, with the 1994 EPA reassessment of dioxin and the agency's admission that industry-produced dioxin has become a major source of domestic contamination, suits against the industry are multiplying. (For example, Syntex faces 350 additional dioxin law suits from those who lived in Times Beach.) Again, the public policy and the national agenda is to protect industry at the expense of human health.

Observing the local media's silence on crucial environmental stories with growing alarm, in 1992, I and a group of Chicago citizen activists formed a group called Chicago Media Watch (CMW). The Environmental Task Force of CMW zeroed in on the IJC biennial meetings. Although the IJC felt there was sufficient evidence to warrant a call for a sunset of chlorine in industrial uses, almost all of the Chicago media kept an astonishing silence. The only outlet that addressed the matter at all was Public Radio's affiliate WBEZ, which produced a half-hour show that was so industry-biased that the serious issues raised by IJC were completely ignored.

As chair of CMW, I wrote the following letter to WBEZ's Adam Davidson, who produced the show:

I decided to wait a day or so before replying to the nearly half-hour discussion on the Great Lakes, January 31, 1994. Frankly, the show was a great disappointment and my only hope is that we can continue the dialogue on some future date. The critical issues surrounding the Great Lakes crisis did not come out.

. . . When I brought the issue of the Great Lakes to your attention in the first place, it was in reference to the International Joint Commission meeting which took place in October 1993. The data coming out of that meeting was enough for me, a journalist and community activist, to believe there was a need for a greater reportage. The IJC is not a group to be dismissed; the commissioners are all very conservative businessmen appointed by our two governments (Reagan, Bush on the U.S. side) to oversee the quality of the Great Lakes basin. They are backed by fact-finding task forces and scientific panels that conduct research and report back their conclusions.

That you chose to ignore the data . . . is to do a great disservice to your listeners. WBEZ is a publicly funded body and rather than serve the taxpayers, you bent over backward to serve industry. The IJC meeting was not even mentioned, an omission I believe was not accidental. The industry spokesperson dominated the conversation and unfortunately was responsible for some serious misinformation.

The IJC has already reported that the Great Lakes ecosystem is in crisis, so polluted from so many sources it's impossible to identify just where all the poisons come from.

The consequences to human health and the wildlife are now being studied and the data tell us there is a human health epidemic. Organochlorines—dioxins, DDT, DDE, PCBs, CFCs, pesticides, PVCs, trichloroethylene, dibenzofurans, and some 50,000 other newly derived, untested chemical compounds are now contaminating the waters. These toxins are invisible, silent, persistent, and very destructive in minute parts per million, billion, and trillion. They bioaccumulate and are stored in the fat of both wildlife and humans.

Women, their children, and future generations are at great risk from exposure to hundreds of these toxins. Their effects can be long-term as in breast cancer, or short-term where children born to mothers eating Great Lakes fish just twice a month are learning disabled and developmentally delayed. Men suffer from reduced sperm count, and small or undescended testicles. In fact, sperm count in men has gone down 50 percent during the last 50 years—an alarming fact, and one we all need to know. Organochlorines bioaccumulate, affecting hormonal functions, and can wreak havoc on a number of systems, from reproductive to immune.

This is the kind of information WBEZ listeners need to hear, not the watered-down conversation presented on Monday. Industry suggests that the toxins are too small to worry about—ignoring the fact that in minute quantities, dioxin, PCBs, DDT, etc. cause incalculable damage. Eventually, these "tiny amounts of toxins" build up. And no one was there to refute industry's distortion.

As for the "billions" industry claims it would cost to reduce their polluting policies, I am grateful that the person from the Great Lakes Initiative was able to suggest their calculations come to millions, not billions. [Greenpeace spokespersons should have been there also to counter industry's inflated and fear-producing figures. But WBEZ rejected outright any spokespersons from Greenpeace.]

As for the EPA, . . . it has rejected outright the IJC position, a fact your listeners should know.

Industry . . . spouts half truths, exaggerates costs, makes questionable claims, and uses their power to intrude upon the public dialogue. They already have been allowed to enter the dialogue in such a way as to threaten and diffuse the IJC position, and postpone any action—although secretly some dioxin-producing paper mills are successfully eliminating chlorine as a bleach. . . . Unfortunately, WBEZ, in its poorly instructed effort to keep "balance" has played right into industry/EPA hands.

... NPR and WBEZ are all the public has. True balance must come from media outlets that do not need to imitate the mainstream, industry-dominated press. Industry does the polluting and gets away with it because so few are informed and enforcement is so lax. The public knows very little about a host of problems that affect us all—you, me, and our children—every day. And they should. If WBEZ doesn't, who will?

More than two years later, after numerous phone calls and a meeting between myself and WBEZ staff, the station has yet to air anything close to an in-depth story on the Great Lakes organochlorine connection or even interview one IJC commissioner.

Let's now look at breast cancer specifically. Is there media coverage on breast cancer? Yes, a great deal. It's good copy, especially in October—declared by some ICI public relations official as "Breast Cancer Awareness Month." Consumers will read about a new drug, or attend an elegant benefit fashion show whose proceeds go to breast cancer research. We'll hear again about the necessity for mammograms. We'll see Supreme Court Justice Sandra Day O'Connor, a survivor of the disease, addressing her fears on TV and we'll watch the profile of Ingrid Bergman, the tragic victim of breast cancer. We'll listen to interviews of women artists who have endured the trauma of mastectomy and how they've turned their own crisis into a possible art form. And because of the media, we'll wear pink ribbons to demonstrate to our friends that we support those with breast cancer.

But, we will not hear about causes, prevention, or alternative treatment, and we will not hear about those corporations that continue to pollute.

Two media events are indicative of media treatment of breast cancer. In April 1993, a major study was published linking DDT to breast cancer. The story got moderate media attention. In May 1993, a study linking breast cancer to alcohol consumption came out, and it received a huge reception in both print and electronic media.

Here's the subtle difference between the two. If the cause is something that can be blamed on the victim's lifestyle, then it gets a big play in the media. Perhaps it is because of our perception that we can "change" our lifestyle and live healthier. However, if uncovering the cause leads to women taking real control of a national issue, publicity is to be shunned. Consumers are not to be told that industry may be liable.

There's no better example of media cooperation and collusion with polluting companies than silicone breast implants. While the ongoing lawsuits against the manufacturers got adequate coverage, little mention was made of the true reasons for their settlement—that the manufacturers were well aware of the problems inherent in their products and the potential dangers these products posed to women. That kind of news was rarely reported by the mainstream press.

However, good news from the manufacturers' point of view easily makes the evening news programs on all three major networks. In 1994, well after the implant lawsuits were settled, a Mayo Clinic study headed by S. E. Gabriel lent credence to the belief that perhaps breast implants may not be as much of a problem as thought. The study was published in the prestigious *New England Journal of Medicine,* and it got eager press coverage. A *Washington Post* story on June 16, 1994 was headlined "Breast Implant Study Finds No Link to Disease." Despite hundreds of pages of incriminating evidence brought out in the implant trials, the media was quick, even anxious to quote the *NEJM* article. But it turns out, as detailed in Chapter 8, that the study deserves some very serious scrutiny.

First of all, as reported in the *Washington Post* article, "As much as $174,000 of the implant study funds could have come from implant manufacturers and medical organizations that had an interest in the outcome." The research was supported by grants from NIH and the Plastic Surgery Educational Foundation.

And the authors admitted that their sample was too small, and that it would require a sample population of 62,000 women with implants and 124,000 women without implants. Lack of a suitable sample size and lack of appropriate follow-up time did not stop the *NEJM* editors from publishing the article.

And if good science reporters had examined the *NEJM* article in detail, they would have found data that did not support the authors' primary conclusion. When the various categories reflective of connective tissue abnormality are *added* together, there is a striking difference in the incidence of connective tissue illnesses. Twelve percent of those in the control group—which included some women who had breast cancer surgery but did not have implants—developed connective tissue illnesses. But 26 percent of those who had implants after cancer surgery developed connective tissue illnesses.

These overall numbers should have raised red alerts for the *NEJM* editors about the veracity of the study.

There were simply too many unanswered questions in this study, too many examples of suspect techniques. The mainstream media did not do its job—as it regularly fails to do when public health is pitted against media-controlling industry. It did not do what it must to keep the public informed about the important issues of the day.

# 12

# WE CAN SAVE LIVES

Gloria Pierzynski is a blond women in her mid-50s who speaks with as much zest as she can muster. When she gets into her story, her red-and-green glass earrings begin to bob and a lovely ray of light dances on her shoulders:

I remember, it was 20 years ago. We lived in a very big house. I used a powder around the baseboards to keep the waterbugs away. Then, we moved to Glen Ellyn. In that house, I sprayed for spider mites. I also gardened and sprayed lawn care products—pesticides and herbicides. I also sprayed for ants. I've also eaten all those things that are wrong for me; I love steak, chocolate, fried potatoes. I rarely ate fresh veggies and fruit. Now I subscribe to *Vegetarian Times*.

I was diagnosed with breast cancer in February 1991. I found it myself—a small lump in my right breast about one-and-a-half centimeters. I had a mammogram about a year and a half before and there was an area in question, but they didn't say it was serious. They told me to come back in eight months.

I did. Afterwards, I went to my regular doctor and he said, "Don't worry." But I did see a local surgeon the next day and he wanted me in the hospital for a biopsy. I thought, "Hey, this is different. I don't want to be in a local hospital in a small suburb." So I dialed 1-800-4-CANCER, and asked them for a specialist and they gave me two names. I chose Dr. Marion Morrow at the University of Chicago. That was one of the best things that ever happened to me. She was knowledgeable and when she felt it, she felt a small lump.

She performed a needle biopsy and found "questionable cells." If it was cancer, she felt it was contained in that lump. She told me the survival chances would be excellent; I would have a 90 percent chance of being cured. She did the lumpectomy. A week later, they took the lymph nodes out. Four of the 22 had cancer. I'm now up to Stage II. I stopped my estrogen therapy immediately and aged ten years in two.

The cancer is very aggressive. Even though I was postmenopausal, they wanted to do chemotherapy, radiation, and tamoxifen. I waited until I healed from the surgery, so I had some time to decide. I debated about the chemo and I read a study that said that postmenopausal women did just as well on tamoxifen. I mentioned this to my oncologist, but I got a lot of pressure to do chemo too, and I did. I took six treatments, three weeks apart, with a combination of drugs.

Chemo made me feel like I had a thousand symptoms. I was so painful just going in. Hot—*hot* feelings in my groin. Then they gave me an anti-nausea drug. I got real sick. There was a huge red line going up my arm from the site of the needle. They decided I was allergic to the anti-nausea drug and stopped that, but I still had most of the symptoms. I could not go through a second session, so I bought a relaxation tape and used it during treatment.

I got sores in my mouth and then a thick white coating; I felt great nausea, my favorite foods tasted horrible. I lost my hair, gained 50 pounds, then lost all my body hair. I was tired all the time, my eyesight got worse, I lost some hearing and my bones ached all the time. I continued on—then lost my energy and felt great back pain.

I wish I had never taken it. I'm not sure if it's the medication or the cancer. I'm still on tamoxifen. My symptoms have continued on—after the chemo. I still have short-term memory loss, severe exhaustion. My mouth sores just stopped four months ago and the terrific back pain is just easing. Now I'm getting headaches. I can't breathe—asthma. And there's palpitations of the heart.

After chemo, I took radiation—some 30 days straight—and felt even more tired. The skin on my breast burned to a crisp—peely, pussy, red. I sustained a third-degree burn. I remember putting on these packs for the burn. It's healed now.

For two years, cancer became my whole life. I'm trying to get my life back now, doing volunteer work. It's making me more normal. I get very depressed at times. Cancer is a time bomb. It takes millions of cells before it shows up anywhere else. I've had a lot of tragedy in my life; lost a child at 18 months. I'm a survivor.

I don't have any plans for the rest of my life. I was seeing three doctors a month at one time. They don't know what's causing these symptoms now. I seriously think I may need more testing. It might have spread to my brain. No oncologist will tell me I'm in remission, even though I have no clinical evidence of cancer now. Tell me my symptoms are a reaction to all these meds; then I would feel safer. No one wants to tell me I'm okay. Once it's in the lymph nodes, it's all over.

I used to dance for hours at a time—social dancing, reggae, exercise class, Caribbean dance classes. I worked 12 hours a day. Now I'm a women who can't get through a mall without a cane. They tried blaming my fatigue on my fat. But what can they say about my right leg, which can't move?

My concern is survival. Will I have insurance after my husband retires? Any more cancer and I'm dead. I need a roof over my head. It's scary. My doctors say I'm going to get better, but I'm not a whole lot better. Now I only need a wheelchair in the airport.

I've been in a support group for a year. I've lost young friends who have died of various cancers. Some of those who are currently in treatment will die. If you're meek, they'll step right on you. Some people just let the doctors do their thing and accept death.

## Traditional Cancer Therapies: They're Poison

No matter how ill we are, humans cling to life. In the face of overwhelming odds, we suffer pain, endure harsh, disfiguring procedures, and loss of body image and various body functions in order to just hang on. And that's what traditional cancer therapies—surgery, radiation, chemotherapy, and hormone—offer.

The first three therapies have been the national standard for cancer treatment for over 40 years and are part and parcel of the vocabulary of medical schools and hospital libraries, doctors' offices, NCI, ACS, major treatment centers, and political organizations created for waging the "war on cancer."

That war on cancer is a failure. The five-year survival rates for the majority of cancers (lung, colon, breast, and stomach) remain essentially what they were 20 years ago (Robert Proctor, *The Sciences,* March/April, 1995). In fact, our ability to cure most advanced cancers has improved scarcely at all since 1971.

Traditional practitioners generally do not acknowledge that traditional treatments are not working. They maintain a rigid medical mindset despite some compelling truths: there is no known "cure" for breast cancer, and the mortality rate for the disease has barely changed in the last 50 years. Based on 1996 figures from ACS, of the more than 185,000 Americans who are diagnosed with breast cancer every year, nearly one quarter will be dead in five years. And according to the Breast Cancer Fund, more than 40 percent will be dead in ten years.

Women undergoing traditional breast cancer therapies pay a price, often a very high price. First there is the surgery, sometimes just a lumpectomy, sometimes more radical mastectomies—always a terrifying, unpleasant experience. If the cancer has spread, women may be subjected to removal of lymph nodes from within the chest cavity. Then comes radiation and chemotherapy, a process that destroys both cancerous and healthy cells because these very powerful, very toxic chemicals cannot distinguish the difference.

More recently, hormone therapy (using tamoxifen and other substances to stop cells from growing), biological therapy (using the body's immune system to fight cancer), and now bone marrow transplantation are being introduced into treatment at selected cancer centers. Hormone therapy brings its own dangers: recent studies have concluded that after a certain time it is no longer effective; in fact, beyond that limit, other cancers may develop. And since each woman has a unique response to the hormones, too much or too little can cause its own unique set of problems.

The following limited discussion is just a sampling of the traditional therapies that are available. Any therapy may or may not work depending on a number of factors, including the advancement of the cancer and the individual's tolerance of radiation and chemotherapy.

### *Surgery*

The Burton Goldberg Group, who compiled the comprehensive tome *Alternative Medicine: The Definitive Guide,* says this about cancer surgery:

> Surgery to remove cancerous tumors grew out of the premise, since discarded, that localized tumors were isolated manifestations of the disease and that removal of the diseased body part, if caught in time, would prevent the cancer from spreading. Surgery removes as much of the cancer as possible (very often leaving dangerous cancer cells behind) but does not correct the underlying cause of the cancer. Consequently, the tumor often re-occurs. Physicians now know as well that a cancer may already have spread to distant parts of the body long before it becomes detected elsewhere as a lump. This has been borne out by studies which show that mastectomy presents no advantage, in terms of survival, over a lumpectomy and radiation.

If premenopausal women elect surgery, timing is a key issue. W. L. McGuire published a study of 283 premenopausal women who had breast cancer operations in a 1992 issue of *Journal of the NCI*. McGuire found that cancer recurred in twice as many women who had surgery in the first half of their menstrual cycle compared to those who had surgery in the second half. And Seifert and Grant, writing in the *International Journal of Cancer* in 1992, confirmed these results in a five-year analysis of 385 premenopausal women.

During a normal 28-day menstrual cycle, estrogen levels increase in the first two weeks until an egg is released from the ovaries. Estrogen declines in the second two weeks as progesterone is released to prepare the uterus for implantation of a fertilized egg. High levels of estrogen are associated with increased cell division in breast tissue and lowered immunity, two factors that are significant for increased breast cancer risk. Thus, if surgery is performed during the first two weeks, when cancer cells are dividing more rapidly, there's a greater risk they will spread to other tissue, such as the lymph nodes.

Age seems to be an important factor in the results of surgery, as well. A randomized study by Jacques Borger, et al., in Amsterdam comparing breast conservation therapy (lumpectomy) with mastectomy showed equal survival rates for the two therapies, with slightly higher recurrence rates in patients younger than 40 years of age (*Journal of Clinical Oncology,* 1994).

For younger women who undergo surgery, the survival rate for some whose lymph nodes are not involved can reach 90 percent. The prognosis worsens when malignant cells are found in the lymph nodes. That's when doctors recommend radiation and chemotherapy, or drugs that circulate throughout the body in an effort to kill local and distant malignant cells.

The Amsterdam study also indicated that vascular invasion of the cancer site is also important. According to Dr. Judah Folkman, keynote speaker at the Cambridge Healthtech Institute's conference on angiogenesis: "All tumors require increased vascularization (blood supply), or angiogenesis, in order to continue to grow." (This newer understanding of how cancer metastasizes is fundamental to treatment. It will be discussed at greater length under "Inhibiting Angiogenesis" below.) The cancer cells use the blood system as a highway to move to other sites. Microvessel density is the most significant predictor of metastatic sites. Thus, if there are a number of vessels surrounding the cancer cells on one site, chances are the cells will move to other places in the body. This makes surgery less effective.

### *Radiation*

Radiation after surgery does appear to have some salubrious effects. An Austrian study of 420 breast cancer patients, reported in the January 23, 1994 *Chicago Sun-Times,* showed that 92 percent of those who had received traditional external radiation survived for five years with no recurrence of cancer. Of those patients who received an implant of high-dose radiation after breast cancer surgery, 96 percent were alive and cancer-free after five years.

The greatest difference between the two groups of patients in the Austrian study was cosmetic. After five years, 91 percent of the radiation implant group had what the researchers termed "good to excellent" results—little or no skin reddening due to enlarged blood vessels, or growth of fibrous tissue. Only 70 percent of the traditional radiation group reached the same level. The Austrian researchers said that their high-dose implant method was faster and more convenient than the low-dose implant method currently used in France, Great Britain, and other European countries. The high-dose method involved implanting 12-14 needles containing radioactive material in the area of the breast where the tumor had occurred. The entire procedure took 45 minutes to an hour, whereas the low-dose method involves radioactive wires implanted for 2-5 days, which takes five or more separate days.

* * *

### *Chemotherapy*

An editorial in the May 5, 1994 *New England Journal of Medicine* stated, "Randomized clinical trials have shown that chemotherapy, tamoxifen and ovarian ablation [surgically removing or chemically ablating the ovaries] can each reduce the frequency of relapses and prolong survival among patients with operable breast cancer and ipsilateral [other side] ... metastases." The editorial continues with this recommendation: "Multi-agent chemotherapy is the present treatment of choice for premenopausal women with node-positive breast cancer; for postmenopausal women, endocrine therapy, alone or in combination with chemotherapy is advantageous."

But chemotherapy is actually a questionable treatment at best. A German cancer biostatistician, Dr. Ulrich Abel, showed just how impoverished this approach is. In a 1990 article entitled "Chemotherapy of Advanced Epithelial Cancer," Dr. Abel stated, "A sober and unprejudiced analysis of the literature has rarely revealed any therapeutic success by the regimens in question in treating advanced epithelial cancer. ... These cancers originating in the epithelial layer of the body, lung, breast, prostate, colon, etc. account for at least 80 percent of cancer deaths in advanced industrial countries. There is no evidence for the vast majority of cancers that treatment with these drugs exerts any positive influence on survival or quality of life in patients with advanced disease. . . . The almost dogmatic belief in the efficacy of chemotherapy is usually based on false conclusions from inappropriate data."

Abel then polled 350 oncologists and research units around the world, trying to gauge the true feelings of doctors who use chemotherapy in advanced cancers. He received 150 replies, and found that the personal views of many oncologists were in striking contrast to communications intended for the public. Abel cited studies that indicate many oncologists would not take chemotherapy themselves if they had cancer. And he concluded that in the case of breast cancer, there is "no direct evidence that chemotherapy prolongs survival. Its use is ethically questionable."

While Dr. Abel's statements were publicized in *Der Spiegel,* the German equivalent of *Time,* the U.S. chemotherapy establishment has maintained a discreet silence, reinforcing the American dependence on chemotherapy. Other studies indicate that employing chemotherapy for metastasized cancer may even be a mistake. ACS's 1994 *Cancer Facts and Figures* states, "The five year survival rate . . . for persons with distant metastases at the time of diagnosis is 18 percent. And also in 1994, in the February issue of the *Journal of Clinical Oncology,* A. Romero, et al. found, "During the last few years, no substantial improvement has been noted in the outcome of chemotherapeutic treatment of metastatic breast cancer." How many women will elect to receive radiation and chemotherapy, having to endure the hair loss, nausea, loss of appetite, pain, immune suppression, and fatigue, in the anguished hope that they will be in that 18 percent group?

These are bad odds and the price of mere survival is very high. In fact, doctors admit that it's possible to kill patients with chemotherapy without ever getting rid of the cancer. "Contrary to popular opinion, a reduction of tumor mass does not prolong expected survival. Sometimes, in fact, the cancer returns more aggressively than before because killing off 99 percent of a mass fosters the growth of resistant cell lines," stated Ralph Moss in the December 1990 *Cancer Chronicles Newsletter.* The 1994 NCI summary of treatment actually states, "Breast cancer that recurs can often be treated but usually cannot be cured when the breast cancer recurs in another part of the body." And according to Dr. John Cairns of Harvard University School of Public Health, of the approximately half a million people who die each year of cancer, only about 2-3 percent gain any benefit from chemotherapy.

The chemotherapeutic drugs themselves offer one explanation for their ineffectiveness—many of them are capable of inducing a second cancer at an entirely different site. Chemotherapy agents weaken the immune system, allowing the cancer to spread and infection to develop, further weakening an already sick woman. Immune system damage is almost universal in chemotherapy patients. So in curing cancer at one site, traditional treatment may make the body too weak to fight off an infection or a secondary cancer elsewhere.

And chemotherapy is a two-edged sword. The drugs are intended to take advantage of a cancerous cell's rapid growth and division, and either block a key metabolic process or interfere with cell division. Some agents work by damaging the DNA of fast-growing cells, thereby inhibiting growth potential. However, when introduced to a patient's body, these poisonous agents cannot distinguish between cancerous cells and normal cells, so many normal cells are injured in the process. It's little wonder that the Breast Cancer Fund has stated, "Chemotherapy . . . unleashes such a barbaric assault on the human body that we at the . . . Fund are commited to breaking from the status quo of searching for yet another toxic 'cocktail' and seeking, instead, more effective, more humane, and less damaging treatments."

Toxicity is a factor in chemotherapy treatment and countless reports in the standard medical literature openly admit this. Articles abound on how to minimize or diminish the poisonous side effects, with suggestions ranging from marijuana to different and additional drugs, many with their own side effects and a few with cancer-promoting effects. Without exception, all chemotherapeutic agents have serious side effects. No patient is free of these toxic effects. It is the hope that in killing the cancer cells, the patient won't also die. Clearly she will be pushed to her limit.

Normal cells particularly susceptible to chemotherapy agents are those which divide rapidly—hair, the lining of the gut, and the bone marrow—leading to the symptoms we all recognize in chemotherapy patients: hair loss, nausea, vomiting, diarrhea, anemia, increased susceptibility to infection, and profound fatigue. There is also bone marrow depression, organ and nerve damage, early menopause, and other severe toxic reactions. Add to all this the woman's psychological distress waiting for the results of her treatment, the anticipated fear of recurrence, her fear of the adverse effects of treatment, and the risk of a false-positive report leading to invasive diagnostic procedures and possibly over-treatment.

In a tacit admission of treatment bankruptcy, some medical institutions actually repeat the same series of drugs to the patient, even after the patient has shown no response the first time. Stated G. Falkson, et al., in a 1994 *Journal of Clinical Oncology* paper, "It is concluded that, although reinduction with the same cytostatic regimen yielded disappointing results, . . . no other salvage regimens are known to provide good results after relapse. The results of this study underscore the importance of developing new regimens for the treatment of metastatic breast cancer."

### *Additional Establishment Therapies*

Because chemotherapy is failing to get desired results, more and more drastic (and costly) treatment measures are being employed by traditional practitioners. An article appearing in the Diagnostic and Therapeutic Technology Assessment (DATTA) section of a 1994 issue of *JAMA* discussed hyperthermia as adjuvant treatment for recurrent breast cancer. For the most part, the doctors were guessing with this procedure. They could not predict response rates; they did not know the temperatures except at locations where sensors had been inserted. Nor could they evaluate temperature distribution in the target tissue.

While hyperthermia sounds like a plausible idea—the heat speeds up reactions, theoretically making cancer cells more susceptible to chemotherapy agents—the application as presented does not give patients very good odds, and are questionable considering the trauma and uncertainty of the treatment.

Perhaps one of the most traumatic, costly, and controversial treatment approaches is to use the patient's bone marrow—the body's crucial blood-and-immune-system factory. If the cancer has metastasized, doctors may remove, treat, and freeze about a quart of the patient's own marrow. Then they administer high-dose whole body radiation—10 to 50 times the normal dose—to kill all the cancer cells. As the patient hovers on the brink of death, doctors return her marrow to her body, hoping that it will rebuild the immune system. Not all of these patients respond.

There is much criticism of this procedure. "The procedure is considered experimental for . . . breast cancer," states Jane Zones, whose article "Autologous Bone Marrow Transplant: What Is the Price of Hope?" was published at the end of 1995 in *Network News:*

> Although many women have been offered [these procedures] as "promising" treatment, not one study has been published that compares conventional chemotherapy to high-dose chemotherapy (HDC) with autologous bone marrow transplant (ABMT/BCT) in patients with metastatic breast cancer in the fifteen years the procedure has been used. The research that has been published has serious flaws that make it extremely difficult to determine the therapy's safety and effectiveness. In the past two years, ECRI, an independent technology assessment organization, has reviewed the published literature . . . for Stage IV breast cancer patients and conducted a "meta-analysis" of the studies' pooled results to assess its relative effectiveness compared to conventional chemotherapies. . . .
>
> The group found that patients in conventional chemotherapy studies were more likely to have a longer disease-free and overall survival time than were patients with HDC with ABMT/BCT studies. . . . If those patients who died shortly after the experimental treatment had been counted in the reported outcomes of the studies, survival figures would have been significantly worse.

\* \* \*

In October 1994, doctors at the University of Chicago announced a new procedure called blood cell transplantation (BCT). The technique consists of extracting blood from the patient and taking from it millions of stem cells—the root of all mature cells—to grow billions of infection-fighting white cells in the laboratory, and then reintroducing this enriched blood mixture into the patient after chemotherapy. The hope is that growing white cells outside the patient's body will reduce the time during which transplant patients are at great risk of life-threatening infections.

"The goal is to determine whether we can make bone-marrow transplantation safer and less expensive by hastening the functional recovery of the patient's immune system," said Dr. Stephanie Williams, director of the autologous bone marrow transplant program at the University of Chicago hospitals. "That would allow us to reduce the number and severity of infections, cut antibiotic use, lessen the need for transfusions and shorten the average hospital stay," reported Tom McNamee, in the October 19, 1994 *Chicago Sun-Times*. The *Chicago Tribune* described the controversial procedure as "agonizing, dangerous, and expensive—$60,000 to $250,000—depending on the length of hospitalization."

No doctor wants to do nothing. A caring physician facing a patient with a life-threatening disease is often in the ambiguous position of having only the merest hope to offer. A desperate patient's imperative to hold onto life and the physician's desire "to do something" often sways the physician to recommend a drastic therapy in the hope that it may be of some help. They fail to ask: At what cost, monetarily and in quality of life?

Why is the cancer establishment so uncritical of chemotherapy's continued use? Ethics demand those entrenched within the traditional system undertake an impartial review of the true effectiveness of these therapies. Why aren't more doctors of conscience demanding why we aren't getting better results? Cracking open the door just a bit by adding immune enhancing agents to conventional therapies, or advocating a natural alternative to conventional methods is considered no less than heresy.

Good sense suggests that treatment for cancer should not be so toxic, so painful, and so ineffective. But the hardened systems and mindsets of the established order are in place. The past will continue to be the guide for the future, meaning that research will focus on some new combination of drugs developed by a well-connected pharmaceutical company that has spent over $200 million to bring the product to market in anticipation of even greater profits.

At best, all these efforts will be variations by the same players within the same game. The same accepted approaches are moved around on the chess board, or perhaps a newly patented piece is periodically added to the board. But, the parameters of the board never change.

In 1991, the Office of Technology Assessment found almost 200 scientific studies supporting alternative treatment methods. OTA urged NCI to investigate, states Sam Epstein. But NCI would not. Both the cancer establishment and industry resist alternative therapies and vigorously attack them—especially those where the therapy holds no possibility for a patentable product—whether or not evidence indicates the alternative therapies may be working. The establishment, protected by medical tradition, large corporate profits, and a compliant media, makes nearly impossible the study of or introduction of alternative therapies into the medical mainstream.

Doctors applying conventional cancer treatment are not bad people. Most oncologists are sincere, dedicated, and deeply concerned about their patients. But they've been trained in the traditional system and have spent untold thousands of dollars in getting that training. All the while, they are bombarded by messages from the pharmaceutical companies, whose sales forces enjoy easy access to medical centers and whose ads fill the oncology journals with the latest "breakthrough."

It takes a great deal of independence to pursue alternatives to entrenched practices taught in medical schools and residency programs. And it takes a very strong woman, upon discovering she has breast cancer, to fight her terror (and her doctor's valued, but possibly limited, advice) and to learn about alternative treatments. The issues here are information, choice, and courage.

In the case of breast cancer, rather than considering it a localized disease, more physicians are suggesting that it is systemic. This creates enormous implications for understanding the growth and treatment of the disease. If breast cancer is indeed systemic, its appearance in another part of the body years after the initial tumor has been cut or shrunk can be explained. The likelihood of metastasis in that case is substantial, if nothing is done to help the entire body strengthen itself.

Therefore, it makes sense for doctors and patients to consider not just the cancer in its site, but the entire body as well. Failure to understand this is one compelling reason why standard medical treatment has shown no breakthroughs. Traditional treatment has yet to deal with the whole body. We need a different emphasis, a new kind of research and funding that explores treatment that enhances rather than damages the patient.

## Choosing a Healthy Body

There is a new category of doctors who, eschewing the gridlock in traditional medicine, practice environmental and alternative medicine. They understand it is just as important to enhance immune function to prevent tumor growth as it is to kill cancer cells (as well as healthy cells!) with toxic chemotherapy. The mysterious "spontaneous remission" is simply the return of a healthy immune system.

*Alternative Medicine: The Definitive Guide,* introduces its chapter on cancer therapy with the following:

Conventional medicine rarely treats cancer as a systemic illness. Alternative medicine, by contrast, regards cancer as the manifestation of an unhealthy body whose defenses are so imbalanced that they can no longer destroy cells that turn cancerous—as would normally occur in a state of health. Its essential premise is that healthy bodies do not develop cancer, and that cancer is a reflection of the body as a whole, rather than a localized disease in one particular part of the body. . . . Shunning the use of highly toxic modalities, such as radiation and chemotherapy, . . . they prefer to heal the entire body and employ a multifaceted, nontoxic approach to doing so, incorporating treatments which rely on biopharmaceutical, immune enhancement, metabolic, nutritional, and and herbal methods. Because cancer is a disease with multiple causes, it is important to realize that the best chance of treating it lies in an approach which addresses all of the factors involved.

Mainstream medicine does not answer all our problems and many people—including a number of doctors—know this. A few hospitals now offer alternative medical departments, and the nation's first government-run natural medicine clinic is scheduled to open in Seattle in Fall 1996. The American College for the Advancement of Medicine in Laguna Hills, California refers callers to physicians across the country who practice nonconventional treatment. The American Academy of Environmental Medicine in Kansas is a newer organization whose members work with those who have developed chemical sensitivities to environmental pollution. Another field emerging as viable in the area of both prevention and treatment are nutritionists (as opposed to dietitians), who are experts in developing specific diets for surviving in our toxic world.

Of course, many mainstream practitioners discourage their patients from seeking alternative therapies, and the cancer establishment disapproves of them. However, in this century, more than 100 different alternatives to conventional treatments have been advanced, according to Robert G. Houston in his book *Repression and Reform in the Evaluation of Alternative*

*Cancer Therapies.* He wrote, "hundreds of researchers are now working on different aspects of natural, nontoxic therapies. With few exceptions, these efforts have met with official disapproval from the cancer treatment establishment, concerned to keep patients oriented to standard therapeutic options."

There is nothing unique about the establishment's intolerance of alternative therapies, for "a different way" has been the route to most medical advancements in history. Countless procedures, from Louis Pasteur's germ theory of disease to Sir Joseph Lister's antiseptic surgery, were denounced and the creators considered quacks. Lumpectomy for breast cancer patients was considered unacceptable treatment by American surgeons as late as 1948 (David Steinman, ed., *Life Extenders and Memory Boosters!* Health Quest Publications, 1994). Dr. Emile Grubbe was bitterly denounced by leading surgeons and it was not until the 1930s, after decades of official scorn, that the treatment of cancer by radiation was finally accepted by the American College of Surgery. When systems, profits, and orthodoxy are in place, it takes time and pressure for the new to become accepted.

With a number of available alternative therapies, I have chosen just four to discuss. They shore up the immune system, isolate the cancer, get rid of toxins, and improve state of mind—all part of a bona fide anti-cancer program. The medical theories behind these three are compelling and completely sensible.

### Antigen Treatment as Immune Therapy

Because the immune system is compromised by traditional cancer treatments, Dr. Georg F. Springer, Professor and Head of the Heather M. Bligh Cancer Research Labs at the Chicago Medical School, has developed a program using T antigen cells that has shown some promising results in patients who are undergoing chemotherapy. Springer's letter to prospective patients explains the procedure:

This investigation is designed to stimulate your immune system to fight cancer. We intend to accomplish this by injecting into your skin small amounts of antigen prepared by rigorous chemical degradation from healthy human group O red cells (T antigen) and free of any viruses, bacteria, and pyrogens.

T antigen, which occurs normally only masked in healthy cells, has been found uncovered on the surface of cancer cells. Since the T antigen does not normally occur uncovered, the body recognizes it as foreign and fights it immunologically, just as it does invading microbes. We bolster this fighting power. . . .

In 1994, Springer wrote about his work in an article entitled "T/Tn Antigen Vaccine Is Effective and Safe in Preventing Recurrence of Advanced Human Breast Carcinoma" appearing in *Cancer Biotherapy*: "For nearly 20 years, we used T/Tn antigen vaccine in safe, specific, effective, long-term intradermal vaccine against recurrence of advanced breast carcinoma. Treatment is ad infinitum. All 18 breast carcinoma patients treated (Stages IV [6], III [6], and II [6]), survived more than 5 years postoperatively; 10 survived more then 10 to 18 years. Of the latter, three patients each are Stages III and IV. Five additional 5-year survivors have not yet reached 10 years. . . . There were no untoward side effects." The increase in survival times when compared with patients undergoing standard therapy is statistically astounding when you consider that only 18 percent of women with metastasized breast cancer who undergo traditional treatment are alive five years later, and Dr. Springer believes the vaccine may find its most beneficial use as a preventive agent.

Not every patient qualifies for this treatment; they have to meet certain blood chemistry requirements. And though Springer's office receives hundreds of phone calls from potential candidates and constant physician referrals, they are able to add only one or two new patients per month. The vaccine is made in their own lab, and it is not patented. The program does not charge for the treatment (the lab is privately endowed and donations come from the private sector). A number of oncologists and researchers are now looking into similar vaccines.

### Inhibiting Angiogenesis

Angiogenesis is the development of blood vessels both to and from the cancer site. Cancer growth depends upon a supply of blood. If the blood supply is stopped, the cancer cells dry up. There is significant evidence showing that tumor growth and metastasis are dependent upon angiogenesis.

Dr. William Stetler-Stevenson, Chief, Extracellular Matrix Pathology Section, Laboratory of Pathology at the NCI, makes a strong statement about angiogenesis:"Metastasis formation is the most deadly aspect of tumor progression. There is a direct correlation between the number of blood vessels around the tumor site and the frequency of metastasis."

Stetler-Stevenson explained that, for a metastasis to occur, there must be three processes: the cancer cells must *attack* the glue, a substance called matrix, that holds the cells of a blood vessel together; then the cancer cells must *degrade* it—or make a hole; then the cancer cells must move forward—or *migrate* to the next site. Companies are now researching and developing drugs that block the process. These drugs are called "matrix metallo proteinases"—tissue inhibitors of the metallo protein or TIMPs. They are not yet approved by FDA.

When asked about shark cartilage, the natural substance that has been reported by *60 Minutes* to be effective in dealing with angiogenesis, Stetler-Stevenson replied, "Shark cartilage has been shown to be a rich source of metallo proteinases, and it may be of value. However, there are a lot of other things in there [impurities], so we can't do quality control. I feel a synthetic inhibitor will prove safer for patients since we can control the dosage and test for concentrations in the blood."

In the meantime, a variety of brands of shark cartilage are being advertised and bought in health food stores and cata-

logues across the country by consumers looking to enhance
their immune systems and stop their own metastasis. BeneFin,
one of the purest of the products, is being tested in the United
States, Chile, China, and Japan. In Chile, Japan, and China, breast
cancer is included in the trials.

American companies are already conducting clinical trials on
various other substances that look promising for inhibiting
angiogenesis. Dr. Henrik Rasmussen, vice president of British
BioTech, says his company is working on the very substance that
blocks the matrix metallo proteinase inhibitors. "Tumors produce huge amounts of enzymes," he said. "We make an analog,
similar in composition to the natural enzyme, but which will
bind to the site instead of the original enzyme. The synthetic
enzyme will form a capsule around the tumor and the tumor will
not grow. We are presently testing classes of compounds that are
specific for various cancers in medical centers across the United
States. In the animal models, the findings have been very positive; we are stopping the enzymes that promote tumor growth
and we are stopping the creation of new blood vessels."

### Detoxification

One of the very few effective treatment regimens for patients
with high levels of fat-soluble toxins in their bodies is detoxification: change of diet, increased mobilization of chemicals from
fat stores, and increased excretion. A good detoxification program aids in eliminating unwanted chemicals from our bodies.
Such a program could be useful before any cancer shows up, and
is certainly a sensible approach to add to any therapy once cancer has been diagnosed.

One notable detox program has been devised by Dr. William
Rea of the Environmental Health Center in Dallas, Texas. Rea has
demonstrated a lessening of the chemical burden in a number of
patients. He does so by eliminating pesticides and other toxic
chemicals from the diet, and by adding clean, carefully managed
food to the diet. He also recommends sauna to increase mobi-

lization of toxic chemicals from fat stores.

The clinic also offers nutritional supplementation, exercise, vitamin and mineral replacement, administration of xenobiotic binding substances, osteopathic manipulation, and immunotherapy. Its brochure states, "surgery and medication are used when indicated, but the Center's goal is to minimize their use and ultimately to decrease the patient's need for them."

The results of his detox program are impressive. Writing in the journal *Clinical Ecology*, Rea stated, "All the patients [staying at the center] improved their signs and symptoms, producing an improvement rate of 100 percent. Seventy percent of outpatients improved through a mean treatment time of 8.8 months, while 80 percent of the sauna/physical therapy patients improved through a mean treatment time of 7 weeks...."

### Support Groups

They're important. Research shows that patients with cancer who participate in support groups do better than those who struggle with illness on their own. Women with breast cancer have found great comfort and shared community with other women suffering the same fears, pains, and anxiety. If you have a local support group within your neighborhood, sponsored by your local hospital, by all means join. Your life expectancy will increase.

The American public knows there are more weapons in the fight against cancer than the establishment is willing to give them, and it is spending millions of dollars outside the medical mainstream. Unfortunately, patients must search out alternatives for themselves, a difficult and sometimes costly procedure, for "unapproved" treatments are generally not covered by insurance.

Yet there are cracks in the establishment walls. Because of public interest, NIH allocated $2 million for an Office of Alternative Therapy (OAM) in 1992. The 1995 budget for the

OAM was $6 million, or only 0.05 percent of NIH's total appropriations, but the increase hopefully shows that pressure from advocates who are challenging the business-as-usual mindset is having an effect. Even private foundations are sponsoring research into unconventional therapies: chiropractic and nutrition therapies, and how electromagnetic signals affect immune activity.

In his 1992 book *Cancer Therapy: The Independent Consumer's Guide to Non-toxic Treatment and Prevention,* Ralph Moss lists 36 alternative therapies specifically for breast cancer. Many of these therapies complement each other or work in tandem with conventional drugs to boost the immune system in patients undergoing chemotherapy and radiation. Some of them can help reduce the dosage of conventional treatments.

For further information on alternative therapies, read the following books: *Alternative Medicine: The Definitive Guide* and *Alternative Medicine Yellow Pages,* both published by Future Medicine Publishing (800-818-6777); *Sharks Don't Get Cancer,* by Dr. I. William Lane and *Third Opinion: An International Directory to Alternative Therapy Centers for the Treatment and Prevention of Cancer* compiled by John Fink, both published by Avery Publishing Group. You might also subscribe to *Health and Healing,* a monthly newsletter on alternative medical news written by Dr. Julian Whitaker (Phillips Publishing, 800-539-8219).

The alternative movement is growing vigorously and may very well leave behind those physicians who practice "the old way," no matter how "state of the art" that old way may be. An article printed in the World Health Organization publication *Emerging Forces in Cancer Care* stated, "The mainstream of scientific research is moving toward increasing recognition of the limits of conventional therapies and cautious optimism about the potential for new biological therapies. This situation has given rise to a social phenomenon among cancer patients. Today, in many parts of the world, a significant minority has chosen to engage actively in the fight for recovery. This minority searches for an intelligent integration of efficacious conventional therapies and complementary therapies involving personal trials of intensive health promotion.... It appears that 10 percent among those patients achieve exceptional results, another 10 percent fail, and 80 percent become healthy cancer patients."

# 13

# PUBLIC ACTION TO PROTECT OUR NATION'S HEALTH

**W**hat is the state of our environment in the 1990s? Thanks to Congressional underfunding and deregulation, the situation is deteriorating: unpolluted water is growing scarcer; persistent toxic chemicals continue to be spewed out as part of industry's formula for financial viability.

## The Threats of the 1990s

Our very food sources are dwindling, exemplified in the loss of stock in both the Pacific and Atlantic fisheries. What fish are left are contaminated by hormones, pesticides, antibiotics, and industrial chemicals. Chronic diseases are accelerating throughout the world. Asthma deaths are up in the United States, and life expectancy has dropped precipitously in Rumania, Poland, and the area surrounding Chernobyl in Russia.

Various important environmental bills died in Congress in 1994 and were not revived in 1995. They included the Clean Water Act and legislation to reform the Superfund.

The consequences of backtracking on environmental protection are serious. According to the "27th Environmental Quality Review" published by the National Wildlife Federation in

February 1995, EPA acknowledged that "Thirty percent of the nation's rivers, 42 percent of lakes, and 32 percent of estuaries continue to be degraded, mainly by silt and nutrients from farm and urban runoff, combined sewer overflows, and municipal sewage. EPA Administrator Carol Browner said . . . that 22 years after the law was originally passed, an estimated 40 percent of the country's freshwater is still unusable in terms of public health and safety. . . .

"There are 200,000 public water systems in this country, a substantial percentage of which are basket cases that cannot even meet the most basic microbiological standards," continues the National Wildlife article.

The 1994 "Year End Review" of *The Earth Times* was even more negative: ". . . it can be safely said that the White House's environmental policy is in shambles. Throughout the entire course of the recently concluded 103rd Congress, the administration managed to get just one environmental bill passed into law, the California Desert Protection Act. All other administration initiatives—including Superfund reform as well as reform of the nation's mining, grazing, and pesticide laws—fell by the wayside. And, in a clear sign of EPA's diminished stature on Capitol Hill, efforts to elevate the agency to cabinet-level status were torpedoed by a bipartisan coalition of the House of Representatives."

Why did the Clinton administration and its allies in the environmental movement do so poorly? According to the author of this story, "The answer lies in a dramatic shift in public attitudes toward the way in which the federal government provides for environmental protection—a shift the White House, EPA, and the environmental community failed to recognize until it was too late."

Protecting the environment is a political act. Early on, the Clinton administration did not perceive it was getting sufficient public support for its election promises on the environment; Clinton himself was too beholden to certain industries that had helped him win. The Wise Use Movement, using corporate-trained citizens fearful of job loss or the rising price of grazing on government lands, also stopped environmental activity with intimidation and threats of violence. And vast and convincing public relations campaigns were waged on behalf of polluting industries. The public bought in. The mantra, "Getting government off our backs," first chanted by Reagan supporters, had taken the place of reasoned thought.

Abetting the anti-environmental movement is the inordinate amount of money contributed to business-as-usual, anti- environmental candidates and initiatives. The March 16, 1995 *Rachel's Environment & Health Weekly* tells what happened to a citizen-sponsored ballot initiative in Massachusetts in 1992 to reduce wasteful packaging and require packaging materials to be reusable or made of recycled or recyclable materials. The measure was defeated, 59 percent to 41 percent. Out-of-state corporations funded the anti-initiative forces to the tune of $4.8 million. The largest contributor was the American Paper Institute, which gave $854,564; others included Dow Chemical, Occidental Petroleum, Exxon, Union Carbide, Philip Morris, Chevron, Mobil Chemical, and Kodak, each of which contributed $100,000 or more.

President Clinton is also doing his own compromising. Two major producers of methyl bromide (a poisonous, ozone-depleting gas used to kill bugs) with a long history of political contributions to Clinton house their very large plants in Arkansas. Clinton has supported changes in the Clean Air Act that would allow continued production of methyl bromide.

In the 1994 "How to Defend Our Environmental Laws: A Citizen Action Guide," a coalition of environmental groups including the Sierra Club Legal Defense Fund, the Wilderness Society, and the National Audubon Society, offered the following analysis:

> Thanks to political pressure, federal funding for state and local environmental protection has dropped over the past 15 years. One reason for the decline was a deliberate effort by the

Reagan administration to gut environmental programs. The most serious effort, backed by 1995 Republican-dominated Congress has been to pass a law that exempts states and cities from all federal laws and regulations that are not fully funded by Congress. The battle cry of some state and local officials has been: "No money—no mandates." While this sound bite has deceptive appeal, it ignores several key factors:

Providing a safe and healthy environment is a basic duty of all levels of government. Congress should not have to pay cities and states to provide their citizens with clean air to breathe and clean water to drink.

Most environmental laws apply to states and cities in the same way as they do to private business. We don't pay industry not to dump chemicals into a river; we should not have to pay a city not to dump raw sewage either.

Pollution knows no geographic boundaries. [Poisons] from one city can close beaches or contaminate drinking water downstream. Air pollution can cross city and state boundaries and affect people and property downwind.

It is not fair that some states and cities do a good job of protecting citizens and others will be let off the hook. It is not fair for citizens in some areas to be exposed to significantly higher risks from pollution than in others. It is especially not fair to the people in the poorest cities who will breathe the dirtiest air and drink the dirtiest water.

There is no end to what the anti-environmental crowd can come up with. Fueled by their early success at gutting reforms for the Drinking Water Act, the Clean Water Act, and Superfund, the House of Representatives passed far-reaching changes in how federal agencies enforce health, safety, and environmental laws in February 1995. Title III of H.R. 9 places reducing costs for industry above protecting public health. It directs regulatory agencies to base rules primarily on economic calculations of costs and benefits, not the health-based standards at the heart of many existing environmental laws. The act would give environmental violators an arsenal of new weapons with which to dodge prosecution.

The bill passed with enough votes to suggest the House could override a presidential veto. (President Clinton has vowed to veto the bill, and the Senate has not yet acted upon it.) The legislation supersedes existing laws. Any business subject to federal regulations could at its discretion challenge the rules and require the relevant agency to undertake time-consuming risk assessment and cost-benefit analysis. That means placing dollar values on such things as avoiding cancer or birth defects, reducing infertility, or preventing a child's learning disability.

EPA Administrator Carol Browner reacted strongly against the bill. In National Wildlife Federation's "Action Alert" of February 15, 1995, she said, "The risk bill purports to be an application of sound science; in truth, it perverts not just science but also common sense. Twenty years of protection for our children and our air, our land and our water are being rolled back in the dead of night without even a thoughtful debate in Congress." Rick Spencer of the National Wildlife Federation adds:

> The bill is part of the Contract strategy. It came out of committee late at night and there were but four business days to get public comment on it. There has been no press coverage, no debate.
>
> There will be 23 levels of risk analysis, cost benefits, and peer reviews before any action can be taken, and then, the bill calls for a polluting company to take the issue before the courts if it is not happy with a regulatory decision. Polluters now have a right to sue the EPA before it proposes a rule, when it proposes a rule, and after the rule is issued and when the rule is enforced. This delay tactic will tie up enforcement, waste valuable financial resources in lawsuits, and allows the polluter to keep on polluting.
>
> Sponsors of this risk assessment legislation have made it clear that their purpose is to minimize liability for polluters and reckless business, while putting the American people at risk.

Does all this mean citizens are powerless? No. The nation's concern for the environment is much stronger than some ideologues had anticipated. Recent polls indicate that the Republican-led Congress is vulnerable on this issue. It seems that, after the first flush of excitement engendered by the Republican Contract's radicalism, the American public has realized the bill of goods they have been sold.

The scene is set for action. Since women are the ones who are most worried about nuclear waste, chemical pollution, and food poisoning, it is appropriate that women are the ones addressing the future of this planet. Assimilating tough information, learning the science, women are engaged in political action reminiscent of the public health, antislavery, Suffragette, and feminist movements, all of which had great female leaders. Woman are addressing the entire landscape of pollution/profits, sickness/profits, and women as fair game for medical excesses. Woman are revealing the seductive and powerful social, political, and economic structures that block change and keep the system going.

What unites us is the fact that breast cancer is an equal opportunity disease. Women are united by the toxic assaults to our bodies. In that universality, there is power.

## Changing the Corporate State

With the deterioration of our environment, with the industrial status quo protected by government and the law, we need radical action to protect our health. Cleaning up the environment and changing the way we do business has not happened under any administration, Republican or Democrat. And despite the promises of Vice President Gore and our hopes for President Clinton, environmental progress has taken several steps backward. Those who understand the issues must also understand that our national priorities need radical revision.

Whatever we want to believe, we no longer live in a democracy. Instead, we live in a corporate state in which corporate influence at all levels of government can override voters' wishes. We will never be able to stop the pollution and live healthy lives under the present system, so clearly something very big must change. If the sovereignty of the people is to be recaptured, if the people are to regain this democracy, our new advocacy must fight for fundamental reforms.

We must look at corporations in a new way, not as the benign, socially concerned organizations that well-crafted ad campaigns make them out to be. On TV, Dow "Makes You Do Great Things" and GE "Brings Good Things to Life." But no one brings us the message of these companies' pollution records, their political leverage, and their true power. Very few delve into what happens when a wealthy company buys out a competitor. This is as true of the health care field as it is for any other. A new slogan is coined, a new logo is prepared, and press releases go out trumpeting the improved ability of the new conglomerate to provide services to old and new customers. In addition, however, power is consolidated. If competition is eliminated, there is no alternative if the new powerhouse does not live up to its promises. And bitter experience has taught us that when profit and concern for humanity are in the balance, profit almost always wins.

Enough of the image. It's time we understand corporate structures as the invisible powerhouses that they are, controlling what they want through ownership of mainstream media, an interlocking network with powerful government bureaucrats, memberships on federal advisory boards, and just plain money. The consequence is the corruption of the political process and the erosion of democratic procedures underneath our own unsuspecting noses. Corporate power has gotten way out of balance.

### *Penalizing Offending Corporations*

To redress this balance, it is necessary for corporations to feel pain. For more than 100 years, American corporations have enjoyed many of the rights and constitutional protections that individual citizens enjoy. However, they have not been subject to the same types of penalties when they break the law. How can a corporation be thrown in jail? How can you prosecute managers who do what they are legally bound to do—and what their bosses tell them to do? Peter Montague framed the problem concisely in the May 5, 1994 issue of *Rachel's Environment & Health Weekly:*

> Corporations are legal fictions created by law to engage in business for the purpose of returning a percentage on investors' capital. This legal purpose requires that sufficient growth must occur each year (on average) to produce a surplus that can be returned to investors; and it requires that costs must be "externalized" (passed along to outside parties such as workers or the general public) to the extent possible. As former Ronald Reagan economist Robert Monks has said, "Despite attempts to provide balance and accountability, the corporation as an entity became so powerful that it quickly outstripped the limitations of accountability and became something of an externalizing machine, in the same way that a shark is a killing machine—no malevolence, no intentional harm, just something designed with sublime efficiency for self-preservation." . . .

> Individuals who make decisions for corporations are not free to do what they personally believe is right. . . . If corporate decision-makers make decisions contrary to these narrowly and legally defined corporate goals, they can be sued by shareholders for breach of fiduciary trust. . . . These corporations are chartered to pump out chemicals profitably; legally that is about all they can do.

> . . . The most important aspect of the corporation—individual investors and managers are legally protected from liability for the corporation's actions. Indeed, limiting individual liability was the purpose for which the corporation was invented. . . .

> Because corporations cannot feel pain when the corporation hurts someone or damages the environment, the fundamental constraint on human behavior (personal pain) is missing from the corporate form. . . . It is principally through pain

that humans learn to control themselves and civilize their behavior.

Montague believes that we must rethink our legal attitude toward corporations. Instead of their being organizations that can go on forever even though individual managers may be prosecuted and removed, they should operate under the ultimate threat of death. For instance, if a corporation receives three felony convictions, its charter would be revoked. The state would remove the company's privilege to do business.

"Outfitting corporations with a perpetual threat of death would concentrate the minds of management, shareholders and workers wonderfully, providing a strong, continuing incentive for ethical behavior. Such a perpetual threat would humanize and civilize the corporate form, which in recent years has arguably emerged as our most rogue and dangerous institution," Montague concludes.

If innocent citizens are under a constant death threat from corporate irresponsibility and misconduct, then fundamental justice requires that the polluting companies live under threat of termination as well.

### *Encouraging Good Corporate Behavior*

Besides being threatened, business can also be enticed. Paul Hawken, successful entrepreneur and author of *The Ecology of Commerce,* actually sees big business as the most promising lever for bringing about a sustainable future. In the Fall 1994 issue of the *Rocky Mountain Institute Newsletter,* he wrote, "The world's 500 largest companies control 25 percent of the world's output. Like it or not, there's not much hope in achieving sustainability without them on board." He issued a call to "turn industry on its head" in the next 20 years by creating an environment where people will no longer work for, invest in, or buy from unsustainable companies. Hawken believes that business leaders and employees are ready to countenance change, for they are recognizing that the "growth economy" that they set so much faith in forces them to use more resources, produce more waste, and compromise their children's lifestyle. "The way to sell sustainability," Hawken says, "is by demonstrating how *reducing* throughput can *increase* profits and productivity, *create* jobs, and *make* a healthier environment."

Curtis Moore and Alan Miller, authors of *Green Gold,* are optimistic for a different reason: businesses do not like to lose out to others. "In the United States, decisions are too often driven by the outmoded and false view that the environment can be protected only at the cost of the economy, when the truth is precisely the opposite," Moore wrote in a letter to the Society of Environmental Journalists. Moore and Miller surveyed the rapidly growing global market for environmental goods, ranging from better light bulbs to zero-polluting fuel cells, and they say that the United States is falling behind the rest of the world in the development of environmentally friendly technology. In the long run, that will cost us jobs and money.

> We're considered the environmental laggards in the world's economy. . . . Other countries, particularly Germany and Japan, are rapidly becoming competitors with California for the worldwide "green technology" market. Tough environmental regulations create more jobs. . . . The U.S. is foreclosing itself from those markets. Other nations have environmental standards at least as tough as ours. If we can't meet their standards, why would they even look at our products?
>
> If we don't have the products, we're locked out. Increasingly, we don't have the products. . . . Without tougher environmental standards, clean technology simply won't be developed. Environmental issues aside, if the technology isn't developed, countries looking for environmentally friendly products will make their purchases elsewhere.
>
> [This is] a fundamental truth understood by Germans, Japanese, Swedes, Dutch, and others around the world, but not by U.S. politicians: namely that better and stronger products, companies, and national economies are created because of

environmental protection, not despite it. . . .

America has already lost tens of billions in income and tens of thousands of jobs because of the environmental hostility of the 1980s, an animosity that drove made-in-the-U.S.A. technologies overseas and straight into the open arms of foreign governments and business who understand the trillions in profits to be realized from clean goods. "The potential profits," said one senior Japanese official, "are limitless."

There you have it: the carrot and the stick. Citizens can work with businesses to start, showing them the advantages of being first in the race for environmentally friendly products and processes. And we can organize to put pressure on our legal representatives—Congress, the Justice Department, state district attorneys, and others—to make repeat offenders feel real pain for their antisocial behavior.

## Refusing the Seductions

Do women know there is a breast cancer epidemic? Of course. Breast cancer awareness is springing up as a cottage industry—new groups and organizations that serve as avenues of support, education about the disease, fundraising, and advocacy. Many awareness groups offer needed emotional support to fellow sufferers. Women share their stories, their concerns about their treatments, their fears. Some men receive training in support for their wives. Some groups offer education; others offer an opportunity to contribute money and time for the sake of those who are ill and who have fewer resources for help.

However, sometimes these well-meaning groups unwittingly serve the interests of others. Corporations that pollute have a special knack for hiding their actions from the public, or for supporting front groups that serve their true interests.

General Electric is the company that brought us the leaking radioactivity at the Hanford, Washington nuclear weapons site and other toxic nightmares, according to INFACT, a Boston consumer watchdog group. Yet, GE is a major player in philanthropy, giving generously to support a number of causes, including breast cancer fundraisers. The company is a strong supporter of National Mammography Day, which is sponsored primarily by the American College of Radiology and ACS. GE makes mammography machines.

Mobil Oil gives money to the Heritage Foundation, a right-wing think tank that has proposed opening designated federal wildernesses to strip mining. Joel Bleifuss reported in the November 29, 1993 *In These Times* that "Heritage has called upon conservative activists to 'strangle the environmental movement' and thereby put an end to 'the greatest single threat to the American economy.' . . . Mobil helps fund Citizens for the Environment, a Washington-based lobbying group that believes environmental problems would be solved if only corporations were deregulated."

It's a cynical game: corporate sponsors of good causes may turn out to be the very companies that poison. In supporting a cause, companies have much to gain—a good reputationand an opportunity to influence a group's agenda. This allows them to pay for respectability while continuing to pollute.

Waste Management, Inc. (now called WMX Technologies, Inc.) of Oak Brook, Illinois, is one of the largest waste management companies in the United States, if not the world. In 1990, its revenues were more than $6 billion. A 1991 Greenpeace report entitled "Waste Management, Inc.: An Encyclopedia of Environmental Crimes & Other Misdeeds" states:

> Waste Management, Inc. (WMI) has become a primary actor in and accessory to the process of global contamination. The technologies employed by WMI are all inherently destructive; the company's only major line of business—waste disposal— severely damages the environment. . . . An in-depth history of its corporate conduct reveals a history of environmental and antitrust law violations, a history of attempts to gain illegitimate political influence, and a history of disrespect for the communities where the company conducts business. . . . WMI

not only destroys the natural environment, but also under-mines democratic decision-making at the local level.

...In many instances, the company has reportedly used ille-gal competitive tactics—bid-rigging, price-fixing, and alleged-ly even physical threats—resulting in criminal and civil law-suits.... Since 1980, WMI, its subsidiaries, and its employees have paid more than $28 million in fines or settlements.

The company is a major contributor to a number of Chicago-area cultural organizations, including Chicago's Symphony Orchestra and Lyric Opera. Former CEO Dean Buntrock served on the Orchestral Association's executive committee in 1994, and received grateful acknowledgment in the opera's program for his generosity. He and his wife are part of the elite of Chicago's opening-night world; each time they make the society pages, WMX adds to its image as a major supporter of some of the most exciting cultural activities and important social ser-vices groups in the area.

The company has also contributed thousands of dollars to the National Audubon Society, the Center for Environmental Education, the California Environmental Trust, the Nature Conservancy, the Sierra Club of California, the Wilderness Society, and the National Wildlife Federation. Additionally, WMX or one of its subsidiaries has been reported by Environmental Action as contributing to the Center for Marine Conservation, Defenders of Wildlife, Environmental Law Institute, Izaak Walton League, National Parks and Conservation Association, National Wildlife Federation, World Resources Institute, and the World Wildlife Fund. Who knows what kinds of decisions are made about environmental action with the specter of thousands of dollars of corporate gifts looming in the background?

Supporting breast cancer is good business and a cynical market-ing tool as well. There certainly will be women hooked by the slogan "Help Support Breast Cancer Research" at Evans Furs, one of the largest furriers in the Chicago area. In one ad, Evans promised to donate $10 for each mink coat sold (they retail between $3,000 and $15,000) to the Friends of Fur Fashion Breast Cancer Fund, which benefits the Susan Komen Breast Cancer Foundation. Women who buy an Evans fur will receive a pink mink ribbon to wear in order to "raise awareness about this devastating disease."

Perhaps Evans might have reconsidered its decision to support the Komen Foundation if it had known about the Chlorine Chemistry Council's involvement. According to *Executive Newsline,* published by the CCC, the organization has become a national underwriter of the Komen Foundation in order to further its work in "research, education, awareness, and patient advocacy." (The CCC also sponsored a table at the Komen Foundation's October 2, 1994 awards luncheon in Dallas, which featured former First Lady Barbara Bush and Foundation awardee J. Roger Hirl, head of Occidental Chemical.)

And then there is Breast Cancer Awareness Month (BCAM), held annually in October. According to "BCAM Scam," an expose published in the November 15, 1993 *Nation,* the idea of BCAM "was conceived and paid for by a British chemical company that both profits from this epidemic and may be contributing to its cause."

> Imperial Chemical Industries (ICI), along with two non-profit groups, co-founded BCAM nine years ago. The event has grown in influence—the thirteen institutions now on its board include the American Cancer Society and the National Cancer Institute—and has become fashionable: Avon, Estee Lauder, and Hanes lead the corporate parade. But, since the beginning, all BCAM's bills have been paid by Zeneca Pharmaceuticals, the new name of ICI's U.S. subsidiary. Altogether, ICI has spent several million dollars on BCAM, according to [a] Zeneca spokeswoman.
>
> In return, ICI has been allowed to control the message conveyed on every one of BCAM's hundreds of thousands of posters, pamphlets, radio spots, newspaper ads, and promo-

tional videos. And ICI's consistent message is: "Early detection is your best protection."

There's nothing wrong with the message, as far as it goes. Like other cancers, breast cancer is more curable before it has spread. But, detection is not prevention. And ICI's motives for promoting early detection are suspect. . . . ICI's principal business [is] the production of the synthetic chemicals [connected to the epidemic]. With annual sales well in excess of $18 billion, ICI is one of the world's largest producers and users of chlorine. Chlorine is used to make many products including paper, plastic, paint, and pesticides.

Judy Brady of the Cancer Prevention Coalition charged that BCAM "is a public relations invention by a major polluter which puts women in the position of being unwitting allies of the very people who are making them sick." The ICI/BCAM public relations campaign effectively keeps information of what causes cancer from the public. Carcinogens are never mentioned in BCAM literature.

The Women's Community Cancer Project suggests that October be renamed "Cancer Industry Awareness Month." Co-sponsors of BCAM include NCI, ACS, the American College of Radiology, Dow Chemical, Du Pont, and GE—all heavily invested in the cancer business. The more women concentrate on detection and treatment—rather than actual prevention—the more profits flow into the hands of these organizations.

Perhaps this explains the priorities of such groups as Y-ME. The organization is working so hard to support those with breast cancer, but it has taken no stand on alternative treatments or cancer prevention.

Y-ME's booklet states, "Women need to turn to other women who have undergone surgery and follow-up treatment for breast cancer. There are several different treatments . . . and women need information about their choices so they can make decisions that are best for them. They also need to learn skills for coping successfully with the emotional trauma of their illness.

Women are often sent home after surgery to face cancer, possible breast loss, and sometimes dreaded chemotherapy or radiation treatments, without any support other than that provided by their bewildered, frightened families."

A very valuable contribution, but they can do so much more. They can join in the fight for prevention instead of parroting the cancer industry's mantras.

During 1994's BCAM, a private home in Illinois was the scene of a special Y-ME fundraiser. In a spacious, well-appointed living room (large enough to hold 106 guests) in an affluent suburb of Chicago, contributors listened to well-known author Dr. Susan Love, director of the Revlon/UCLA Breast Center, say, "There are 1.5 million women living with breast cancer and a million more who don't know they have it. *We have no clue what causes it and no cure for it and no way to prevent it.*"

It's difficult to understand why Dr. Love would make such a claim, for the statement is flat-out wrong. Not once did Dr. Love mention the carcinogens that are connected to breast cancer. Rather, Love spent her time preaching about the breast cancer gene.

Dr. Love was speaking to members of the board of directors of Y-ME and their guests. She was there to help launch a $150,000 campaign for Y-ME, $10,000 of which has been earmarked for advocacy to improve public policy on breast cancer issues. But unless Y-ME is willing to direct that money to the issues of prevention—which include bucking ICI's influence and control and avoiding their toxic chemicals—that $10,000 will be spent in vain.

Industry has been co-opting environmental and citizen action groups for years; it's part of their strategy. Many of the same companies that fund anti-environmental extremists also pour money into mainstream environmental groups. Frank Boren, former president of the Nature Conservancy and a board member of ARCO Petroleum, advocates corporate co-optation of mainstream environmental organizations. As he told his colleagues,

"One good thing about this is that while we're working with them, they don't have time to sue us." (Quoted by Stauber, Pampton, and Green, *Environmental Action Magazine,* Winter, 1996.) Besides avoiding lawsuits, the corporations get to influence the decision-makers in these groups. And the environmental groups, it seems, seduced by the pleasant access to power and money, let the corporations in! No matter how you slice it, it becomes a compromise.

There will always be people who will identify with the establishment—however outrageous that establishment is. It's not easy to buck the trappings of glamorous luncheons and elegant dinners in someone's stunning suburban home, because it represents money, authority, and achievement.

But, once hooked, some of us will buy into the limitations of that status-quo world, a world which then co-opts us, controls our questions, and makes us followers in an established and controlled system. It becomes the ultimate manipulation—ignoring our own human needs and identities while allowing others to define us.

But we can do something about it.

Women can use their time and money to learn about what causes breast cancer and then join the growing community of activists in working for real change. Breast cancer might have made it into fashionable ads but, the laws protecting polluters still remain in place.

Women need to liberate themselves from the false allure of the rich and powerful, from products that only add to our contaminated lives. Women need to find their independence, their own voices, and their own visions. We can learn to say no to tainted money.

## The Women's Health Movement

After Rachel Carson's *Silent Spring* was published in 1962, many critics from the chemical industry asked, "Why should Rachel

Carson be concerned? She doesn't have any children."

The answer to this question came in February 1994 at a Greenpeace/WEDO-sponsored conference in Austin, Texas of 35 leaders in the feminist/environmental movement to plan action about breast cancer.

Half the women had been victims of breast cancer. There were disabled factory workers, community activists, and organizers from Long Island and Toronto; from poor, contaminated, African American communities in California and Alabama; from poor, contaminated, maquilladora communities in Texas and New Mexico; and from the "cancer corridor" in Louisiana.

We heard experts like Devra Lee Davis, Rosalie Bertell, and Vladimir Chernousenko speak about the effects of organochlorines and nuclear radiation. We heard about how we are exposed to toxic estrogens and fission products through the food chain and the atmosphere. We shared conversations about our families; and we spoke with hope about our growing power and responsibilities. We left Austin to carry the word to others—including the powerful statement entitled "Rachel's Children":

> We are Rachel's Children, named in honor of Rachel Carson, who was first to sound the alarm on the link between pesticides and cancer. We are women representing groups from Canada, Mexico, and the United States, dedicated to ending the silence about the deterioration of women's health and its connection to the environment.
>
> We are initiating a worldwide campaign to take action to prevent cancer, particularly breast cancer, as well as other diseases caused or triggered by environmental pollution. We do not accept the fact that one out of three people will get cancer and one in every four will eventually die from it. . . .
>
> We demand accountability from corporate polluters who are sacrificing the health of millions for billions in profit. As a beginning, we call for the phaseout of the entire class of chlorinated organic chemicals and an end to the production and use of all nuclear power and weapons. With careful transition planning, the use of hazardous materials and toxins can and

must be replaced with clean production, renewable energy and health workplaces.

Women's lives and health have been compromised by the cancer establishment. We hold these agencies and institutions responsible for their inaction and failure to prevent cancer. We demand immediate action with a priority on prevention in all programs, policy, and research areas.

We hold accountable our governments that are supposed to be protecting us. We challenge them to confront the polluters who are poisoning us and to stop them before millions more die. For too long, women have been excluded from decisions that profoundly affect our lives and our families. We demand our right to participate in all stages of decision-making about health and environmental issues.

We have the right to live in communities where the air we breathe, the water we drink, the food we eat and the places we work are clean and poison-free. We invite you to join us in our campaign to achieve these most basic of human rights.

Together, with effort, we can create the political will and awareness necessary to address the urgency of these issues.

It took the father of Russia's environmental movement, Alexei V. Yablokov (present head of the Russian equivalent of our EPA) to say it: "It's now up to the women. The very future of this planet is at stake."

Women understand. The "Dominator Model" described so eloquently by Riane Eisler in her cutting-edge book, *The Chalice and the Blade,* has seized the political and social world of the mid-1990s. Rather than partner with women who want to nurture and educate the young, our lawmakers and media spout aggressive, violent, mean-spirited messages. Laws eviscerating environmental oversight and regulation, education, and child care are promulgated, eroding our safety and our inner strength. Violence and the celebration of war fill the airwaves, befouling the minds and spirits of our young. Children are learning domination, cruelty, betrayal, brutality, exclusion, and the conquest of nature. They are not learning sacrifice, patience, commitment, compassion, tolerage, courage, and concern for the future. It's a dangerous time.

Yet women understand. We are coming together fast, fired with anger and concern. It's happening around the United States, in Canada, England, Europe, Russia, and China.

In the United States, women are coalescing to fight the pollutants causing the health epidemic in themselves and their children. We are gathering in places from the cold reaches of the Canadian border to impoverished towns near Mexico. The leaders, research scientists, and physicians represent thousands of others—women who are scared and scarred, angry and ready to act. For too long, male-dominated industry and government have made decisions negatively impacting our health. Now, women are starting to take back control of the dialogue.

Men have excluded human values in their rush to make weapons and to make products for profit, regardless of potential toxicity. Conversely, women lead with their hearts; they are the nurturers and sustainers. Women see environmental degradation as an issue of profound self-interest. Women are looking for a sustainable and just world.

In the United States, there has been a burst of activity: conferences, "awareness" marches, and petitions to the president. More women are learning, defining the issues, and becoming active every day.

The word is spreading. On March 1, 1994, I attended a conference sponsored by Chicago's Women's Issues Network (WIN), a group of leaders and opinion-makers. Professionals, legislators, business heads, suburban women of privilege—well over 100 women came for a briefing on the issues of women's health. An EPA representative told the gathering off the record, "Congress listens to those with the biggest noise. Get busy, get clout. Don't let the energy die." The phone calls have not stopped since; Chicago women are networking, are taking action.

The Washington, D.C. National Breast Cancer Coalition conference which took place in May 1994 pulled over 400 women from across the country to address the issues surrounding breast cancer. The focus was first on education and then on political action—the women were trained in mounting the Capitol steps to advocate for more research funding.

NBCC includes 250 organizations nationwide and represents several million patients, professionals, women, their families, and friends. The thousands who are members of the Coalition's National Action Network gathered 2.6 million signatures demanding that President Clinton put forth a coordinated strategy for this disease.

Taking seriously their mandate as leaders, NBCC has initiated a national effort—Project LEAD—to develop local leadership. "A cornerstone of our mission is to involve consumers—breast cancer advocates—at every level of the breast cancer research process. Our efforts so far have established a model which allows for open dialogue, exchange of information with the scientific community, and an openness to listen and learn," states the application sent to all those attending the May 1994 conference.

In the Midwest, the Great Lakes Women's Leadership Network came together to address issues such as the toxic soup of contaminants in those lakes and their health consequences. The Network has developed a structure to educate women and promote smart political action. The conference organized by the Network in September 1994 was called, "Women Setting the Agenda." This group continued its activism, conducting activities around the September 1995 IJC meeting held in Duluth, Minnesota. (The IJC meetings attract a host of activists, who come to testify, share information, and apply pressure.)

In the San Francisco area, a number of breast cancer and environmental groups formed the Toxic Links Coalition. Their motto is, "Stop Cancer Where It Starts." Among the events planned by the Coalition for Breast Cancer Awareness Month, 1994, was a "Toxic Tour Protest." The coalition identified and visited corporate polluters responsible for the cancer epidemic. In the San Francisco area they visited Chevron, Bechtel, *Time* magazine, ACS, and the EPA.

More conferences and public hearings on cancer and the environment, and on the influence of corporate-funded science in misleading public opinion on cancer risks were held in 1995 and 1996 in Atlanta, Indianapolis, Minneapolis, New Orleans, Madison, Raleigh, and again in San Francisco. Canadian women are also becoming active. In 1995 and 1996, a consortium of women sponsored a number of conferences on breast cancer; the June 1996 effort was a world conference in Kingston, Ontario. (Another will be held in the same city in July 1997.)

The seeds we have planted are bearing fruit. At meetings, individuals and groups are forging partnerships to collectively advocate for effective breast cancer policies that have prevention as their centerpiece. They are going home and reinvigorating their organizations or starting new initiatives to extend their influence.

Dianne Dillon-Ridgley, co-chair of the Citizens' Network for Sustainable Development and one of the coordinators of the nationwide WEDO/Greenpeace regional conferences, sees the environmental movement as *the* agenda of the future. "This movement is evolving," she said in an interview:

> People are making connections; they're also emerging out of the civil rights movement—where Gloria Steinem, Bella Abzug, Barbara Jordan, Rosa Parks, and a host of others made early contributions.
>
> The breakdown of the Soviet Union has meant there is no longer an East-West polarity. There's a shift in the activist community. Add the Earth Summit, the World Women's Conference for a Healthy Planet with 1,500 women from 83 countries, and I see these issues becoming global. Energy is growing outward in every country on the planet. In the United States, state by state, we're getting out real information.
>
> Breast cancer is a political disease. The medical research

community refuses to say what we now all know. The elite, they're not living outside this planet. At this point, they don't—or won't—get it. But, we can't wait for the crisis, which we know is coming. When the crisis is evident to a far broader spectrum of people, it will be too late.

Industry can no longer profit off our backs. We women can be passive for ourselves, but when it comes to our children, we just may become proactive. Women have been the caretakers for our own and for the children of others. The nurturers now must turn it on the world. The world and its processes are on trial. Women have to set the agenda for the world.

Devra Lee Davis summed it all up. "This may be the start of the most important movement in history—a combination of feminists, environmentalists, and the social/environmental justice movement coming together. It's a new women's network accessible by cable TV, conferences, video, E-mail, and Congressional hearings. Yes, it's spreading."

## The Activist Agenda

While citizens are developing the organized power to confront the corporate state, there are achievable, short-term goals that can be pursued on an individual or group basis.

*Ban on Chlorine.* We can work for a ban on chlorine—an important first step. Joan D'Argo, formerly of Greenpeace, says, "We must eliminate organochlorines in our society. Plans are in the works to pressure a phaseout of these chemicals and substitute far less toxic, but effective, products and processes."

There are substitutes for much that presently depends on chlorine. "Totally chlorine-free" (TCF) paper is available to printers now. We must demand a standard of zero dioxin release by paper mills. And we can create a market for nonchlorinated paper by demanding that all government agencies buy chlorine-free paper.

A strict control on the manufacture of PVCs is essential, as is a moratorium on the construction of any new PVC generating facilities. We also need to phase out PVC packaging and disposable products, and PVC in products that are recycled in smelters, like copper cables and cars.

If we would stop allowing sewerage and farm runoff (including pesticides, herbicides, and rBGH) from entering our water sources, we would need far less in the way of chlorine disinfection. Chlorine in drinking water has been shown to cause some forms of cancer.

*Incineration.* We must call for an immediate ban on incineration as a waste disposal tool. EPA aggressively backs incineration, and only when communities bring tremendous political pressure to bear have they been successful in preventing burning. Alternatives to incineration already exist, although they receive scant attention by EPA because of the vested interests of the incineration industry.

One splendid alternative is Eco Logic, a Michigan-based incinerator company that uses a patented gas-phase chemical reduction process for the destruction of high-hazard organic chemicals. The company has the distinction of providing the only process for destruction of hazardous organic wastes, including dioxins, that is regularly recommended by environmentally concerned individuals or groups. Destruction efficiencies of 99.9999 percent are obtained—currently an impossibility with the open stack technologies that EPA continues to support.

*Nuclear Power.* Nuclear power plants are dangerous and consumers have a right to safer alternative energy sources. So much information is available on this subject already, it serves us all to start advocating for full-scale federal support of wind and solar power immediately. Older nuclear plants must be phased out and replaced with safe energy sources. Spent fuel rods and nuclear waste must be stored in a way that prevents contamination of the public and their food and water sources.

*EPA.* The EPA is under the aegis of the White House and as a result, the EPA administrator forms and executes environmental policies with the approval of the president, who is subject to the political pressure of campaign contributions from polluting industries. Since the EPA was established in 1971, no president has aggressively enforced environmental laws. In fact, some have worked to weaken environmental regulations with the result that we are exposed to more untested, unregulated toxins than ever.

Congress created the EPA and Congress can change its status. The EPA and its director can be placed in a position that is above politics, that is completely independent of pressure, as was done with the Federal Reserve.

*Campaign Reform.* Political action committees (PACs) and the millions of dollars they raise and disburse each year turn our government representatives into friends of polluting companies. Tough laws that ban corporate, civic, educational, and charitable PAC money from going to any legislator at any time are long overdue. Violators could be prosecuted as felons for subverting the democratic process. Our elected representatives must be free to vote that which is in the best interests of the people, not a polluting corporation.

PAC money destroys our democracy, because it makes almost impossible any but the richest to be heard in the halls of our legislatures. Thus, serious campaign reform is a must, including total public financing of elections. This would allow voters to choose candidates on the merits of their ideas and on the vigor with which they fight for the common good, not because they can raise money from the wealthy. Public financing would cost each taxpayer $5-$10 a year, according to Peter Montague, which is a small price for regaining control of our democracy. Think of the savings and loan bailout, Montague chides: that $500 billion "is enough money to finance all federal elections for more than 1,000 years."

Once election reform takes hold, there will be much less coddling of polluters, for legislators will not have been bought. The American public will be able to demand zero tolerance for official denials and delays; zero tolerance for the release of dioxins,

PCBs, and other toxic chemicals; zero tolerance for risk assessments and cost-benefit analyses. The public might begin to force industries to clean up their own discharges, rather than letting them do it with taxpayer money.

An important step was taken when President Clinton signed a bill in December 1995 that required lobbyists to register and disclose their activities. The law broadens the definition of who is a lobbyist. Supporters of the bill claim decades of gridlock was broken, but it's only a first step. While the law would require that lobbyists report how much they are paid and the specific issues on which they are working, it still allows gifts to members of Congress.

*Personal Injury Caps.* Citizens must advocate against a push to set limits on personal injury claims. Heavily supported by Republicans in Congress, the effort is spreading across the country to state legislatures. The effort may eventually influence the amount of damages claimed by anyone who has been poisoned by toxic chemicals or by products such as silicone gel breast implants. Companies will be able to continue to contaminate our lives knowingly, make their profits, and figure the limited damages into the cost of doing business.

*Research Money.* Women must stop blindly advocating "more research" for breast cancer, and start demanding that more money be spent on identifying environmental toxins and preventing their release. Considering the accumulated knowledge already linking chemical contamination of the environment to cancer, any further research must focus on environmental factors.

*Government/Industry Revolving Door.* People who work for regulatory agencies are compromised if they believe their government positions will lead to jobs with the industries they are supposed to regulate; no industry will hire you if you've been too tough on them. Public health automatically takes a back seat to a government employee's private ambitions.

New laws making such professional opportunism impossible—at least for a specific and lengthy time—are essential. There are already laws prohibiting former employees of the State and Commerce departments from working for a foreign government or a lobby group for at least two years. Such a prohibition must be part of any reform for regulatory employees.

*Medical Schools.* Medical schools play an important role in the cancer story. The medical school paradigm still emphasizes cure over prevention, drugs over natural substances, low-fat diets over toxin-free diets. We must encourage medical schools to spend more time on prevention. Of the 125 medical schools in the United States, only 30 require a course in nutrition.

These are some of the major goals for which any citizen—even if you are not part of a group—can work. Pick one or two and become educated. Then let your legislators, both local and national, know that you believe the status quo must be changed. Join marches, meet others who feel the same way you do. Be a part of the movement to save the environment, and very possibly your own life.

# 14

# PRIVATE ACTION TO PROTECT YOUR OWN HEALTH

**B**ecoming an activist for the public good is a fine thing, but what can you do to protect yourself and your family from environmental toxins? After all, breast cancer can strike anyone, no matter how involved she may be in the fight against it.

There are common-sense alternatives to the toxin-laden products that supposedly make our modern lives so easy. Switching back to nontoxic materials requires some thought and some effort, but not as much as the endless commercials for unnecessary products imply. And as demand for safe products has grown, those products have become cheaper, more accessible, and easier to use.

## Substitutes for Contaminated Products

There are substitutes for many of the products you use in your home that are made with chlorine. For instance, you can buy writing paper that has been lightened using nonchlorine methods. Its color may be a pleasing tan or gray, which is very easy on the eyes. On the market are unbleached coffee filters—the color of the filter does not affect the taste of the drink. You don't need chlorine-bleached diapers or toilet paper, either. Find cotton tampons bleached with hydrogen peroxide, which are developing a niche in the marketplace.

When you go to the grocery store, speak up to the manager. Demand foods that are packaged in cellophane or glass, which can be recycled. Find a paint store that stocks nonchlorinated paints and solvents. And use alternatives to PVC in your home remodeling projects—wood, metal, and glass can take its place for most uses. We must wean ourselves from reliance on plastics: they are derived from petroleum, and all produce toxins during production and disposal.

Stay away from chemical pesticides: most household insects can be controlled by cleanliness, barriers to their movement, containment of food and wastes, and the strategic placement of such natural ingredients as boric acid, washing soda, ammonia, and white vinegar, which are far cheaper and safer. As for herbicides, stepping on common garden weeds will not make your children sick, but their romping over freshly sprayed grass sets the stage for breast and other cancers 15 or 20 years later. If you want a pretty garden, use simple elbow grease.

As a thoughtful person, you do not need to buy mindlessly. We pay a very high price for comforts that emphasize ease but take away thoughtful choice. There's too much plastic packaging, too many prepared convenient foods, too many frozen TV dinners and seductive snacks—overpackaged and full of artificial chemicals and sodium. If enough people stop buying harmful products, the incentive to produce them will diminish. Pollution-free products can be made to cost less—when consumers understand the issues, when consumer demand grows, and when corporations see opportunities to profit.

You can be your own radical consumer advocate. Tell your supermarket that you want to buy pesticide-free vegetables and fruit, and milk products that are free of rBGH. If you choose meat, buy uncontaminated, hormone-free, drug-free meat and tell your supermarket that this is the only meat you'll buy. Then explain to your friends and neighbors that they should do the same. Pretty soon, enough people will walk through the doors looking for toxin-free products, and the supermarket will stock them.

Boycott products made by the companies identified in this book (or through other reading) as major polluters—Dow, ICI, Monsanto, General Electric, and others. Resist the false allure of buying products made by Dow and other polluters that say they will contribute to charities, some of which are fighting diseases that these corporations have created. A lot of other people are doing the same thing. (For instance, INFACT, the consumer advocacy group, spearheaded an international boycott of GE products because the company was making nuclear warheads. The company lost so many millions of dollars because of the boycott that it sold off its military weapons division.)

Conversely, support companies that make alternative products which do not add to the environmental burden. And tell your merchants why you are making these buying choices so that they know they are dealing with informed consumers.

Until we can stop the production of environmental poisons, what you eat and drink may be your best defense against breast cancer, both prospective and realized. Back in 1987, in the preface to his book *Healing Nutrients,* Dr. Patrick Quillin stated, "A new era in health care is emerging. We are beginning to work with nature to restore health, rather than antagonizing nature by subduing symptoms. . . . Nutrition is no longer shotgun-in-the-dark therapy. It is specific. And it works. The next step is to incorporate it into the health care system of America."

If diet is to play a part in your health program, you must be willing to accept a significant lifestyle change. No, you will not have to go back to stirring a stewpot over an open fire. But you will have to recognize the intense cultural, social, familial, and emotional messages that food carries for most people. Eating a meal is a social act. Certain foods evoke memories of family, celebrations, cultural identity. It's hard to let go of these feelings, but let go we must if we are to stay healthy in a minefield of toxic traps.

## Food Choices in Treatment of Breast Cancer

Dr. Keith Block of Evanston, Illinois bases his medical practice on the diet-cancer connection. In the chapter he contributed to the 1993 book *Adjuvant Nutrition in Cancer Treatment,* Block stated, "Our understanding of the pharmacological effects of foods has been growing during the past decade, led largely by the increasing awareness of the role of diet in cancer prevention. With this growing understanding has come the recognition that dietary habits may indeed have some impact on the growth of tumors once they have been diagnosed, as well as during the preclinical period explored in cancer prevention studies."

Block identified numerous studies showing a connection between the intake of fat and breast cancer. One showed that breast cancer patients with surgery will have a recurrence if their diets are over 40 percent saturated fat. Other studies demonstrate the greater health of Japanese women, who have low-fat, high-carbohydrate diets, compared to those in Western countries.

Block uses several approaches to his breast cancer patients. One is the macrobiotic diet: patients consume diets with 10-13 percent fat. The macrobiotic diet is, in principle, nothing more than the traditional Japanese diet, recast somewhat for Western tastes and sensibilities. He recommends a general dietary pattern for cancer patients that has 15-18 percent fat content. "We have been using a program whose nutritional base is the 15-18 percent fat diet in clinical practice for well over a decade," Block says. "The major thrust of the program is improving the overall fitness of cancer patients with a multidimensional intervention that addresses biomedical, biophysical, nutritional, and psychosocial aspects of disease and health care."

Block uses primary fats like canola and olive oils, along with limited intake of seeds and nuts, long-chain omega-3 fatty acids found in cold-water fish and fish-oil supplements. He also recommends gamma linolenic acid (available in health food stores) as a supplement and protein from vegetables. He stresses soy foods, carbohydrate sources like whole grains, vegetables, and fruits along with sea vegetables (seaweed), and miso soups.

He urges that patients avoid red meats, poultry, polished grains, refined flour, sugar, artificial sweeteners, carbonated beverages, alcohol, eggs, and dairy products, as well as any food that may further compromise the intestine. Dr. Block adds a number of nutritional supplements for his patients: shiitake mushroom, garlic, echinacea, astragalus, carotenoid, antioxidant vitamins, and acidophilus. He also advocates a full-spectrum multivitamin as well.

For women who have been diagnosed with breast cancer, antioxidants—especially vitamins A, C, E, and co-enzyme Q10 (CoQ10)—are important supplements. These supplements are immune enhancers that help produce more natural killer T-cells, more lymphocytes, more interleukin and interferon. This reduces the chance for abnormal cells to multiply into a cancer.

An article in *U.S. News and World Report* on May 24, 1993 reported on the effects of these antioxidants. Work at the Pacific Northwest Research Foundation and the University of Washington at Seattle indicated that DNA from cells in cancerous breasts had much more oxidation damage than did DNA from normal breasts. A test based on this knowledge could be an early warning sign. Women with oxidation damage likely will be advised to eat more fruits and vegetables rich in beta carotene and vitamins C and E, or take large doses of the vitamins.

## Food Choices to Prevent Breast Cancer

For millions of Americans, eating "healthy" is part of the accepted 1990s lifestyle. Rich cream sauces, deep-fried foods, and steak are out; herbs and spices that bring out natural flavors, nonfat cooking sprays, and pastas are in. Conscious consumers are wisely buying food that is low in sodium, salt-free, and fat-free, and manufacturers are coming out with more and more products to suit these choices. There is low-fat and no-fat mayonnaise and salad dressings. There are a variety of olive and fish oils rather than lard or corn oil. Even pork and beef are leaner now, and people are just eating less of those protein sources.

It has taken us years to gain access to a full-range of low-fat products in our supermarkets. The demand drove the supply—more people were asking for these types of products. What drove the demand was improved knowledge about the dangers of high-fat diets and a general rise in consciousness about health.

Now that we have come this far, the next step is for more non-toxic foods to appear in our pantries. As consumers become more aware of the poisons in the food supply, of the weakened environmental oversight, of the deceptions foisted upon us by polluting companies, they will begin to look more closely for clean foods. When this demand reaches a critical point, organic, nontoxic food will make its way in abundance from the farmers to the supermarkets to our kitchens.

Until that time, you will have to take special care when you shop for your family's food. Start at a store that features organic food—food that is grown or raised under certified organic standards without pesticides or herbicides, antibiotics or growth hormones. Whole industries are awakening to this growing market, and thousands of consumers already shop in health food stores and vegetable stands where a wide variety of pesticide-free vegetables are offered. They buy free-range chickens and beef free of hormones; organic raisins and other snacks for themselves and their kids. They're juicing and gulping down vitamin supplements with rigorous discipline.

They browse the magazine racks where new age magazines and health and nutrition information are displayed for education. They subscribe to newsletters that devote entire pages to vegetarian recipes and natural health remedies.

Many nutrition counselors advocate a vegetarian diet, with the substitution of nuts, legumes, and soy products for meat. In view of the contaminants and the increasing incidence of bacterial contamination of meat, it is sound advice. Many health-conscious consumers now avoid milk products, too—including butter, sour cream, cottage cheese, cream cheese, ice cream, and even skim milk. It makes sense, for most of these products are made from milk laden with pesticides, dioxin, and rBGH.

Fish have always been considered a low-cost, tasty source of protein, but these days, more and more fish are contaminated with PCBs, pesticides, and heavy metals. Thus, if you eat fish, choose small ones in which the toxic-laden fat has had less chance to accumulate, and cut away any fat before cooking. David Steinman, in his book *Diet for a Poisoned Planet,* has developed a comprehensive list of fish that are "virtually pollution free."

It's entirely possible to live healthy lives with no meat or milk products. Soy milk is a great substitute for cow's milk. You can buy brown rice and seitan—a wheat product that is a protein substitute. You can buy soy-based veggie burgers and cereals made from organic wheat, rice, or bran that are low in sodium and need very little sweetening. You can buy lima, pinto, kidney, and great northern beans that are protein-rich and filling. They're great in soups, salads, and side dishes.

Taking these measures just occasionally won't do, for short flings with toxin-free diets will not reduce the dioxin concentrations in your body. This means health-conscious consumers must begin meal planning very early and stay the course. It's a lifetime choice.

## Cooking for Health

It's hard for most of us to break away from the security of long-held beliefs and patterns, for food is an important part of socializing and a significant part of our cultural and ethnic backgrounds. You don't have to change everything you do right from the start. Rather, ease gently into the new regime. Explore and experiment to discover what you and your family like. After a while, you will be amazed at the number of old-time standards that you no longer crave.

There will be certain situations in which you will be faced with unhealthy choices—particularly when you are not in charge of the food preparation. Holiday feasts, for example—Christmas, Easter, Thanksgiving, Passover—bring turkey, ham, fish, cream sauces, cheese, and fried foods. Don't get crazy about eating these foods a few days out of the year, for if you are otherwise consistent with your diet, breaking the health pattern on holidays won't do much damage. Or, you can bring a couple of your creations to the table and share them with your family. But make extra, or you may find that there won't be enough left for you.

You'll need some new equipment. Buy nonstick frying pans so you can cut down on cooking oil. Buy a juicer (there are a variety on the market) and juice as many fresh raw vegetables and fresh fruits as you can. Make up your own cocktails—carrots-celery-spinach is good, as is apples-bananas-kiwi fruit. Carrot juice is especially healthy. Drink all juice fresh so that the newly released enzymes can go to work in your body.

Reduce the amount of oil you use in cooking. Eliminate margarine and animal fats. It is easy enough to change recipes so that they don't need oil, and you can use cooking sprays to coat your pan when you have to saute something. There are many oil-free salad dressings in the supermarkets, or you can make your own using olive oil, rice vinegar, and a variety of herbs.

Instead of using chicken or steak as the centerpiece of your meal planning, make it a meatless chili, a rich fish chowder, or a vegetable casserole. With those basics in your refrigerator, you can easily vary the meal with side dishes of grains, pastas, or fresh vegetable combinations. With judicious use of herbs and spices, your meals will look beautiful, smell wonderful, and taste sensational. They will provide all the satisfaction of the high-salt, heavy-fat pork chops-mashed potatoes-gravy meals that you have left behind.

Make whole-grain products staples at the table, for they have far more nutrients than those made from refined flour. Wheat bran helps usher cancer-stimulating estrogen out of the body, presumably cutting the risk of breast cancer. (The American Health Foundation found that about 15 grams of wheat bran fibers daily lowered estrogen levels 17 percent in pre-menopausal women. The *USA Weekend Magazine* of November 3, 1995 reported that Tufts University researchers found that wheat fiber suppressed circulating estrogen better than a simple low-fat diet did.) For breakfast, muffins, pancakes, waffles, and bread are all easily available in whole wheat form in your super-market. They come ready-made, frozen, or as mixes. There are also a number of whole-grain cereals you can buy.

Increase your consumption of complex carbohydrates: brown rice, potatoes, pastas. Foods made with wheat bran, rye flour, and flax seeds have fat-decreasing effects. Researchers advise women to eat foods rich in isoflavanoids and lignins: tofu, tempeh, rye bread, and other soybean products.

Vegetables and fruits are crucial to your diet plan. "Tomatoes are rich in *p*-coumaric acid and chlorogenic acid, which hook onto nitric oxides in the foods we eat and spirit them out of the body before they can form cancer-causing nitrosamines," reports Peter Jaret in the March 1995 issue of *Health*. Add broccoli, cau-liflower, greens, kale, cabbage, and green peppers—all rich in vit-amin C. People who eat a lot of cabbage and other cruciferous vegetables have less cancer. Cabbage chemicals called indoles induce the body to burn off a form of estrogen that promotes breast cancer, according to research by H. Leon Bradlow at the Strang Cornell Cancer Research Laboratory in New York City. "Getting rid of this estrogen," he says, "lowers women's risk of breast cancer. These indoles are also in broccoli, cauliflower and Brussels sprouts. In tests, eating the indoles in one-fifth of a head of cabbage revved up estrogen removal in 85 percent of women

(Jean Carper, *USA Weekend,* February 3, 1995). And Paul Talalay at Johns Hopkins University discovered a potent anticancer chemical in broccoli called sulphoraphane. In laboratory rats, it slashed the breast cancer rate by two-thirds.

Beta carotene is a natural chemical found in many fruits and vegetables, especially brightly colored ones like tomatoes, red peppers, watermelons, carrots, mangos, papayas, and yams. Sweet potatoes, winter squash, and spinach are also very good sources of beta carotene.

(For those suffering with cancer, there is some debate about citrus fruits. Oranges and lemons both contain limonene, which raises the naturally occurring enzymes thought to break down carcinogens and stimulate cancer-killing immune cells. Citrus fruits also contain glucarase, which inactivates carcinogens and speeds them out of the body. However, citrus fruits contain acid, and certain cancers thrive in an acidic environment. Thus, some therapists prefer to avoid citrus juices and fruits.)

Drink at least one quart of good quality water per day—either distilled water bought from the store or water you have run through your own filter. Trusting the American public water supply may be a mistake, for thousands of water treatment plants need updating and remodeling. The water from your tap may be bacteria-free, but not all municipalities have purification systems that can detect and remove the hundreds of pollutants contaminating our groundwater. Also, public systems use huge amounts of chlorine too kill bacteria (not always successfully), and a good deal of that chlorine is passed on to you. Substitute fruit and vegetable juices for tea, coffee, and artificially sweetened soft drinks.

Decrease your consumption of refined sugars such as sucrose and fructose. Its more than an empty calorie, for sugar gravitates to cancer sites and nourishes them. Commercial sugar substitutes like saccharin and aspartame have their own negative side effects. Substitute fresh fruits, which have natural sugars, in your cooking and baking, and encourage your family to eat them as snacks. Health food stores also offer substitutes such as rice sugar.

When preparing vegetables, cook them as little as possible. For the most anticancer activity, eat crucifers raw or lightly cooked, still crunchy. Light steaming or stir-frying helps to hold in the nutrients. Never deep-fry; if you need to "fry" something, coat the food with seasoned wheat bread crumbs and bake or broil it.

Eat foods that keep your bowel movements regular, because moving toxins out of the body regularly is basic to good health. As David Williams noted in the September 1993 issue of *Alternatives for the Health Conscious Individual,* "Literally, correcting constipation is one very important step in preventing breast cancer or one of the other estrogen-dependent cancers."

Eat food that is rich in phytoestrogens—plant compounds that have a chemical structure very similar to estrogen. In fact, they are weak natural estrogens; in the presence of more potent estrogens, they exhibit anti-estrogen activity. For estrogens to do their work, they must bind with certain cell receptors. Phytoestrogens bind with these cell receptors and keep estrogen from doing so. This helps keep estrogen from promoting cell growth and reproduction in sexual organs, like the breast. Legumes (peas, beans, clovers) are the main source of phytoestrogens. Soybeans and soy products are another good source.

Trim all visible fat from anything you eat. If you must choose meat, stick to small portions of very lean, skinned white meat chicken, cornish hen, or turkey. And avoid smoking. Nothing anyone can recommend to fight cancer will counter the negative effects of smoking. It's not even debatable.

## Food Supplements

Most everyone is familiar with vitamins and food supplements, even if only from the one-a-day supplements that are sold off the shelf at supermarkets. But a one-a-day does not provide enough protection. First, they are produced for the "average" man, woman, or child, and so will not cover your specific nutritional needs. Second, they generally do not give the dosages that you need to help your body fight off cancer.

More and more research indicates that certain supplements strengthen the body's defenses. A core group of supplements, which are discussed below, comes up again and again. All these supplements are available from health food stores and from mail order catalogues.

Doctors have found one natural substance that specifically helps in fighting cancer. The newsletter *Alternatives* describes the amino acid L-arginine, which in England, has been used as a supplement by doctors in combination with conventional forms of treatment. They call it "nutritional pharmacology." "They discovered that oral doses of L-arginine can accentuate the cancer-killing effects of radiation and chemotherapy on breast tumors," the newsletter stated.

What makes L-arginine effective is its ability to inhibit angiogenesis through the creation of nitric oxide. It also improves the ability of the body's white blood cells or macrophages to destroy invading organisms and parasites. The amino acid has also been found to strengthen the immune system in the elderly by stopping the atrophy of the thymus gland.

Flaxseed or flaxseed oil contain a group of compounds called lignins. David Williams stated, "When ingested, these lignins are broken down by intestinal bacteria into compounds that have anti-estrogenic properties—counteracting the effects of estrogen. High levels of converted lignins appear to protect against cancer. In vitro studies have shown that lignins can inhibit both estrogen synthesis and estrogen-stimulated breast cancer cell growth. Flaxseed is the most concentrated food source of lignins. Consuming flaxseed or the oil results in over 100 times more lignin production than any other oilseed, grain, or legume tested. . . . When processed correctly it has a very pleasant nutty flavor. Recommended daily dosage is usually around a tablespoon a day."

Vitamin C is a powerful antioxidant. It destroys harmful chemicals called "free radicals," which are atoms that carry an unpaired electron but no charge. They are very short-lived but can cause serious damage in the body. They are counteracted by free radical scavengers such as Vitamin C, which is found in many foods including lemons, oranges, and green peppers. Vitamin C is also considered one of the most promising items in the anticancer arsenal and countless studies affirm this. It is considered the most effective antioxidant in human blood plasma, for certain chemical reactions that cause cancer simply cannot take place when vitamin C is present.

Take vitamins A, beta carotene, E, and B-6 in much larger dosages than the recommended daily amounts. The *American Journal of Clinical Nutrition* reported in 1990 that low blood levels of beta carotene are associated with increased risk of breast cancer. Add vitamin D, which acts in breast cancer prevention, as do CoQ10, carnitine, and the fatty acids EPA from cold-water fish oil. Garlic, as a food or in pill form, seems to have preventive value also.

Algae is also a powerful help. Ralph Moss notes that a new anticancer agent—turbinaric acid—has been found in various algaes. In addition, Moss says, "Algae have proved to be among the richest sources of carotenes. Japanese scientists studying a beta-carotene-rich algae named *Dunaliella bardawil* found that it markedly inhibited spontaneous breast cancers in mice. In a 1991 paper, they reported that it not only stopped breast cancer, but normalized the mice's glucose tolerance and lactic acid levels. Japanese scientists concluded that the results strongly suggest that *D. bardawil* inhibited breast cancer by this stabilization of body chemistry as well as the antioxidant activity of beta-carotene. Other forms of algae—Chlorella and Spirulina extract—boost the immune response.

Kelp is a proven breast cancer preventive, especially in Japanese women who eat it as a food rather than as a supplement. In *Life Extenders and Memory Boosters!* David Steinman writes, "The exact mode of action is not known but researchers have observed that kelp protects against radiation. Algin, the important ingredient in kelp, can prevent living tissue from absorbing radioactive materials including strontium-90, barium, mercury, zinc, tin, cadmium, and manganese. The algin in kelp also increases fecal bulk and alters the nature of fecal contaminants and perhaps renders harmless bacteria that could be carcinogenic."

Minerals like zinc, selenium, and chromium are important for the immune system, and herbal extracts like echinacea, ginseng, Pau D'arco, and astragalus also have value. And recently, capsaicin—the compound that makes chile peppers hot—has been shown to have anticancer effects. "It seems capsaicin may neutralize the carcinogenic effects of nitrosamines too. The hotter the pepper, the more capsaicin it contains," says Peter Jaret.

These are some of the choices that you can make to protect yourself and your family against our dangerous environment. It is up to you to pick the ones that make the most sense to you.

Buy cookbooks that will show you how to make vegetarian meals. They are filled with creative recipes that can stretch your food budget. If you have any land, or even a balcony that gets good sunlight, plant your own vegetables. Tomatoes, beans, peas, carrots, and kale all grow well with relatively little care using organic fertilizer and natural pest deterrents.

Get together with your friends, neighbors, and relatives to form communities and alliances of concern. That might mean a neighborhood co-op that buys produce from environmentally conscious farmers. Each member pays a yearly fee, and the farmers bring in clean food (often to a central location) throughout the growing season. The more in the group, the less the individual costs and the easier it is to delegate responsibility.

As I said before, ease into your new program. You are training for the long haul, so you don't want to burn out quickly. Eliminating most meat and all convenience food from your grocery list will free up a great deal of cash for your healthful purchases. Buy in bulk. Watch for specials at your organic store. When you eat out, stand up for your rights as a consumer to have well-prepared, enticing vegetarian meals. Don't be diverted by the seductive ads in which beautiful people have milk moustaches or are talking about how they like their steak done.

If we want to be healthy, we must become rebels; we must give ourselves permission to act on our own behalf. Taking back our lives—from advertisers, from social pressures, and from easy convenience—is what we must do to survive.

# 15

# REDISCOVERING ETHICS: THE HIGH ROAD TO HEALTH

If we have learned anything about the breast cancer epidemic, it is that our lives are being controlled by others: by corporations that put profits ahead of human health, by corporate-owned media, by seductive public relations promotions and campaigns. Polluting corporations control legislators' and regulators' decision-making and the national dialogue, keeping the American public complacent and misinformed.

Morality and ethics disappear in business. In the name of control, in the name of business and convenience, polluters take away life. Gone is our right to live as we wish in an unpolluted country. It's unethical.

Scientific consensus is mounting. Unless we make changes in public policy and personal behavior, we may very well witness a global environmental and human health catastrophe. We don't like to think about this—who wants to contemplate such bad news—and so we push it aside with the help of industry-paid scientists who tell us not to worry.

As Dr. Eric Chivian, professor of psychiatry at Harvard Medical School, said at a 1994 conference sponsored by Physicians for Social Responsibility, "Most people do not understand that they are an integral part of global ecosystems, and that it is not possible to tamper with the atmosphere, to destroy major habitats and extinguish countless numbers of species, to contaminate the air, water, and soil with toxic substances without these changes somehow, somewhere, sometime, affecting human beings." As long as the public dialogue is dominated by the likes of ICI, Dow, Monsanto, GE, and other polluters and their abettors, Americans will remain ignorant.

Since the national dialogue is controlled by business, the human element of it has been obscured. We humans are defined as consumers, markets to be manipulated and exploited. We are the "labor force," the "unemployed," the "baby boomers," or so many ratings points—faceless, with no individual value. There is no reason to enlighten us, for we are simply to be seduced by an overabundance of advertisements and enticed to buy. This applies to health care as well. Hospitals and HMOs now advertise for customers just like any retail store. They compete for patients with the promise of the most caring treatment, the most up-to-date technologies, the best "cures" at the most convenient times.

This tendency runs deep in our consumerized, industrialized society. But tendencies can change, especially when enough citizens band together to demand it.

The dangers outlined in this book are not potential; they are clear and they are present. There is no more time for self-delusion. We must break the bonds of public relations seductions and social regimentation and say to ourselves, "I will not be poisoned!"

We must do it for ourselves and our families, for no one else will do it for us. When I spoke about the breast cancer epidemic to a nursing class at a local college, many in the class asked with disbelief, "Don't they care? Don't polluters know they're hurting themselves as well? What about their own wives and children?"

No, they don't care. They have little sense of social responsibility, or social justice, or the future of this country.

"I'm dedicating myself to caring for people who are the victims of all this?" blurted out one of the nurses, red and angry. "It's evil."

Yes, it's evil. It's evil for government regulators to subvert the law, look away from the consequences of poisonous products or practices, close their eyes when wrong is done—all because of the power of corporate wrongdoers, their PACs, and their political bedfellows. That bureaucrat hiding behind a federal ID number is just as responsible, just as compromised, even if "everybody does it." The same holds true for the corporations.

And yet, in our corporate state, rarely are there consequences for those with power. When one person kills another person, that is called murder and the law demands that the convicted murderer pay the consequences. But when a corporation's actions result in the death of a person (or a whole group) for the sake of greater profits, that is called cost-benefit analysis, and the corporation pays little if any penalty. In fact, its stock price commonly rises.

That is a horrible double standard that must be corrected. Murder is murder whether it is done by individuals or multinationals. Corporations are composed of human beings, and some of these humans make the decisions to release dioxin, sell faulty implants, and dump toxic wastes. No longer should those corporate directors be allowed to hide behind a logo, behind some misbegotten idea of corporate secrecy, or some skewed corporate ethic. There are higher-order issues here, issues that we expect our business and government leaders to tackle.

Clearly, something is missing from the leadership ethic in our country. As potential leaders enter business school for that coveted MBA, as they strive to climb up the corporate ladder, their vision is narrowed by the slavish commitment to corporate mindthink and bottom-line considerations. This excludes concern for the future and the greater good of the community. Not just the future of the physical community in which the business is based (think of Love Canal or Hanford, Washington), but the future of the contaminated workers who may be left behind if the plant shuts down, and the future of the innocent neighbors who must deal with the consequences of a corporation's mindless polluting practices. It excludes an absolutely essential element from corporate decisions—human pain.

We do not have to accept cancer as the price of modern life. That simple truth must be brought back into the public dialogue. "The universal human rights framework provides all individuals with a practical means of defending themselves against environmental degradation. Environmentalists are good at coming up with scientifically sound ways of reducing pollution and slowing resource depletion, but they need human rights activists to uphold people's ability to get such reforms implemented." So states Aaron Sachs in the December 1995 issue of *Worldwatch Paper.*

The readers of this book can become personal emissaries. We can do so through massive public re-education to counter the obfuscations and downright lies of the polluters and their apologists. We can do so through calls to our elected representatives for new laws and regulations that will truly protect us. And we can do so through the power of our own pocketbooks—millions and millions of them.

In the Nuremburg trials after World War II, those Germans who led the mass extermination of innocent humans in Europe were made to answer for their crimes against humanity. It's time to apply this concept—responsibility for crime—to our corporate state. Corporate decisions are not resulting in masses of people being gassed in chambers or American villages being napalmed, but they are resulting in deaths. The deaths may not be as quick, but they are just as sure.

Crimes should not go unpunished because they are slow and silent or protected by power. Crimes of profit and crimes of malfeasance (government employees who violate the public trust) are just as evil, and the perpetrators must be held accountable just as any other criminal.

Our government must be accountable to the citizens. If bureaucrats are discovered defying or undermining the law they are supposed to uphold, they should be fired or prosecuted. Our laws must make individuals responsible for corporate actions. If a corporation is proven to be a polluter, not only the corporation but the individuals responsible for approving the pollution must be heavily fined or jailed.

Corporations should have to operate under the threat of extinction: after a certain number of violations, their charters should be revoked. In his publication "Taking Care of Business: Citizenship and the Charter of Incorporation," historian/activist Richard Grossman explains that citizens have the Constitutional right to seek the revocation of corporate charters:

> We need to know what each charter prohibits, especially if it is an old charter. Armed with our evidence of corporate misuse or abuse, we can amend or revoke charters and certificates of authority. When corporations violate our Constitutional guarantees, we can take them to court ourselves. Corporate officers can be forced to give us depositions under oath, just as elected officials who spurned the Constitution were forced to obey the civil rights movement— often in the courtroom packed with angry citizens.

A democracy establishes and upholds just laws, where the highest interest is the protection of the citizens. Any breakdown in this bodes ill for the democracy, which ultimately depends upon its citizens for its viability. Granting power to corporations to control our lives and to pollute at will means that our internal strength is diminished and our viability as a democracy deeply compromised. Countries that endure are not just well-armed; they have a strong, educated, involved, and healthy citizenry. Our ultimate security lies in our nation's inner strength.

Thus, our most basic principles are these: We have a right to eat clean food, drink uncontaminated water, and breathe uncontaminated air. We must instill a new system of thought for sustainable, clean enterprise. We must help producers and consumers understand that to select anything but the least-damaging product is unethical.

There are points of light on the industrial and governmental horizon. Some are bright beacons to give us hope; others are struggling to stay lit.

A report in the March 12, 1995 *Chicago Tribune* stated, "American drinking water would taste better and be better for us if we used less chlorine to purify it." The article quoted a report from the American Water Works Association that sand, stones, carbon, or modern biofilms purify water very well, sharply reducing the amount of chlorine needed. Paris now uses biological techniques to purify water from the Seine River, and Amsterdam has eliminated chlorine from its water purification.

In November 1995, environmental ministers from 110 nations signed the Washington Declaration, proposing to draft a binding treaty to sunset 12 organochlorine chemicals and pesticides worldwide.

The EPA has targeted the paper industry in a bid to reduce dioxin. A proposed EPA rule would require that paper mills decrease chlorine used in bleaching. Some American companies are changing over already, but other companies are resisting. The changeover is in full swing in Sweden, Austria, Germany, Switzerland, and British Columbia, where many paper mills have stopped bleaching with chorine gas or chlorine dioxide. According to *20/20 Vision,* "By 1996, chlorine-free paper will account for 70 percent of all printing and writing paper in Germany and Scandinavia. Companies in the United States that continue to deny the growing market for chlorine-free paper and fail to update their mills to new international standards will jeopardize their competitive advantage in the world market."

Research is ongoing to develop replacements for plastics. According to a report in the January 1995 *Environmental Health Perspectives,* a team of chemists at the University of

North Carolina at Chapel Hill has devised a new process for producing polymers, the basic component of plastic. The process eliminates many of the toxic by-products generated in conventional polymer manufacturing, much of which result from the present use of hazardous organic solvents in polymer production. This is an important breakthrough, for the U.S. plastics industry produces more than 500 million pounds of toxic waste a year, according to the EPA. One quarter of this waste goes back into the environment.

The 2,000-member organization of Canadian organic growers are supporting organic agricultural research and promoting techniques to build long-term soil fertility and reduce fossil fuel use. The U.S. Organic Farmers Association is a forward-thinking group committed to farming without pesticides. The certification process is very rigorous; farmers are not certified until they are inspected.

German industries are bypassing chlorine completely, selling refrigeration products that use "old-fashioned" propane, butane, and cyclopentane. They are finding such technology quite effective in a growing international market.

Chrysler of Canada has eliminated chlorinated solvents in its manufacturing plant and finds the alternative cleaners cheaper and more efficient. They've eliminated chlorofluorocarbons in air conditioning units installed in all Chrysler cars and vans.

In Vienna, Austria, new hospitals are being built with no PVCs at a much cheaper price. All Vienna hospitals are also using chlorine-free paper, cotton uniforms, heat to clean bedpans, and no spray cans.

The Great Lakes Protection Fund, established in 1988 by the Council of Great Lakes Governors and the Center for the Great Lakes, has a mission to "identify and/or demonstrate, and/or promote regional action to enhance Great Lakes ecosystem health." With a $100 million endowment, the Fund underwrites local groups that seek to prevent toxic pollution and support effective cleanup.

The EPA is actually getting involved with certain industries in helping to facilitate change. Through their Design for the Environment program, EPA has initiated several projects, including minimizing hazardous substances in the production of industrial chemicals, developing curricula for pollution prevention, and using environmentally friendly cleaning products in government-owned buildings.

Over the last 50 years, we have witnessed and even approved an experiment in flawed, polluting technologies that has brought wealth and power to the few at the expense of the many. But now, as we enter the new millennium, the world is ready for a shift in attitudes and technologies. In fact, the world requires such a shift. As Dr. Chivian said, "Human health must be at the center of the environmental debate, not because we are more deserving of life on this planet than any of the other 100 or so million other species, but because people are the destroyers of the environment and people will act to protect it only when they understand the dangers from not doing so to their health and their lives, and especially to those of their children. This is what is at stake."

Living beings can no longer bear the toxic assault of manufacturing driven by profit alone and organized by inhumane, amoral corporations. The only way to get environmental justice and a wholesome, healthy planet is to champion sustainable, healthy manufacturing practices run by companies enjoying profits from ethical, humane choices; and a society whose values celebrate life within a community of concern.

It's time to clear the decks for action.

# APPENDIX A

# GREENPEACE SUMMARY OF CHLORINE PHASEOUT

The purpose of this . . . is to show that society can realize significant economic gains in the transition to a chlorine-free economy, if the process is guided by careful planning to minimize costs, maximize benefits, and insure that both are distributed equitably.

The chlorine industry has argued that phasing out chlorine will result in exorbitant costs to the U.S. and Canadian economies and massive job losses. The industry's scenario, however, is based upon invalid assumptions that drastically overestimate the costs and underestimate the benefits of a well-planned transition.

The industry's calculations are based upon a methodology that assumes the chlorine phaseout will be implemented instantaneously, without thought, planning, or prioritization. The industry assumes that the alternatives that will replace chlorine will be processes that perform poorly, are unreasonably expensive, or are not the cost-effective substitutes the market would select. In fact, chlorine-free alternatives are frequently more efficient and productive than the chlorine-based processes they replace. Finally, the industry's scenario looks only at costs and burdens and fails to explore the benefits and savings associated with the transition to a chlorine-free economy. The actual costs of phasing out chlorine are likely to be only a small fraction of those calculated by the industry and the benefits of the transition are expected to outweigh these costs.

Implemented with careful planning, the transition to a chlorine-free economy can be economically beneficial and socially just. It can save money and create new jobs. Further, it can provide a model for how to undertake major economic change—especially that driven by an environmental imperative, in a way that is humane and equitable for those most directly affected.

A complete estimate of the economic benefits of the transition is beyond the scope of this document. Even the following preliminary information . . . makes clear that *the net savings associated with a chlorine phaseout would outweigh the costs of a well-planned transition.*

By prioritizing major chlorine use-sectors, the cost of the phaseout can be substantially reduced. Even according to the industry's own inflated cost estimates, 97 percent of chlorine use could be phased out for just $22 billion per year. These costs are much lower than the savings associated with phasing out chlorine, with initial estimates beginning at $80 to 160 billion annually. . . .

Current health care costs associated with the effects of persistent organochlorines in the U.S. and Ontario have been estimated at $50-$100 billion per year, according to the International Joint Commission on the Great Lakes. These costs to societies would be saved if chlorine were phased out.

In the pulp and paper industry, converting to totally chlorine-free bleaching process would save the industry $185 million per year in chemical costs; $108-$189 million per year in energy costs, according to industry estimates; and additional millions or billions in reduced expenditures for water use, effluent treatment, disposal of contaminated sludge; and reduced costs for lawsuits, remediation, and liability.

Mills that adopt chlorine-free bleaching process can realize additional cost savings by installing a closed-loop system for chemicals and effluents. Such a system can be built for $40 million less capital than a conventional mill; if all U.S. and Canadian mills built such systems, savings on water, energy, and chemical costs would total $1.4 billion per year.

As the international paper market increasingly demands chlorine-free paper, European producers are converting their production processes to meet this demand. Industry analysts have noted that if the North American industry continues to refuse to change to meet a changing market, it will be left permanently behind with lower market share; revenues and jobs will be jeopardized.

In dry cleaning, a recent U.S. EPA report shows that chlorine-based solvents can be replaced with a water-based system that is equally effective and results in a 42 percent lower capital investment to install, a 78 percent better return on investment, a 5 percent increase in profits, and a 21 percent increase in jobs. Implemented throughout the U.S., the system would create 33,170 new jobs with wages of $606 million a year.

Manufacturing industries can replace chlorinated solvents with cleaner production processes that have been shown to result in large savings, as much as several million dollars per company, due to reduced costs for chemical procurement, control, and disposal. Often these processes also substitute new jobs for chemicals.

Even in the pharmaceutical industry, the majority of organochlorines could be easily eliminated in favor of existing safer alternatives. . . . Most organochlorines are used as manufacturing process aids—i.e., solvents, extractants, and intermediates—that do not appear in the final medicine. Studies by industry and by the Metropolitan Water District of Southern California have found that effective alternatives are available now to replace those organochlorines.

Alternative agricultural systems that reduce or eliminate pesticide use have been shown to increase crop yields, lower farm-ers' costs, increase financial returns, and create new jobs by sub-stituting labor for chemicals, according to the National Academy of Sciences. Estimated cost savings associated with the chlorine phaseout in this sector are up to $8 billion per year in the U.S. and Canada.

About half of the jobs associated with chlorine are in the fab-rication of PVC plastic products. Because flooring, toys, pipes, and other such products will continue to be made when chlo-rine is phased out—but simply with traditional or nonchlorinat-ed plastics—no net reduction in jobs is expected in this large sector.

For workers producing the feedstocks or resins for these plas-tics, growth in production of the alternative materials—fre-quently in the same facilities or regions—are expected to offset reductions in the PVC sector. Because there may be some job dis-placement in this area, . . . careful transition planning is necessary to insure that new investment, job creation, and assistance funds are targeted specifically to minimize the dislocation.

Phasing out chlorine and organochlorines will substantially reduce industry's costs for pollution control and disposal, which can represent a major drag on the economy. Estimated savings from the chlorine phaseout in this sector are estimated at $22-$43 billion per year, based on U.S. EPA figures, using a very con-servative estimate.

Phasing out chlorine will prevent the continuation of a lega-cy of contaminated sites with clean-up estimated at up to $1 tril-lion. Preventing organochlorine discharges that would occur over a 20-year period are estimated to result in $20-$100 billion in obviated remediation costs.

The transition to a chlorine-free economy would require an investment in new construction and new technologies that would provide a powerful economic stimulus. Based on the chemical industry's estimate of this investment at $67 billion, the transition would create about 925,000 job-years of new employment, or 92,500 permanent jobs over a 10-year period.

In order to insure an effective transition, the chlorine phase-out should include the following steps.

1. Priority phaseout sectors: Timelines should be immediately set for phaseout in the following large sectors for which alternatives have been proven effective and affordable: pulp and paper; solvents and dry cleaning; PVC and pesticides—or about 55 percent of all chlorine used in the U.S. and Canada.

2. Secondary sectors: Timelines to sunset other uses should be established based on the quantity of chlorine used and the availability of alternatives. Special attention should be paid to the following sizable sectors for which alternatives are feasible: chlorinated intermediates used to produce isocyanates and propylene oxide; chlorine used to produce titanium dioxide; chlorine used in wastewater disinfection. Together with the priority sectors, these uses consume 68 percent of all chlorine now produced.

3. Chlorine tax: The U.S. and Canada should institute a tax on the chlor-alkali process and on offshore imports of chlorine-containing products and alkali produced through the chlor-alkali process. Chlor-alkali plants should no longer be allowed to purchase government-subsidized electric power, or purchase regulated electric power at less than average market rates.

4. Transition fund to protect workers and communities: Revenues equal to those generated by the chlorine tax should be held in a fund to aid the transition to a chlorine-free society. In particular, the fund should be used for exploring and demonstrating economically viable alternatives and for easing dislocations among affected workers and communities, particularly those associated with the chemical manufacturing industry itself. Funds should be targeted so that investment in cleaner production process-

es is concentrated in locations where chlorine-based processes have been phased out, so that new jobs are created where old jobs are eliminated. Funds should also be used to insure income protection, health care coverage, and educational opportunities for workers whose jobs are eliminated in the transition. A board should be established to help set the policy of the fund and should include representatives of various stakeholder groups.

By admitting that alternatives are available for all major chlorine uses, the chemical industry validates the feasibility of a society without chlorine. By raising the specter of job loss and economic dislocation, the industry declares itself concerned with the interests of chlorine workers, users, and communities where facilities are located. With this declaration of concern, the chlorine industry opens up a new debate about the most effective and equitable way to implement the transition. With a careful planning process, the transition to a chlorine-free future can provide a model for truly sustainable development, and all the environmental, economic, and social benefits that accompany it.

# HOW OUR LAWS
# ARE SUBVERTED

Since the late 1970s, we have increasingly heard in our political campaigns how "deregulation" will set loose the caged tiger that is the American economy, and then all of our economic problems will melt away in a boom like we have never seen. But the plain facts are that, in many instances, polluting industries have already been deregulated, despite some very important laws.

## Delaney Clause

The Delaney Clause was a 1958 amendment to the 1954 Food, Drug and Cosmetic Act. The clause required zero tolerance for carcinogenic pesticides in processed foods, regardless of any commercial benefits such additives might have. However, the history of the Delaney Clause is one of conflict between regulatory officials on one hand and the politically powerful pesticide and oil companies (pesticides are oil-based) on the other.

In 1965, the National Academy of Sciences concluded that the concept of zero tolerance was scientifically and administratively untenable and should be abandoned.

According to Peter Montague, the FDA and USDA adopted the NAS recommendation and in 1966 began establishing allowable levels of pesticide residues, called "tolerances." One section of the law allowed officials to balance the value of cheaper food with cancer deaths.

The food chemicals industry applied relentless pressure on the regulators to allow more poisons into the food supply. In 1987 the NAS recommended a uniform standard that would allow one out of every million citizens to be killed by each use of each pesticide.

Taking its lead from the NAS, the EPA refused to ban processed foods, particularly those registered before 1978, which contained pesticide residues. By 1988, instead of vigorous enforcement, the EPA developed a numbers game called "negligible risk tolerances" for all carcinogenic pesticides on all foods, making cancer prevention secondary to the "benefits" accruing to pesticide manufacturers. Sam Epstein calls this form of risk-benefit analysis "at best a pseudo-science and at worst a smoke screen for the numbers used to prop up politically predetermined decisions." It doesn't consider the cumulative effects of numerous pesticides in the total diet, risks from carcinogenic food additives, animal-feed additives, and food-wrapping chemicals and contaminants.

Because of EPA/FDA unwillingness to enforce Delaney, the law was ignored—until 1992, when a court battle over the negligible risk tolerances started. In July of that year, the Ninth Circuit Court of Appeals ruled that the EPA had to remove from the market any pesticides that are potential oncogens and which leave residues in processed foods. Although the EPA had maintained that the pesticides were not covered by Delaney, the court found that they were. This was backed up by the Supreme Court, which on February 22, 1993, refused to respond to a petition brought by the Grocery Manufacturers and National Agricultural Chemicals associations.

However, Carol Browner, President Clinton's EPA Administrator, made it clear that she had little intention of enforcing Delaney. And in 1996, the clause's tortured life was ended when Congress voted to strike it from the law.

## FIFRA

The EPA is the primary federal regulator of pesticides. Its authority comes from the Federal Insecticide, Fungicide and Rodenticide Act (FIFRA)—a comprehensive regulatory program for pesticides and herbicides originally enacted in 1972. The goal of FIFRA is to regulate the use of pesticides through their registration.

Section 3 of the law mandates that before a product is registered, EPA must determine that the product "will perform its intended function without unreasonable adverse effects on the environment." FIFRA defines adverse effects as "any unreasonable effects on man or the environment, taking into account the economic, social and environmental costs and benefits of using any pesticide." To further this objective, Congress placed a number of regulatory tools at the disposal of the EPA, and made it clear that the public was not to bear the risk of uncertainty concerning the safety of a pesticide. The burden rests on the manufacturer to provide the data needed to support registration for use on a particular crop.

FIFRA is a licensing law. Pesticides may enter commerce only after they are approved or "registered following an evaluation against statutory risk/benefit standards." The EPA Administrator may take action to terminate any approval whenever it appears that, on the basis of new information, that the pesticide no longer meets the statutory standard. These decisions are made on a use-by-use basis since the risks and benefits of a pesticide vary from one use to another.

FIFRA is also a control law. Special precautions and instructions may be imposed. For example, applicators may be required to wear protective clothing, or the use of certain pesticides may be restricted to trained and certified applicators. Instructions, warnings, and prohibitions are incorporated into the labels on the products, labels which may not be altered or removed.

Licensing decisions are usually based on tests furnished by an applicant for registration. The tests are performed by the petitioning company in accordance with guidelines prescribed by EPA. Current requirements can be met only through the expenditure of several millions of dollars and up to four years of laboratory and field testing.

However, major changes in test standards, advances in testing methodology, and the heightened awareness of the potential health effects of long-term, low-level exposure to chemicals which have come into the marketplace within the past several decades brought the need to update the pesticide registry. Thus, Congress directed that the EPA reevaluate its licensing decisions through re-registration. Thus, long-profitable pesticides were in danger of being de-listed, or banned from commercial sale, or at least suspended pending further studies.

This seemed to put the pesticide manufacturers on the spot, but they and the powers in EPA found ways to circumvent Congress's intent.

## Section 18

Section 18 of FIFRA is the slick way industry has been given to avoid re-registration of many toxic chemicals.

Section 18 allows for the use of unregistered pesticides in certain emergency situations:

> The Administrator may, at his discretion, exempt any Federal or State agency from any provisions of this subchapter if he determines that emergency conditions exist which require such exemption. The Administrator, in determining whether or not such emergency conditions exist, shall consult with the Secretary of Agriculture and the Governor of any state concerned if they request such determination.

From 1978 to 1983, the GAO and the House Subcommittee on Department Operations, Research and Foreign Agriculture of the Committee on Agriculture (DORFA) thoroughly examined the

EPA's implementation of Section 18. Under the auspices of Representative George Brown, Jr., DORFA held a series of hearings which revealed that numerous abuses plagued the EPA's administration of Section 18. A report was issued in 1982 and reprinted as part of the subcommittee's 1983 hearings.

The subcommittee found that "the rapid increase in the number and volume of pesticides applied under Section 18 was clearly the most pronounced trend in the EPA's pesticide regulatory program." According to the subcommittee report, "a primary cause of the increase in the number of Section 18 exemptions derived from the difficulty the Agency had in registering chemicals under Section 3 of FIFRA in a timely manner." DORFA stated:

> Regulatory actions involving suspect human carcinogens which meet or exceed the statute's "unreasonable adverse effects" criterion for chronic toxicity often become stalled in the Section 3 review process for several years. The risk assessment procedures required by States requesting Section 18 actions, and by EPA in approving them, are generally less strict. For example, a relatively new insecticide, first widely used in 1977, was granted some 140 Section 18 emergency exemptions and over 300 [Section 24c] Special Local Needs registrations in the next four years while the Agency debated the significance to man of positive evidence of oncogenicity in laboratory animals.

EPA's regulatory practices changed little during the Reagan/ Bush years. In the spring of 1990, the Subcommittee on Environment of the House Science, Space and Technology Committee, chaired by Representative James Scheuer, re-investigated EPA's procedures under Section 18 and found that the problem had gotten worse. Their report stated, "Since 1973, more than 4,000 emergency exemptions have been granted for the use of pesticides on crops for which there is no registration." A large number of these emergency exemptions were granted repeatedly for up to 14 years. The subcommittee's report continued:

The continuing reliance on pesticides is now considered harmful to public health and the environment, and it is also detrimental to the development of innovative, less toxic pesticides. EPA's review of the chemicals under the exemption program entails significantly less complete and rigorous data requirements and analyses than the process required under Section 3 registration. Emergency exemptions, therefore, increase risks to human health and also increase the chances of adverse environmental and wildlife impacts.

. . . The existence of such large numbers of emergency exemptions is primarily caused by the EPA's failure to implement its own regulations. For instance, numerous exemptions are granted despite the fact that the applicant has not made the requisite showing, as provided by regulation, that "significant economic loss" will occur without the use of the unregistered pesticide. Similarly, the EPA often grants exemptions despite the fact that the applicant has not shown, in accordance with the regulations, that the chemical substance is making "reasonable progress toward registration" for that crop. Further, the EPA frequently fails to examine whether or not "effective [registered] alternatives" are available, although the regulations specify that the existence of effective registered substitutes should prevent the use of Section 18.

The subcommittee identified some of the so-called "emergencies" that EPA accepted as reasons to invoke Section 18:"Routine predicted outbreaks and foreign competition and . . . a company's need to gain market access for use of a pesticide on a new crop, although the company often never intends to submit adequate data to register the chemical for use."

As for the re-registration requirement, the subcommittee concluded:

EPA's reliance on Section 18 may be related to the Agency's difficulty in re-registering older chemical substances. Often, Section 18 requests are made for the use of older chemicals on crops for which they are not registered. These older chemicals receive repetitive exemptions for use despite the fact that many of these substances may have difficulty obtaining re-registration since they have been identified as potentially carcinogenic. Thus, by liberally and repetitively granting exemptions to potentially carcinogenic substances, little incentive is provided to encourage companies to invest in the development of newer, safer pesticides or alternative agricultural practices.

...Allowing these exemptions year after year in predictable situations provides "back-door" preregistration market access to potentially dangerous chemicals.

# SELECTED WOMEN'S ORGANIZATIONS

The following is a list of selected women's organizations dedicated to preventing breast cancer by exploring the relationship of the environment to breast cancer. These groups are aggressively alerting women about the problems involved with such issues as the tamoxifen trials. (Groups that do not address prevention or the environmental connection are not included.)

Action for Women's Health
144 Harvard, S.E.
Albuquerque, NM 87106
505-242-6124

African American Breast Cancer Alliance
1 West Lake Street, #423
Minneapolis, MN 55408

Bay Area Breast Cancer Network
4010 Moore Park Avenue
San Jose, CA 95117
408-261-1425

Black Women's Health Project
1237 Gordon Street, S.W.
Atlanta, GA 30310
404-681-4554

Boston Women's Health Book Collective
240A Elm
Sommerville, MA 02144
617-625-0277

Breast Cancer Action
55 New Montgomery Street, #624
San Francisco, CA 94105
415-243-9301
Fax: 415-243-3996

Breast Cancer Fund
282 Second Street, 3rd Floor
San Francisco, CA 94105
415-543-2979
Fax: 415-543-2975

Breast Cancer HELP (Healthy Environment for a Living Planet)
400 Montauk Highway #100
West Islip, NY 11795
516-661-6500
Fax: 516-661-6678

Cleveland Women's Cancer Project
2853 Berkshire
Cleveland Heights, OH 45241
216-321-0442

Foundation for a Compassionate Society
227 Congress Avenue
Austin, TX 78701
512-472-0131

Greenpeace
847 West Jackson Boulevard
Chicago, IL 60607
312-563-6060

Lesbian Community Cancer Project
2524 North Lincoln Avenue, Apt. 199
Chicago, IL 60614
312-549-4729

Long Island Breast Cancer Action Coalition
Nassau County Medical Center
2201 Hempstead Turnpike
East Meadow, NY 11554
516-357-9622

Massachusetts Breast Cancer Coalition
85 Merrimac Street
Boston, MA 02114
617-624-0180
Fax: 617-642-0176

National Black Women's Health Project
1211 Connecticut Avenue, N.W. #310
Washington, DC 20036
202-835-0117

National Coalition for Health and Environmental Justice
860 Pine Grove Avenue
Traverse City, MI 49686
616-933-0121/312-563-6060 (voice mail)

National Women's Health Network
514 10th Street, N.W. #400
Washington, DC 20004
202-347-1140/202-628-7814 (information clearinghouse)
Fax: 202-347-1168

One-in-Nine
Nassau County Medical Center #204
2201 Hempstead Turnpike
East Meadow, NY 11554
516-357-9622
Fax: 516-357-9658

# INDEX